OUR LIVING EVANGELISTS

OF

THE CHURCH OF CHRIST.

EDITED BY

H. C. PATTERSON.

ST. LOUIS:
CHRISTIAN PUBLISHING COMPANY.
1894.

TO MY DEAR WIFE

AND

MY AFFECTIONATE CHILDREN,

WHO HAVE SHARED WITH ME THE JOYS AND SORROWS
OF MY EVENTFUL LIFE, AND HAVE BEEN A
SOURCE OF GREAT STRENGTH UNTO ME,

THIS BOOK

IS AFFECTIONATELY DEDICATED.

PREFACE.

THERE is no class of men in whose work Christian people take greater interest than that of Evangelists. The people everywhere, having heard of the wonderful success attending their labors, have a desire to see and hear them all. But, as this is impossible, I thought they would hail with delight a book which would give them a reasonably correct idea of the physical appearance, mental capabilities and style of address of each of our most successful Evangelists. After consulting with scores of pastors, and corresponding with many others, and receiving nothing but words of encouragement, I at last decided to issue this book.

We have scores of Evangelists whose names do not appear in this book, who are doing faithful work for the Master, but the eyes of the whole brotherhood have been fixed, for some years, upon most of those whose sermons we compile; consequently they will be more interested in reading after them.

As I was walking toward Mr. Spurgeon's tabernacle, in London, one beautiful Lord's day morning, I remarked to an aged gentleman that I had long had a great desire to see and hear the illustrious Mr. Spurgeon. Turning toward me, and placing his hand upon my shoulder, he said: " My dear sir, there are too many who are coming to see and hear Mr. *Spurgeon*, and too few coming to hear *Christ*. Now, sir, I hope you will this day hear *Christ* speaking *through* Mr. Spurgeon." I kindly accepted the mild rebuke, and perhaps thought more of what was said by reason of it. To my readers, therefore, I would say, these are only weak men, after all, and without Christ they are nothing. It is Christ speaking through them that makes them powerful. So, while you read of and admire their push and energy, think not that this is the secret of their success. No, it is Christ *in* them. If one of these were to commit a gross sin this day he would be shorn of his power for winning souls for Christ, as surely as was Samson when his locks fell to the ground. Follow them as they follow Christ and you will be strong.

As you read after these men of God, my prayer is that you may receive new courage for more determined and heroic efforts in building up the cause of our blessed Master.

THE AUTHOR.

CONTENTS.

(7)

BIOGRAPHICAL SKETCHES AND PORTRAITS.

Our Living Evangelists.

THE EVANGELIST AND HIS WORK.

J. V. COOMBS.

PAUL commands Timothy to do the work of an evangelist. 2 Tim. 4: 5. In this one sentence he recognizes the evangelist and his work.

That the evangelist's is a scriptural office, and as permanent and defined as that of the elder or deacon, no one who knows God's word can deny. The divine writers state clearly the evangelist's duties and privileges. God called some to be teachers, others to be shepherds, and still others to be evangelists.

No religious society can dispense with any of these offices and hope for success. Some have tried it and died, as they should. "God's ways are not man's ways."

THE EVANGELIST'S QUALIFICATION.

He must be a diligent student of the word of truth. "Study to show thyself approved unto God, a workman that needeth not to be ashamed, rightly dividing the word of truth." 2 Tim. 2: 15. No man is an evangelist that does not diligently study the word of truth. He must be qualified to divide the word. He must be a man of faith, charity, and peace, and flee youthful lust. He must put away foolish questions, for they engender. strife. He must be thoroughly furnished unto all good works.

WHAT HE SHOULD PREACH.

The evangelist has his work outlined. "I charge thee, preach the word, reprove, rebuke, exhort with all long-suffering and doctrine; for the time will come when they will not endure sound doctrine." 2 Tim. 4: 1-3. "Hold fast the form of sound words."

"There are many unruly and vain talkers and deceivers whose mouths must be stopped." Titus 1: 10, 11. He must use "sound speech that can not be condemned." "Them that sin rebuke before *all*, that others also may fear." 1 Tim. 5:20.

In these Scriptures we find what an evangelist must preach and also how he must preach.

1. He must preach sound doctrine. Yet, there are some so-called evangelists who refuse to preach any doctrine or allow others to preach it. Even among us we find some people who say: "Don't preach any doctrinal discourses. Preach evangelistic sermons." Now a sermon is not evangelistic unless it is doctrinal.

2. He is also commanded to *exhort*. Some people object to exhorting, but God Almighty says to

the evangelist, *exhort.* Much of the power of a preacher is gone if he cannot exhort.

3. The evangelist must also reprove. It is not an easy task to reprove, but the Spirit says, "reprove."

4. *Rebuke* is also enjoined upon the evangelist, and that if necessary "before all," that others may fear. The evangelist cannot be true to his calling and let sin go unrebuked. It is much easier to apologize than to rebuke, yet God says rebuke. A preacher will let sin grow up in the front pews and vice prevail without lifting his voice against them. Should he happen to say anything that does refer to his congregation he always covers it up with the flimsy coat of apology by saying, "Oh, well, I don't mean to say that any of my congregation are guilty of such things, but they are practiced in other places." The evangelist should persuade men to be reconciled to God, not to science and reason. Some preachers spend more time reconciling science and Revelation than they do in reconciling men.

Instead of seeking the lost, they are hunting for the missing link between the man and the monkey. *Preach the word* and let the monkey play the fool. It is not enjoined upon the preacher to play the monkey.

OBJECTIONS TO REVIVALS.

I will notice some of the most common objections offered against protracted meetings:

1. The converts do not *hold out.* The writer has preached from ocean to ocean, and from the lakes to the gulf, and he is satisfied that the best workers in all the churches are those who have been converted during the gospel meetings. Those who are born into the kingdom under the warm influence of a great meeting are ready to go to work. It is better to be born in a hot-house than in an ice-house.

In an audience of 800 people the writer asked all who were members of the church to arise. Not fewer than 500 arose. Out of that number all but about 30 united with the church during a revival. Among the 470 who were converted during revivals was nearly every preacher, deacon and elder who was present. In a men's meeting in Virginia, I asked all who were church members to arise. About 1,200 stood. Then I asked all who were converted during a revival to be seated. All but about 175 sat down; 1,025 to 175 converted in a series of meetings, and among the 1,025 was every preacher and church officer present. Nearly all the best preachers of the land united with the church during revivals, and they *hold out* fairly.

2. The next objection is, The revival interferes with the regular work. If the regular work is to save souls and build Christian manhood and womanhood, then the revival does not hinder, but helps.

Meetings are arranged too often to attract people and amuse them. The church has arranged for reunions, festivals, fairs, sociables and concerts. The revival crosses the track of these festivities, hence would be as objectionable to society people as a prairie fire would be to the frontier settler.

3. The evangelists may supplant the pastor and carry off the hearts of the people. That there are evangelists who do supplant the regular minister, I am compelled to admit, but they are few. Upon this point the evangelist should be careful. He has it largely in his power to make or kill the pastor. Always hold him up and help him. On the other hand, let the pastor be not over sensitive. If the evangelist preaches a good sermon, the people will likely tell him so, but in doing so they do not underrate the work of the pastor. Let the preacher and pastor be co-workers.

If both will lose sight of self and hide behind the cross, there will be no trouble. A true evangelist will never strive to be popular.

The custom of giving farewell banquets to evangelists is a pernicious one. Let the last act of the evangelist be an effort to save souls. All receptions and banquets given in his honor are wrong and fraught with evil. Let the evangelist finish his work by a sensible talk to the young converts, and then, as quietly as possible, take his departure. This is much better than to get them to cry over him, and tell him that he is such a dear, good preacher, and that they want him to locate with them.

1. The best way to prepare for a revival is to have one week of prayer. Prayer is the mighty right arm of evangelism. Without prayer God will not give the increase. Get every one possible to pray. Let the prayers be direct and short. This week of prayer should be held before any preaching is done.

2. Have a meeting in which all are urged to talk. Discuss the topics : " What do I want this revival to accomplish ?" " What will *I* do for these meetings ?"

3. Select a committee of the most earnest members and through them secure a list of persons who may be induced to come into the church.

4. Secure a good band of singers and have a song book for every person in the house. Let the music be simple and that which is easily sung. Avoid all dazzle and show. A few operatic songs may badly cripple a meeting. Anything that draws attention from Christ and him crucified positively hinders. An egotistic leader of music and a band of instruments are entirely out of place.

HOW TO SUCCEED.

1. Preach the word of truth fearlessly but lovingly. The preaching that leaves love out leaves

all out. Love is greater than faith or hope. Better have weak faith and great love than strong faith and no love. The evangelist can preach the primitive gospel without abusing any one.

2. Preach every sermon as if you knew that there were men before you who would never have another opportunity to obey. Tell them plainly that upon this winged moment eternity depends.

3. Preach mightily against sin. Make men sick of sin, and they will take the medicine.

4. The committee on personal work should be carefully drilled. There should be from house to house visitation. Personal members should plead relentlessly for souls. Don't be afraid of over-persuading. If the personal workers have the gospel plan in their minds, and give a Bible answer to all inquirers, there is no danger of over-persuading. At the first call for soldiers in the late war, many promptly went to the front. But when there was a call for enlisting for life, men hesitated. But the recruiting officer went to them personally and told them that their homes were in danger. Reluctantly these men were persuaded to enlist. Gen. Grant says : "These men who were persuaded to go into the ranks were the best soldiers." The Lord pleads earnestly for souls. We must do so if we live for him.

5. The way to make a protracted meeting a success is to *protract it till it is a success.* Short meetings are usually failures. In a meeting of 200

accessions conducted by the writer, at the end of nine days there was but one confession. Toward the end of the meeting there were 81 in one week, and nearly all were men.

THE IMPORTANCE OF HIS WORK.

Let the evangelist realize the greatness of his profession. Let him realize that primitive Christianity cannot triumph without his efforts. He should not underrate the importance of the work of the pastor. The pastor has his work. The evangelist is the recruiting officer. The pastor trains these recruits for life's battle. The evangelist cannot overestimate the importance of his work. Let the evangelist abandon the field and the current reformation would come to a stand-still. The old school Baptists neglected evangelistic work, and they are rapidly going to the wall. Presbyterianism for the last twenty-five years, with few exceptions, has neglected the work of the evangelist. In proportion to their members and wealth within the last thirty years we have outstripped them in numbers of ingatherings ten to one. If all our preachers would catch the evangelistic fever, we could double our membership in one year. The preacher who does not have the evangelistic spirit will soon be a back number. Then, with buoyant heart, untiring energy, sleepless zeal and fervent hope, let the evangelist realize the high importance of his work, its wide-reaching influence stretching far beyond the stars, to breathless eternity. Let him recognize that to save souls is the grandest calling allotted to men.

Should an angel wing its way from earth back to heaven, and announce that there was one poor sinner on earth to whom no one had ever preached the gospel, and the Son of God should call an angelic council and say, " Who will volunteer to go to earth and save that man ?" I believe all the angels in heaven would shout, " Lord, send me, send me." Evangelist, it is your blessed privilege to carry this message of love.

2

B. F. HILL.

B. F. HILL was born in Moniteau county, Mo., March 11, 1860. He was brought up on a farm, with all the usual environments of rural life. He took the literary course of study in Aurora High School, California, Mo.; confessed his faith in his Savior, who is now so precious to him, at the age of sixteen, and began life as a teacher in the public school of the district in which he was born and raised.

He was married at the age of twenty to Miss Dora Cloninges, an amiable and most worthy lady, whom everyone loves and highly esteems, upon forming her acquaintance.

At the age of twenty-two he decided to enter upon the work of the ministry, and to more thoroughly prepare himself for the work, he at once entered the Christian University at Canton, Mo. He began preaching at the age of twenty-five, for churches near California, Mo., where he was brought up. In December of that year he was called to the pastorate of the church at Valley Center, Kan., where he remained fifteen months, when he took charge of the work at Malta Bend and Miami, in Saline county, Mo. At the close of

B. F. HILL.

the year the church at Miami called him for his
entire time. During his three years' labor with
this church the membership was increased by 184,
and a mission of 75 members was built up, and a
house of worship for them was erected at Miami
Station, across the river.

At this time the State Sunday-school Board secured him as an evangelist of the Northwestern District of Missouri. During the six months' work as
evangelist he delivered 193 addresses, organized
five schools and one church, had 132 additions, and
raised $2,318 for church and Sunday-school sup-
port.

He was called to the church at Clarksville, Mo.,
immediately upon leaving the Sunday-school work.
During his pastorate of one year at this place
there were about fifty added to the membership;
the Y. P. S. C. E. reached an enrollment of eighty,
and the Sunday-school was greatly strengthened.
His work here was highly satisfactory, both as a
preacher and a pastor.

In February, 1891, the church at Fulton, Mo.,
gave him a unanimous call, and after careful and
prayerful consideration, he tendered his resigna-
tion at Clarksville, and accepted the proposition
made by this church, to begin work the first of
April of the same year.

As a preacher and pastor, Bro. Hill's superior
has not been among us. He makes the church's
troubles his troubles, and their joys his joys. He

glories in the Cross of Christ and preaches Christ
and him crucified. He takes the lead and members follow; cheers the broken-hearted and distressed in their afflictions; visits the sick and
ministers to their wants, and does all in his power
to make men and women truer, better and nobler
in the work of the Master.

Since he came among us the church has experienced a wonderful growth, financially, numerically
and spiritually. More than one hundred have been
added to its membership.   A Y. P. S. C. E. has
been built up that is a credit to the church and
city.   When Bro. Hill came to our city the Y. P.
S. C. E. had a membership of seventeen, and I find
on page 37 of the secretary's record her report for
the year 1891, which reads as follows: "At the
close of the year (1891) we had eighty-two active,
and twenty-one associate members; total membership 103.   These, once associate members, have
all united with the church and have been trans-
ferred on the list as active members.   The society
is educating one young lady in the Orphan School
at this place, and contributed $13.50 to the
Orphans' Home, St. Louis. This is only one year's
work, with only seventeen members to begin with.
Has not God blessed our efforts?   What will be
done in the future with 103 to work?"

The attendance in our Sunday-school during the
past year has been nearly double that of any previous year, and contributed $150 to the State Sun-

day-school work. Surely we have been blessed in every feature of our work beyond our expectations, and we pray God's blessings upon our leader, that he may be strengthened and encouraged in his labors in the present year. Truly his labors have not been in vain the past year, and we prophesy more good in the future.

A. W. PASLEY.

THE ANGEL'S PROMISE TO MARY.

B. F. HILL.

THEREFORE, also that holy thing which shall be born of thee shall be called the Son of God.—*Luke* 1: 35.

THE historians or evangelists in the Gospels introduce a character to whom *they call attention* as "The Christ, the Son of the living God." (Matt. 16 : 16). They disclose a secret to us concerning the incarnation of Jesus; they reveal the fact that he was begotten as none other before or since.

"Now the birth of Jesus Christ was on this wise: When as his mother Mary was espoused to Joseph, before they came together, she was found with child of the Holy Ghost. Then Joseph her husband, being a just man, and not willing to make her a public example, was minded to put her away privily. But while he thought on these things, behold, the angel of the Lord appeared unto him in a dream, saying, Joseph, thou son of David, fear not to take unto thee Mary thy wife : for that which is conceived in her is of the Holy Ghost. And she shall bring forth a son, and thou shalt call his name Jesus : for he shall save his people from their sins. Now all this was done,

(22)

that it might be fulfilled which was spoken of the
Lord by the prophet, saying, Behold, a virgin
shall be with child, and shall bring forth a son,
and they shall call his name Emmanuel, which
being interpreted is, God with us." (Matt. 18 : 23).

"And the angel said unto her, Fear not, Mary:
for thou hast found favour with God. And, behold, thou shalt conceive in thy womb, and bring
forth a son, and shalt call his name Jesus. He
shall be great, and shall be called the Son of the
Highest: and the Lord God shall give unto him
the throne of his father David : and he shall
reign over the house of Jacob for ever; and of his
kingdom there shall be no end. Then said Mary
unto the angel, How shall this be, seeing I know
not a man? And the angel answered and said
unto her, The Holy Ghost shall come upon thee,
and the power of the Highest shall overshadow
thee : therefore also that holy thing which shall be
born of thee shall be called the Son of God."
(Luke 1 : 30-35).

"And there were in the same country shepherds
abiding in the field, keeping watch over their
flock by night. And, lo, the angel of the Lord
came upon them, and the glory of the Lord shone
round about them : and they were sore afraid.
And the angel said unto them, Fear not: for, behold, I bring you good tidings of great joy, which
shall be to all people. For unto you is born this
day in the city of David, a Saviour, which is

Christ the Lord. And this shall be a sign unto you; Ye shall find the babe wrapped in swaddling clothes, lying in a manger. And suddenly there was with the angel a multitude of the heavenly host praising God, and saying, Glory to God in the highest, and on earth peace, good will toward men." (Luke 2 : 8-14).

Surely from such an introduction as this the world had a right to expect something above an ordinary character. And if there is that in the teaching, work, and character of Jesus of Nazareth that corresponds to the alleged mysterious conception and circumstances attending the introduction of the infant Jesus, it must have its weight in settling the truthfulness of the angelic PROMISE to Mary. And if Jesus of Nazareth was so distinguished a character as the angel promised, he must be worthy of the admiration of the entire human family. Now let us look at him as he stands before the world : We are told of his perfect humanity ; he hungered, he thirsted, he grew tired and was greatly fatigued, and yet when his disciples came with meat, he said : "I have meat to eat that you know not of." He recognized Mary as his mother and claimed God as his father. He is known to have had none of the advantages of a technical education, yet his wisdom was acknowledged. Again, the Messiah had been the theme for ages. The Jews for more than one thousand years had been expecting the announcement of the arrival of the Messiah, the one who would reign in David's place.

Reader, remember that when Jesus of Nazareth entered upon his ministry HE LAID CLAIM TO THE MESSIAHSHIP. He claimed his position in the world on the ground of fulfilled prophecy: "Search the scriptures; for in them ye think ye have eternal life: and they are they which testify of me." (Jno. 5 : 39). I AM the CHARACTER that your Scriptures treat upon. "The woman saith unto him, I know that Messias cometh, which is called Christ: when he is come, he will tell us all things. Jesus saith unto her, I that speak unto thee am he." (John 4 : 25, 26).

Thus it is clearly manifest that he called attention to himself as the Messiah; and to convince the people of his veracity he manifested his power over animate and inanimate creatures and things. He spake the word and the billowy Galilee was calm and serene. He said, "Put forth thy hand," and the sick of the palsy was healed at his word. He anointed the eyes of one born blind, with saliva and clay, and said to him, "Go and wash." He went and returned seeing. At his command the dead arose. But let us follow after this mysterious person. He said, "I must be about my Father's business." "I am going to establish a kingdom: my kingdom is not of this world." The angel said to Mary: "His kingdom shall be an everlasting kingdom." Yes; HE PROMISED her that Jesus should BE GREAT. Let us institute a careful search for his greatness. May I ask in what did his greatness consist? Could it have been derived from the high social standing of his family? No, for they did not rank in that circle. Was it earthly riches that made him great? No, *he had none.* He became poor that we through his poverty might become rich in faith and glory. When his friend desired to stay all night with him, he said he had no where to pillow his head. Thus we see him poorer than the poorest. Was it his relation to the Aaronic priesthood that made him great? No, he was not of that tribe. But let us look for his greatness in another direction. Turn to the PLAN INSTITUTED by him, for the organization of his kingdom. How did he proceed? Did he call the rich? No. Did he call those of high social and political standing? No. We see him as he passes the Sea of Galilee, and hear him calling to some men of the lower class of humanity, and saying: "Follow me, and I will make you fishers of men."

Instead of going to Jerusalem, and Athens, and Rome, the hubs of the three greatest civilizations on earth in the days of Jesus, and from among those of highest social and political caste selecting his ambassadors and those that were to represent him in the uttermost parts of the globe and carry a message to every creature under the sun, we find him selecting these poor and uncouth fishers and peasants. They were without money and without a knowledge of the affairs of governments and the conditions of humanity; THEY WERE STRANGERS TO THE WORLD and possessed nothing to commend them to the world or that would enable them to attract the attention of men. IF ANYTHING OF NOTE EVER COMES OF SUCH AN ENTERPRISE IT WILL CERTAINLY BE WONDERFUL. Yes, it will be as great a wonder as the alleged mysterious conception and circumstances attending the birth of Jesus. Those men left their nets and followed him. He said to them, "The kingdom of heaven is like to a grain of mustard seed, which a man took and sowed in his field, which indeed is the least of all the seeds: but when it is grown, it is the greatest among herbs, and becometh a tree so that the birds of the air come and lodge in the branches thereof." But in what respect is the kingdom of heaven like to a mustard seed which was planted and became the greatest among herbs? The sequel alone of the kingdom of heaven contains the answer to that question. His kingdom did not begin as the Assyrian kingdom, of which Nebuchadnezzar was the most celebrated of all her kings, 600 B. C. Neither did his kingdom begin as the Medo-Persian Empire, founded by Cyrus the Great, 536 B. C., lasting till 330 B. C., a period of 206 years. His kingdom did not begin as the Macedonian Empire, founded by Alexander the Great, 330 B. C., lasting till 30 B. C., a period

of 300 years. Neither did it begin as the Roman
Empire, founded by Augustus, B. C. 30, lasting till
330 A. D., a period of 360 years. But it began in
an unheard-of and undreamed-of manner. It
seemed, and INDEED WAS, QUITE SMALL in its beginning, but its growth has been marvelous.

After the resurrection of Jesus, the eleven tar-
ried in Jerusalem until they realized the fulfillment of his promise to them when he said, " I will
send you the Comforter." "When he, the spirit of
truth, is come, he will guide you into all truth ;
for he shall not speak of himself; but whatsoever
he shall hear, that shall he speak ; and he will
show you things to come." (Jno. 16 : 13). These
men, after the resurrection and ascension of Jesus,
went into Jerusalem, and there announced the resurrection of Jesus. They did not go over into
Arabia to begin preaching the doctrine of a risen
and crowned Lord, but they began among the people in Jerusalem and Palestine, who were well ac-
quainted with Jesus of Nazareth and who were
familiar with the termination of his life on the
cross of Calvary. His greatness we find in the
power of his teaching and its effect upon the
heart. Napoleon, whom no one has accused of
being a pietist, had this to say of Jesus : " He
was more than a man." While on St. Helena he
asked one of his officers if he could tell him who
Jesus of Nazareth was; to which the officer re-
sponded, No. " Then," said he, " I will tell you,"

and having contrasted himself with Charlemagne,
Cæsar and Alexander, he said : " They and myself have all founded empires, but upon what did
the creations of our genius depend ? FORCE. But
Jesus of Nazareth has established his empire upon
LOVE, and there are millions who will die for him.
Charlemagne, Cæsar, Alexander and myself are
men, but Jesus was more than a man." (I quote from
memory.) Yes, he was and is great, and his kingdom is an everlasting one. It is to Jesus that we
owe our enlightenment. It is the Gospel that has
led us thus far on the road to civilization. There
is in the Gospel of Jesus of Nazareth the panacea
for all that afflicts the human family. It *has built*
hospitals and *asylum* and is civilizing man, and it
is God's appointment to moralize and Christianize
the world. In all this is seen the greatness of his
kingdom, but greater still is the SAVING POWER OF
JESUS and the efficacy of his shed blood in the salvation of man from sin, darkness and eternal despair; for God will save all who will come to him
as directed by Jesus.

When we contemplate eternal separation from
God, unless redeemed, and behold in Jesus our
only possible hope for escape, we must recognize
HIS GREATNESS. His love is great, too much so for
the dull comprehension of sinful man; his sympathy is great; behold his compassion as he ago-
nizes in the garden ; see him upon the cross and

hear him petition God in behalf of his enemies: "Forgive them, Father, for they know not what they do." When the sun was veiled and the earth shook, the centurion said: "Surely this was the Son of God." Yes, my friend, this one is "The only begotten of God," his dear and well-beloved Son, "Hear ye him." He is a "great" physician; will you not send for him and be healed of your malady and live forever? He is a true friend; he has said I will never forsake you. He is a wise counselor; you can never stray if you follow his instruction. He is a "GREAT" captain; he will lead you safely through life's conflicts and bring you off a conqueror at the end of the journey of life. He is the very and eternal King, and will give to you a royal place in his father's house if you will trust him and obey his orders. He says, "Come unto me, and I will give you rest," and "Blessed are they that do his commandments, that they may have a right to the tree of life and may enter through the gates into the city." "The Spirit and the Bride say, Come, and whosoever will, let him come and take of the water of life freely." Let no one say, I cannot come, for Jesus says you may if you will. Come, alien sinner, confess his divinity, acknowledge his sovereignty and obey him *now*, and all through life, and he will be with thee, even in death. There will be no darkness hanging over the tomb, for Jesus went before and lighted up the way, bringing life and immortality to light. Yes, the angel's promise to Mary was fulfilled. "The holy progeny was the Son of God, and of his kingdom there is no end."

BIOGRAPHICAL SKETCH OF EVANGELIST J. V. COOMBS.

J. V. COOMBS was born in Boone County, Ind., in the year 1849. His early life was spent on a farm, learning those lessons of self-dependence which are so essentially necessary to one's success iu life. Being left fatherless at the age of 18 months, he never knew a father's love and guiding care; and, as a natural consequence, grew to manhood with very little education. But possessing, as he does, an indomitable will, there were no obstacles that could offer him more than momentary resistance, so step by step he ascended the hill of knowledge. In the fall of 1875 he entered Butler University, Irvington, Ind., and entered at once upon a classical course of study. That fall the writer also entered the same college. Being poor, I sought an opportunity of boarding myself, in other words, baching it. I was informed that a young man was there desiring some one with whom he could unite his temporal interests for the same purpose. I was taken into the presence of a young man whom they introduced as J. V. Coombs, the celebrated evangelist and lecturer in embryo. We had soon entered into an agree-

J. V. COOMBS.

ment. I was to do the cooking and dish-washing, (sometimes I broke a part of the contract, because I dislike to wash dishes, but prefer to *lick* them). He was to carry the wood and water and run errands. We fitted up our room with second-hand goods, and few at that. Our provisions consisted of soup-bones (which we would boil as long as they would make eyes on the water), crackers, fried liver and molasses. Sometimes we had pepper-sauce for dessert. So scant was our living that it only cost, both of us, $9 during three months. We had a little given us occasionally by dear friends. These were some of the experiences of life for which we have both been thankful all along our way. Bro. Coombs was a good student, and, applying himself closely to his books, made rapid progress. That year he began preaching, and I have known him to walk many miles, preach in the morning, and then walk back, that he might be there to answer to the roll-call in the chapel. For all his preaching he received almost nothing, but this proved no discouragement to him; he was not preaching for money, but from love to God, and sympathy with sinful humanity. Therefore, with Paul, he could say, "Necessity is laid upon me," and "woe is me if I preach not the gospel." In this way he spent three years at Butler University. He then went to Eureka, Ill., where he spent one year, and in 1877 he graduated from the

3

Indiana Normal School.   In 1882 he graduated in
the Classical Department from Chicago University.
He served as President of colleges up to 1886,
when he entered the lecture field, in which he
achieved great notoriety. Having heard his lecture
on "Strange Things and Funny People," I regard
it the equal to any I ever heard from the most
celebrated lecturers in the land. During the two
years he was in the lecture field he visited and
spoke in forty States and Territories. In 1888 he
entered the field as an evangelist, and here his
greatest work has been accomplished. Thousands
have been added under his ministry. He has held
many meetings in which the additions numbered
from 50 to over 200. In the last six months that
he was in the field there were 703 added to the
churches for which he held meetings.

In December 24, 1888, he was married to Miss
Allie Marlatt, an accomplished lady and fine
singer. She accompanied him on his lecture tours,
and has been a helper to him in his evangelistic
efforts. To them has been born one child, a little
girl, now 18 months old.   Bro. Coombs is quite a
musician, and is the author of a song book entitled
"The Gospel Call." This book has had a wonderful sale in the West. Growing tired, as every
man does who loves his home and family, of being
always among strangers and away from his loved
ones, he gave up evangelistic work and entered
upon the duties of a pastor with the church at

Madison, Indiana, where he held a great meeting with more than 200 additions. His work there has been very successful. The house has been made almost new, and all departments of church work have been pushed forward with an enthusiasm begotten of his energy and born of his zeal. His services are in demand all over the land, and he now has over one hundred calls which he cannot accept.

> " Lives of great men all remind us
>   We can make our lives sublime,
> And, departing, leave behind us
>   Footprints on the sands of time;

> " Footprints, that perhaps another,
>   Sailing o'er life's solemn main,
> A forlorn and ship-wrecked brother,
>   Seeing, shall take heart again."

Truly such lives are a benediction sent of God upon the world, to lead it up into higher realms of mental and moral enjoyment. May J. V. Coombs live to a ripe old age, and go through life scattering the sunshine of God's gracious love upon multitudes, is the earnest prayer of his friend, schoolmate and brother in Christ.

H. C. PATTERSON.

WHAT THE CHRISTIAN CHURCH TEACHES;
OR, OUR PLEA.

BY J. V. COOMBS.

MAN, pendulum like, swings from extreme to extreme. We see this tendency in the individual with his hobbies, and trace it in the masses with their ever-varying and unreliable public opinion. We behold this tendency in the rise and fall of religious bodies, in their onward sweep across the centuries. In religion we are likely to overlook the points of agreement in our anxiety to find wherein we differ. Most of the cardinal points of Christianity are held in common by religious bodies. In this sermon I desire to state what we believe as a people. I shall not attempt to discuss these points, but try and state clearly our distinctive peculiarities. We desire to be called Christians, and the church to which we belong to be known as the Church of Christ, or the Christian Church.

The following are some of our distinctive features:

DIVISION OF THE BIBLE.

We believe that the Old and the New Testaments are both the inspired word of God; but that the New Testament is the exclusive book of authority. Everything that is necessary for the unconverted to do in order to become a Christian, and everything that is necessary for the Christian to do in order to go to heaven is found in the New Testament. The Jews were governed by the Law; we by the Gospel. There is no command binding upon us that is not found in the New Testament.

The old law was nailed to the cross. Col. 2 : 14. Our country was once governed by the articles of confederation, but the constitution supersedes these articles, and they now possess no binding force. There are laws now on the statute books of Illinois that are similar to some of the Colonial laws of Pennsylvania; but these laws are binding, not because they are found in the dead law of Pennsylvania, but because they are re-enacted into the new law of Illinois.

Commandments once found in the Old Testament are now found in the New; but they are binding upon us, not because they are found in the Old, but because they are re-enacted in the New.

NO CREED BUT THE BIBLE.

We believe that all human creeds and confessions of faith are wrong and engender strife. All creeds have come out of controversy. We claim that the Bible *alone* is sufficient for our rule of faith and practice. If the creed contains more than is in the Bible, it contains too much; if it contains less than is in the Bible, it does not contain enough; if it contains just what is in the Bible, it is entirely unnecessary. We go to the Bible for our authority in church government, as well as to learn the plan of salvation. Whatever the Bible commands us to do, those things we do; what the Bible forbids, from those things we refrain; where the Bible is silent, freedom of opinion. Tó make a creed is to belittle the Bible. Hundreds of persons have subscribed their names to creeds which they never believed. We rejoice to-day to see the human creeds falling. May God help us take the Bible as our guide.

THE NAME.

We teach that the children of God should be known simply as Christians, and that the church should be called the Church of Christ. Christ said: "Upon this rock I will build my church." This church, not established when Christ spoke, was to be Christ's Church. When we use the phrase "of Christ" we have used a second class element. We can change that second class element to a first class and say "Christian;" hence, the "Church of Christ" and "Christian Church" are synonyms.

There is only one true church, and that is the Church of Christ. It is His church, and should be called the Church of Christ. The followers of Christ should be called Christians. Luke says: "The disciples were first called Christians at Antioch." Peter says: "If any man suffer as a Christian, let him not be ashamed, but let him glorify God on this behalf." 1 Peter 4 : 16. The new version renders it "in this name." That is, glorify God in the name *Christian*. By obeying Christ one becomes simply a Christian. A few days ago Mr. Talmage immersed a man in the River Jordan. No denomination was responsible for it, and hence the man did not belong to any denomination. He was a Christian. Peter makes salvation depend upon a name. Acts 4 : 12. When men say there is nothing in a name, they do not mean it. Should a preacher baptize a candidate in the name of Paul, Luther, or Calvin, it would not be valid baptism. Names are sacred. What would we think of a preacher who would baptize in the name of Beelzebub? If we say to a Methodist brother, "You are not a Baptist," "you are not an Advent," "you are not a Congregationalist," "you are not a Mormon," "you are not a Catholic," to each of which he will pleasantly say "no." But you say, "You are not a Christian," he will quickly resent it. There is something in a name. Christ is the Bridegroom. The church is the Bride. The Bride should wear the name of the Bridegroom.

A lady has no right to wear the name of her betrothed until the marriage ceremony is performed. For her to attempt to live with him or wear his name before marriage would be very objectionable and sinful. But for her to refuse to wear his name after marriage would be an insult. No one has the right to wear the name "Christian" until he is married to Christ by complying to the forms of law. Equally certain is it, that it is an insult to Christ for us to wear any party name after we have complied with the terms of the gospel. All party names are sinful. Hear Paul, 1 Cor. 1 : 12, 13. Hear Luther: "Do not call yourselves Lutherans, but call yourselves Christians." Hear Wesley: "I would to God all party names were forgotten." Hear Campbell: "Abandon all party names and take the name Christian." We dishonor Christ when we accept the name Methodist, Campbellite, Lutheran, etc. We positively reject all party names. We desire to be called simply Christians. Not the only Christians, but Christians only.

BAPTISM.

We are peculiar in reference to baptism.

1. *As to the subject*, we say, "Penitent believers only are proper subjects of baptism." Baptism without repentance is a mockery. A man

might be baptized twenty times without faith, and it would do him no good. Faith and repentance must come first. Baptism alone will save no one. Hence we say, that if you were baptized before you were old enough to believe, you have never received Christian baptism. Hence, we reject infant baptism as unscriptural. When the child dies it goes to heaven. It needs no baptism.

2. *As to the action*, we teach that Christian baptism is the immersion of a penitent believer in the name of the Father, the Son, and the Holy Spirit. That this immersion in water is Christian baptism, and this only. We reject the idea that there is now such a thing as "Holy Spirit baptism." The baptism of the Holy Spirit gave the persons receiving it the power to speak with tongues. It was a miraculous gift. There are only two instances of the baptism of the Holy Spirit recorded in the Bible: On the day of Pentecost and at the home of Cornelius. The baptism of the Holy Spirit passed away after the days of miracles. The baptism of the Holy Spirit was a promise; the baptism of water a command. Christ alone could baptize with the Holy Spirit; men are to baptize penitent believers in water. We claim immersion to be the only action of baptism for these reasons:

1. The word *baptizo*, from which comes our word baptize, never meant *sprinkle* or *pour*.

2. In the Greek literature we find the word

used 230 times, and out of these 230 times it is
never used in the sense of *sprinkle* or *pour*, but
always dip, immerse, plunge or a kindred meaning.

3.   In no Greek dictionary, in any college in
America or Europe, is the word ever defined *sprinkle.* Not one Greek scholar in the world dares
translate the word *sprinkle.*

4.   The Greek Church, with its 85,000,000 members, practices nothing but immersion. This is
not the evidence of billions of men, but of billions
of Greeks, who knew their language and needed
no translator. Billions have been *immersed*, but
not one Greek has been *sprinkled.*

5.   Out of thirty-seven early translators of the
Bible, all translate *baptizo* immerse, dip or plunge,
except three; one of these translates it *wash.* Not
one ever gave *sprinkle* or *pour* as a meaning of the
word.

6.   Christ and the apostles used the word eighty
times. Would they use a word with three meanings, and never explain these meanings ?

7.   All scriptural references point to immersion.

a.   Jesus was baptized in Jordan. Mark 1 : 9.

b.   John baptized in Enon, because there was
much water.

c.   Read Acts 8 : 38, 39 : "And they went down,
both into the water, both Philip and the eunuch,
and he baptized him."

d.   In referring to baptism, Christ says : " Except a man be born of water and of the Spirit, he cannot enter into the kingdom of God." John 3 : 5. *Born of water* is *baptism.* Immersion does represent a *birth.* *Sprinkling* does not.

e. Paul calls baptism a *burial:* "Therefore we are buried with him by baptism." Rom. 6 : 4. Immersion represents a burial. *Sprinkling* does not.

f. All the scholars, historians and commentators of any note have admitted that the primitive practice of the church was immersion.

No one ever acknowledged sprinkling or pouring to be valid baptism prior to 1311. Invalids and sick people were sprinkled, but if they recovered, immersion was demanded. In 1311 the Romish Church claimed the right to *change* the ordinance from *immersion* to *sprinkling.* This change was made, not on scriptural grounds, but on the infallibility of the Pope, who said the church had a right to change the ordinance of God.

The Catholic Church to-day does not claim that the Bible sanctions *sprinkling.* Calvin admits the primitive practice was immersion, that Christ and all that were baptized by the apostles were immersed. Yet he claims the church can change an ordinance.

HOLY SPIRIT.

We believe that the Holy Spirit operates in conversion, but not independent of the word of God. We teach that *faith* comes by hearing, and hearing by the word of God. The Spirit speaks to us through the Bible. We hear and obey. " The Spirit beareth witness with our spirit that we are the children of God." Rom. 8: 16. The proposition to be proven is that you are a child of God. There are two witnesses: "The Spirit of God and your own spirit. The Spirit says you must believe." Mark 16: 15, 16. You say, I do believe. Then your spirit and the Spirit of God testify to the same thing, and that far you are in favor with God. If you say, " I do not believe," then the case is decided against you. The Spirit says you must repent. (Acts 2: 38.) Your spirit says, " I have repented." Then both spirits testify to the same, and you are so far acceptable to God. The Spirit says, " You must be baptized." You say, " I have been baptized." Then your spirit or consciousness and the Spirit of God agree, and you are a Christian. The Spirit says you must live a pious life. Your spirit says, " I am living a Christian life." Then you are a child of God. Our whole plea may be summed up as follows :

1. The union of all God's people upon the Bible.

2. Rational plan of salvation.

WE CANNOT BE WRONG.

The denominations *may* be right. They may be wrong. We are right, and *cannot* be wrong. It *may* be right to make a human creed. It *may* be wrong. We take the Bible as our rule of faith and practice, hence *cannot* be wrong. Human names *may* be right, or they *may* be wrong. All agree it is right to be called Christian. We can not be wrong in wearing that name. If you have a doubt, *you*, and not *God*, are responsible for that doubt. Sprinkling may be right (for argument's sake), or it may be wrong. All admit immersion is valid baptism. We are right and can not be wrong in practicing only immersion. If you doubt your baptism, you can remove that doubt by being immersed, for all accept immersion. Not long ago, while in California, an old lady demanded immersion. She had been sprinkled thirty years before. When she came up out of the water she said, "Now I *know* I am right." If you were baptized when you were an infant, your spirit does not testify to this act. You have only one witness, hence the case is against you. Be on the safe side.

OUR STRENGTH.

The membership of the Christian Church is above 1,000,000 people. We have about 6,000 churches, 5,000 preachers, 40 universities and colleges, 30 church papers, 20 publishing houses and over 100 missionaries, with foreign missions in India, China, Turkey, Japan and the West Indies. Our membership is rapidly increasing in England, Australia and Canada.

We have numbered in our ranks some of the clearest thinkers of the age, among whom may be mentioned Timothy Coop of England, the great philanthropist; James A. Garfield, President of the United States; Judge Jerry S. Black, Secretary of State; Walter Scott, Barton Stone, Alexander Campbell, and many governors and congressmen. In some States we have a larger adult membership than any other church.

No religious movement has increased so rapidly as this current reformation. Fifty years after Wesley started his movement he had 80,000 followers. In the same length of time we numbered 800,000 communicants. In other words, we have increased ten times faster than the Methodists. At the same rate of increase by the time we are as old as the Methodist brethren, we will number 40,000,000 people. We firmly believe that within fifty years 40,000,000 people will wear no name but Christian, and have no rule of faith and practice except the Bible. Creeds and Confessions are falling and the Bible is rapidly becoming the book of authority.

JESUS THE CHRIST.

We teach that Jesus is the Christ, the Son of God; that he is the Savior of the world. That to him *all* authority is given. He is our Lord, King, Savior, Advocate, Good Shepherd, the Light, the Truth, the Way. "Christ is all, and in all." (Col.

3 : 11). The only test of Christian fellowship is faith in Jesus. He is our personal Savior.

We live in an age of intense intellectual activity. The railroad, the steamboat, the printing-press, the mariner's compass, the telegram and cablegram, annihilating time, space and resistance have made the orient the neighbor of the occident.

Law, medicine and theology have been put into the crucible of science, and much dross has been found.

The old calomel doctor, with his saddle-bags and jug of whisky, has been relegated to the past. The leading surgeon of fifty years ago would not be trusted to-day to wrap up the sore finger of an infant. The boisterous lawyer who shed elocutionary tears by the persuasive influence of red pepper, has gone to keep company with the quack doctor. Old theologies have been put into the retort, and have been exploded. Science solves the laws of gravitation, marshals worlds into order, clears up the sun's spots, invades the realms of the king of day, mounts upon wings, cuts her way through the starry zodiac, and gives us glimpses of the world beyond. Thoughts, not bullets, rule the world. This is an age of research, investigation and speculation. Traditions, superstitions and customs hold no authority over us. Old opinions are cast aside as so much rubbish. Under the searching eye of criticism, fables and things once held sacred are hustled out of sight. The question is not, *What did our fathers* believe ? but, *Are these things true?*

He who clings to a falsehood, because his father believed it to be true, stabs his own convictions, slaps his conscience in the face, and bids it keep its mouth shut. Truth and fact will live, but falsehood and tradition must go whirling in the blast.

But under this severe criticism Christianity still stands. Will it stand in the future? The infidel and the skeptic, the higher critic and the lower sensualist, the free-thinker and free-lover, say that Christianity must go. The philosopher and the Christian say Christianity will stand.

To-day Christ is more prominent in history, art, and the hearts of men than at any other period in the world's history. An infidel said a few years ago, " In fifty years the influence of Jesus Christ will be erased from the earth." He who attempts to erase Christ from history and art has on his hands a large contract and very limited capital.

Should you take a red pencil and run a line through every sentence in history and literature that refers to Christ, you would have the reddest books ever seen. Should you take your scissors and cut out all that refers to Christianity, you would have such ragged books that not one could be read. Why, even the arithmetics would be valueless, for you would continually meet with 1840, 1865, etc., which mean in the year of our Lord. Every letter that is written confesses Christ.

1800 years ago a child was born in the village of Bethlehem. As they beheld the child lying in a manger, no one dreamed that his influence would turn the world upside down.

The history of men is written after they die. The history of Christ was written five hundred years before he was born. His history began four thousand years before he was born. Moses, David, Isaiah and Daniel wrote parts of his history. The place of his birth, the time when he was born, the cruel treatment, his trial, the manner of his death, and the words he uttered while dying on the cross, were all read of ¡all men long before Jesus appeared unto the shepherds.

To blot Jesus out of history, you would be compelled to destroy all prophecy and history written before he was born. Suppose ten bowmen with a quiver of ten arrows each, were to stand at different stations and shoot their ten arrows out into the darkness, endeavoring to hit the target. It is inky blackness, and they know not where the target is. Bowman No. 1 stands 1,500 yards from the target. He sends his ten arrows forward into the inky blackness. No. 2 advances and shoots his ten arrows from a station 1,000 yards from the bull's eye. Then comes No. 3 and sends his ten arrows out into the darkness 800 yards from the target. No. 4 from a station 600 yards, and No. 5 400 yards, sends his arrows forward. They call for lights, and all fifty are found in the center of

4

the target. Under these circumstances you would conclude that these arrows were directed by an Almighty hand.

Come to this prophetic history, and there are 500 prophetic arrows centered in Christ. Moses stands 1,500 years from Christ and sends his prophetic arrows forward. Then come David, Isaiah, Daniel and Malachi, and they send their prophetic arrows out into the future which is inky blackness. Call for lights, and you will find all 500 arrows in the center, fulfilled in Jesus Christ. You will necessarily conclude that the hand of God directed these arrows. Remember that these prophecies were upon the walls of the Jewish synagogues and read of all men, Jew, Greek and Gentile, five hundred years before Jesus walked the shores of Galilee. See Deut. 28th and 29th chapters. In Psalm 22, David, 1,000 years before Christ died, used the words Jesus uttered upon the cross.

Then to destroy the influence of Christ on earth, the infidel will be compelled to burn all the Bibles on the face of the earth. Yonder is one far up in the mountains in a ranchman's hut. Climb up and get it. That lonely missionary in India has the old Book. When all are gathered up, let the infidel set them on fire. Black demons laugh, and say that the history of Christ is gone.

Not true. There are commentaries, biographies, and histories. Every verse of the New Testament, except eleven, can be found in the writings of three of the early writers. Send out the hosts of Bible-haters, let them gather all the histories, commentaries, sermon books and Bible works, pile them up two miles high and set them on fire. As the flames leap to the clouds, the black devils will ha! ha! and the despisers of Jesus will say: "Now all trace of Christ is gone." Not true. Look on yonder church. There over the door see written, "Church of Christ." Go inside of the houses of worship, and on walls and windows we see "Jesus." Go to art rooms. Painting and architecture pay tribute to this name that is above all other names. Accumulate all these houses and pictures, and pile them five miles high. Let infidels laugh as the flames shoot toward the stars, but yet the name of Jesus has not been erased from the earth. Look four hundred feet high on that monument; scaffold up, and cut off the name. Yet his name is not gone. See the destroyer of Christianity marching to the graveyard. The leader of the host orders the name Jesus to be chiseled off the grave-stones.

Yonder in a bunch of briers is a little tomb-stone; on it is written "In the arms of Jesus." The champion of infidelity, with chisel and mallet, crawls under the briers, and with fiendish delight hammers off the inscription. With his hands bleeding and his face flushed with delight, he crawls from the briers only to see a wagon bringing a number of grave-stones, to place at the graves of Christians. And while he was under the briers, five hundred sculptors have carved the name Jesus on one thousand monuments. But suppose that all books, paintings and monuments were destroyed, would that destroy Christianity? No. Christ is in the hearts of God's people. The Bible is in the minds of Christians. Yonder is a girl in New York that can repeat every verse in the New Testament. In a few days the Bible would be put together again, and Christianity would still sway the world.

Sinners, this same Jesus that fills all history and art will come into your heart if you will open it to him. Do you believe his word? He says to you, "Come, for all things are now ready."

A son quarreled with his father, and left the old home. Years passed, when the old father wrote his son: "My son, come home. I will give you the old mansion on the hill. Mother and I want you to come. The past is all forgiven. You can have all we possess if you will return. Enclosed find my check for $200. I will make it possible for you to come. Delay not." The son, who had become a poor, drunken wretch, was sitting in the shadow of a western hotel when the letter reached him. As he opened the letter, the check dropped into his hand. As he read the letter tears coursed their way down his cheeks. When the letter was finished he said: "Oh, I want to be at home. I want to see father, but I do not feel like he wants me. If I knew he wanted me I would go at once. True, here is the money. He has made it possible, and says, Come; yet I will go and ask my friends to write father, praying that he will let me come." So he goes to five friends. Each one writes a long petition to the father, asking him to let the son come home. Then the son wrote: "Father, I received your letter and the money. You say, Come home? Father, I do not know that you want me to come. I pray you, let me come."

A large letter in a few days reaches the father. With trembling hand he opens the letter. Here are five petitions from five men, praying to the old father to let his son come home. Then the letter from the son is read, after which the father says to his wife: "Mother, John is either insane, or else he is mocking our word. We asked him to come. We made it possible for him to come, and yet he prays for us to let him come. What else can I do? He does not believe my word."

This is a fair illustration of many persons to-day, who are desirous of becoming Christians. Instead of taking Jesus at his word, and coming at once, they are praying for God to let them come, and even get others to pray for them. Come now. If you believe God's word, come. Accept Jesus and live, reject him and die. He is all and in all.

If you reject him, there is no other sacrifice for

you. A man is sentenced to be hung. The governor desires to pardon him. He sends the pardon, but the convicted man tears it up. The governor then sends his son with the pardon. The convicted man kills the messenger, and says that if he gets out he will kill the governor. Now, you say, the man must die. There is no more sacrifice. The Father sent his Son here to save sinners. If you reject the pardon, there remains no other sacrifice.

MORGAN MORGANS.

MORGAN MORGANS.

THE subject of this sketch was born in Decatur Co., Ind., Jan. 18, 1851. He is of Welsh extraction, hence the peculiarities of the name. His father and mother are living near Pineville, Mo. To them were born six children, three boys and three girls.

His father was a farmer, and in the fall of 1866 moved from Randolph Co., Ind., to Pineville, McDonald Co., Mo. At this time southwest Missouri was, comparatively, a new country, and torn up by the ravages of the civil war. Schools were scarce, and young Morgans had to work hard on the farm, helping to clear away the brush and put in cultivation two farms, one of which he rented, and the other he bought. He is proud of his rail-splitting record, which, in all probability, is not second to that of Mr. Lincoln. Day after day, and year after year, his whole time was occupied in chopping and grubbing, so that his early education was much neglected. From a child he loved books, and after working hard all day would often sit up and read till midnight by the light of a pine fire.

At the age of 16 (September, 1867) he joined the M. E. Church. His mother was a member of that

church, and was a devoted Christian. His father
at that time was not a member of any church, but
a strictly moral and upright man. He often says
he is greatly indebted to the counsels of his father
and the religious training of his mother for the
position he now occupies. Although his parents
were poor in this world's goods, and were unable
to do anything for him by way of an education,
yet from them he received a legacy far greater
than gold and silver. At the age of 17 young
Morgans joined the Christian Church, under the
preaching of Henry Buckmaster, at Pineville, Mo.,
and on the 20th day of March, 1868, he was buried
with Christ by baptism in the Cowskin river.
Naturally of a religious turn of mind, young Morgans turned his attention to a careful study of the
Holy Scriptures, with a view to preaching the
gospel. In April, 1869, he began preaching. During three years he continued to till the soil and to
preach of Lord's days. From that time he has
been actively engaged in the Master's work. He
has lived in southwest Missouri ever since before
he was 16 years old.

On the 3rd day of July, 1870, he was married to
Mrs. Emma Adams, a widow with two children.
God has blessed their happy union with five children. Sister Morgans is a very domestic lady,
and ever ready to make any sacrifices that her
husband may continue in the evangelistic field,
for which he is so well adapted. To her, as well

as to him, belongs much of the credit for the success that has accompanied his untiring efforts. She labored through poverty and loneliness in assisting her husband in obtaining an education. Heaven alone knows the sacrifices she has made. She is an affectionate wife and devoted mother.

After Bro. Morgans was married he attended school at Newtonia, Mo., where he began the study of Latin and other higher branches. After teaching for some time he entered Drury College, Springfield, Mo., where he continued only a short time. Owing to a lack of means he could not complete his college course, which he has ever since regretted. He has always been a hard student, and improved every opportunity, and so closely applied himself to books that he possesses a fairly good education. Knowing the man and all the facts as I do, I unhesitatingly say that he deserves as much credit for what he has done as any other individual within my knowledge.

He has traveled extensively, not only in this country, but in Europe, Egypt and Palestine. In one year he traveled in twenty-two different States, preaching and lecturing, visiting many of the largest cities in the United States. Bro. M. has quite a reputation as a debater, having met quite a number of representative men of the Soul-sleepers, Adventists, Cumberland Presbyterians, Universalists and Baptists. His last discussion was with the Baptist champion, J. B. Moody, D. D., LL. D.

The cause of Christ has never suffered in the hands of Bro. Morgans.

As an evangelist he has a national reputation, and is very successful. During the past twelve years he has done nothing else but evangelize, except one year in which he was employed as one of the editors and proprietors of *The Faithful Witness*, published at Topeka, Kan. His labors have been principally confined to Missouri, Illinois, Kansas, Iowa, Nebraska and Arkansas. He labored two years under the S. W. Missouri district Board, during which time he organized a number of churches which are now the strongest churches in the district. During 1891 he was in the employ of the Western Pennsylvania Mission Board. Of that work he wrote: "It was one of the most pleasant and successful of my life." While he has held several meetings with more than 100 additions, he does not gather in converts as rapidly as some. Yet his work is of a permanent character, and he prefers to follow the scriptural injunction, "Take heed how ye build," that it may not be said of him that he built "wood, hay and stubble." His preaching, while sufficiently learned and profound to interest the most intelligent and critical, is sufficiently plain and simple for the unlearned. There is something about his preaching that never fails to draw large audiences, which listen with almost breathless silence. He is not, in any sense, a sensationalist, but depends

upon the power of the gospel. He is not an orator
in the strict sense of the word, yet he is often so
called. He has a smooth, strong voice; his articu-
lation is distinct and clear; he is very deliberate,
but forcible, in his delivery. He is a lover of
poetry, and quotes as much as any man I ever
heard. He shuns not to declare the whole counsel
of God, but handles vigorously all doctrinal subjects in a gentlemanly manner, and thus attracts,
instead of repelling, those whose tenets of faith
he feels it his duty to antagonize. He is very
sociable and companionable, and having been
intimately associated with him during all our
travels in the Old World, I pronounce him a
prince among men. He makes few enemies, but
many friends, and as a result he is nearly always
recalled again and again to the same place. He is
six feet tall, weighs 160 lbs., has large blue eyes,
large Roman nose, brown hair, where any can be
found, and long beard sprinkled with grey. His
daughter, Miss Nora, who received her musical
education in St. Louis, accompanies him and
assists in the song service. She is a beautiful
and charming young lady, ever ready to do any
thing she can for her Savior. Having been her pastor, I speak knowingly. She has a clear, sweet
voice, and her solos never fail to please. All
things considered, I think Bro. Morgans the equal
of any of our evangelists.

H. C. PATTERSON.

CHRIST THE BASIS OF UNIVERSAL BROTHERHOOD.

MORGAN MORGANS.

"When Jesus came into the coasts of Cæsarea Philippi, he asked his disciples, saying, *Whom do men say that I, the Son man, am?* And they said, Some say that thou art John the Baptist; some, Elias; and others, Jeremias, or one of the prophets. He said unto them, *But whom say ye that I am?* Simon Peter answered and said, Thou art the Christ, the Son of the living God."—Matt. 16: 13-16.

IN this great and smaller catechism are to be found *two* questions, *two* answers, and *two* principles involved. The answer to the first question represents Christ only *as a man;* the answer to the second question represents him as the Son of God. The principle involved in the first is simply *human,* while the principle involved in the second is *Divine.* Upon the one all human institutions rest; on the other all divine organizations are founded. From this point two lines diverge, which, like a parabolic curve, never meet. The lines are as far apart as the heaven and the earth, as the sequel of this discourse will plainly show.

I. "Whom do *men* say that I, the Son of man, am ?"

1. Human conception of Christ. That is, he is only a man.

(1) What the common people say of Christ.

a. Some of them said he was John the Baptist. They saw a similarity between the plain preaching of John and the withering rebukes of the Son of man.

b. Some said he was Elias, or Elijah. They doubtless saw a similarity between the miracles of the old prophet and those of Christ. Hence, this opinion.

c. Others said he was Jeremias, or one of the prophets. Jeremiah was the weeping prophet, and often they saw this distinguished person weeping, hence this answer.

(2) What the Pharisees say of Christ.

"While the Pharisees were gathered together, Jesus asked them, saying, What think ye of Christ? whose son is he? They say unto him, The son of David. He saith unto them, How then doth David in spirit call him Lord, saying, The Lord said unto my Lord, Sit thou on my right hand, till I make thine enemies thy footstool? And no man was able to answer him a word; neither durst any man, from that day forth, ask him any more questions." Matt. 22 : 41-46.

These self-righteous Pharisees were not willing to acknowledge Christ to be God's Son. They were perfectly willing, however, to grant that he was David's son. They looked upon him as only a man. They were willing to acknowledge that he was David's son, and therefore the rightful heir to the Davidic throne. But he was more than that.

He is the son of two kings, heir to two thrones, and therefore divine.

a. In Luke 3 : 23 Christ is called the "son of Joseph," legally or by reputation. Hence Matthew, writing for the Hebrews, traces his genealogy through Joseph, his supposed father.

b. In Rom. 1 : 3 Christ is called the son of David according to the flesh. So we find Luke tracing his genealogy through Heli, the father of Mary, the mother of Jesus. This view sets aside all supposed contradictions between Matthew and Luke on Christ's genealogy.

c. In Rom. 1 : 4 Jesus is called the Son of God according to the Spirit of holiness by the resurrection from the dead. He has a Divine as well as a human nature. God is the father of his spirit, as David was of his flesh. John, in the first chapter, gives the genealogy of his spirit as truly as Matthew and Luke do of his flesh. As God has (John 1 : 14) only one Son in the universe in the sense in which Christ is his Son, there is but one link in this chain of genealogy of Spirit which connects him with the eternal Father. The expression, "Only begotten Son," differentiates Christ from all other sons. The difference is not a measure, but nature difference. Not in degree, but in essence. John's genealogy of the Spirit of Christ is given in these words: "In the beginning was the Word, and the Word was with God, and the Word was God." This Divine Logos was mani-

fest in the flesh. Therefore he was in the beginning with the Father, and by him all things were
created.

(3) The infidel conception of Christ.

a. Some, like Strauss, the great German exe-
gete, regard the immaculate and miraculous conception and birth of Christ as only a myth, like
the fanciful idea that Romulus was born of Rhea
Silvia and the god Mars.

b. Some, like Tom Paine, look upon Christ as
being an impostor.

c. Some, in fact all intelligent infidels at the
present day, look upon Christ not only as having
actually lived upon this earth, but as being the
greatest and best man the world has ever produced. They are willing to place him far above
Moses, Job, Socrates or the Greek sages. But
their highest conception of him, however, is that
he is only a man. Mr. Ingersoll himself, the great
apostle of modern infidelity, is constrained to say:
"I wish I could have lived in the days of Jesus
Christ, and could have mingled my tears with the
tears of him who was a man of sorrows and ac-
quainted with grief, and could have sat at the feet
of the greatest teacher the world has ever known."

2. A wrong principle involved—force.

(1) This principle is seen in the vegetable kingdom.

a. Weeds choke out the vegetables in our gar-
dens. Here we see, not the "survival of the *fittest*,"

but the survival of the *strongest;* for often the fittest must perish.

b.   Often the grain in our fields must give place to briers, thorns and thistles.

c.   The giant oak of the forest, as he lifts up his head, hoary with age, above all the neighboring trees of the forest, is an example of this principle of force everywhere seen in nature.

(2) This same principle is more clearly seen, and more largely developed, in the animal kingdom.

a.   The whale, shark and other large marine animals by force, implanted in the very instincts of their natures, live upon the smaller animals of the great deep.

b.   The eagle, soaring far above all the rest of the feathered tribes of the air, his keen eye guiding the instinct of his nature, darts down upon the victims of his prey and overpowers them.

c.   The king of beasts in the jungles of Asia or Africa, as he leaps from his lair and seizes the victim of his power, is a demonstration of animal force.

(3) Man, guided only by nature, adopts the brute principle of force that might makes right.

a.   The cannibalism of the heathen, without the revelation of God to guide them, is a demonstration of this brute principle, largely developed.

b.   The expulsion of the red man from his own native home by the white man by mere force, is an example of this heathen principle more largely developed than in the lower animals.

c. The clanking of the chains that bound the captive Jews as they were carried from their homes and sold in all nations of the world as slaves, echoes the shame and folly of Rome to the civilized and Christianized nations of to-day.

3. Building on this principle.

(1) All monopolies or powers which are calculated to degrade man are built upon this foundation—a foundation of sand.

a. The political powers of earth which are reaching out for the conquest of other and weaker powers are based on this false principle.

b. The money power, which crushes everything before it as a mighty avalanche in the Alps, is a demonstration of the hog nature in man.

c. The whisky power, which defies God and man, rests on a foundation, the corner-stone of which was laid by the devil himself. This trinity of powers go hand in hand. The principle which actuates the politician who buys a seat in Congress, and then legalizes the selling of intoxicants which robs poor, helpless women and children of the necessaries of life, and sends 60,000 persons every year to premature graves, is conceived in sin and born in iniquity, and cradled in the hands of demons.

(2) All false systems of religion are built on this foundation.

5

a. Paganism, which, in the ten great persecutions, tried to crush out Christianity, and drove Christians to the caves and dens of the earth, killing millions of them, crumbled on its foundation of sand and fell, never to rise again. Under the second great persecution Domitian ordered the total extinction of the whole lineage of David, Jew and Christian, throughout the Roman empire.

b. If Mohammed, the false prophet, had depended upon the same power for the propagation of his religion that Jesus Christ did for his, Mohammedanism would not have been known to-day. The Koran teaches, as we learn from Gibbon, vol. 9, p. 256: "The sword is the key to heaven or hell. A drop of blood shed in the cause of God, a night spent in arms, is of more avail than two months of fasting and prayer. Whosoever falls in battle, his sins are forgiven him in the day of judgment. His wounds shall be resplendent as vermilion, odoriferous as musk, and the loss of his limbs shall be supplanted by the wings of angels and cherubim."

c. How vastly different the religion of the meek and lowly Nazarene and that of the pretentious Pope of Rome. Temporal power is the foundation of this great false system of religion. It is evident from the Word of God that the Babylon of John, the man of sin of Paul, and the empire of the youngest horn of Daniel's sea monster all refer to Papal Rome, who is drunk with the blood of

50,000,000 of martyrs. When the Pope of Rome put his foot on the neck of the king of Germany, it showed the spirit of Catholicism. Only the loss of temporal power prevents him doing the same to-day. The same spirit of intolerance and persecution still exists and manifests itself occasionally yet.

(3) Human governments are built up by sheer force.

a. Alexander the great climbed the dizzy heights of ambition and dipped his chaplets in the heart's blood of countless thousands, and wept for more worlds to conquer.

b. Cæsar conquered 800 cities, dyeing his garments in the blood of a million of his foes.

c. Napoleon, the greatest military chieftain the world has ever known, the conqueror of fifty great battles, whose mandates kings and popes obeyed, built up an empire by force, and by force it went down forever.

This same great conqueror said, as he was chained to the Rock of St. Helena ready to be put to death by the English Oligarchy: "Alexander, Cæsar, Charlemagne and myself founded empires. But upon what did we rest the creations of our own genius? Upon *force*. Jesus Christ alone founded his empire on *love*, and at this hour millions of men would die for him.

"What an abyss between my deep misery and the eternal reign of Christ, which is proclaimed, loved, adored, and which is extending over all the earth.

"Truth should embrace the universe. Such is Christianity, the only religion which destroys sectional prejudice, the only one which proclaims the unity and absolute brotherhood of the whole human family."

II.   "But whom say ye that I am?"

1.   With the impetuosity and impulsiveness which ever characterized the Apostle Peter, he uttered the golden oracle, "Thou art the Christ, the Son of the living God." Around this two-fold proposition gathers the light of ages, from the stellar light of the patriarchs to the full-orbed light of the golden age. How did the apostles get such a conception of Christ as this?

In John 5: 31-39 we learn that there are three witnesses testifying to the divinity of the Christ— the Scriptures, the Father and Christ himself.

(1)   The Scriptures testify.

a.   Isa. 7: 14: "Therefore the Lord himself shall give you a sign: Behold a virgin shall conceive and bear a son, and shall call his name Immanuel." Born of a virgin. No earthly father. As Paul says, made of a woman. The extraordinary generation is a sign. Not born of an empress or princess, but of humble birth. He is called Immanuel, from *Imma*, with, *Nu*, us, *El*, God, or, according to our construction of language, God with us.

b. Micah 5: 2: We learn that he was to be born in Bethlehem of Judah. Bethlehem means house of bread. This seems to be the fittest place for him to be born who is called the Bread of Life. The birthplace of Christ has never been lost to the world. Thousands of people visited it during the first century. Justin Martyr and others visited it in the second century. Origen visited it in the third century. Jerome and Eusebius visited it in the fourth century. In 327 A. D. St. Helena, the mother of Constantine the Great, built a church over the grotto in which Christ was born, called the Church of the Nativity, the oldest piece of Christian architecture in the whole world.

c. In Gen. 49: 10 the old patriarch Jacob, moved by the spirit of prophecy, said, "The scepter shall not depart from Judah, nor a law-giver from between his feet, until Shilo come; and unto him shall the gathering of the people be." Christ was the last rightful heir to the Davidic throne, and the last law-giver Judah ever produced. The scepter departed and Judah fell when the Messiah came. When Christ was lifted up he drew all men unto him. In Jesus Christ alone are all these Scriptures fulfilled.

(2) God testifies to his divinity.

a. By angels. At his birth angels testified he was Christ the Lord. At his resurrection angels testified he had power over the grave. At his ascension angels, as they escorted him back to his native heaven, said he was the King of Glory, the Lord of Hosts.

b. God testified by a voice from heaven. At his baptism an audible voice from the excellent glory, rending the murky clouds, said: "This is my beloved Son, in whom I am well pleased." On the mount of transfiguration the silence of heaven was again broken, saying, "This is my beloved Son, in whom I am well pleased; hear ye him." In John 12: 28-30 we learn that while Jesus was in Jerusalem in the temple, a voice came from heaven in approval. Some thought it thundered, others thought an angel spake to him from heaven.

c. God testified to the Sonship of Jesus by miracle. At his crucifixion the earth did quake, and the rocks were rent, in sympathy with the great tragedy. The great rents in the rocks are to be seen by every visitor to the Holy Land. Geologist Royal, of England, though an infidel, when he saw this threw up his hands and exclaimed, "Surely Jesus Christ was the Son of God."

From twelve until three o'clock there was darkness all over the land. The early Christian writers speak of this. In Amos 8: 9 we read, "The sun shall go down at noon." When Dionysius, the Areopagite, in the city of On in Egypt, saw the darkness which veiled the great sacrifice on Calvary, he exclaimed, "A god has died," corroborating the Bible record. Phlegon, a Greek historian, a freedman of the Emperor Adrain, in 120 A. D., says that in the 202d Olympiad, which corresponds exactly with the time of the crucifixion, a great darkness covered the earth. Some infidels have tried to account for this great darkness by saying that it was an eclipse of the sun. But Gibbon, one of the most unrelenting haters of Christianity that ever wrote against it, but a true historian, says that there was no eclipse of the sun at the time of the crucifixion. Christ was crucified at the passover, which was always at the full of the moon; and there could be no eclipse of the sun at the full of the moon. Everything, both in nature and history, corroborates the Bible statements.

(3) The works of Christ testify to his divinity.

a. There are recorded in the Scriptures thirty-six miracles of the Savior. Eighteen of these are miracles over all kinds of diseases. Ten of these are miracles over the elements of nature. Five of these were miracles over evil spirits. Three of these were miracles over death. He cleansed the lepers, cast out demons, walked the billowy deep, and restored Lazarus to the weeping sisters of Bethany.

b. His miraculous and superhuman life attests his divinity. He grew away from his own family, tribe and nation. He blessed the daughter of the Syro-Phœnician woman, and restored the son of the nobleman, and taught the erring daughter of Jacob at the well of Shechem. His apostles saw something in him more than man. Hence their divine conception of the Messiah.

c. His works, as seen in all Christian lands to-day, prove his divinity. We judge a tree by its fruits. In him are all the families of the earth blessed. Christianity is a tree of marvelous growth and power. Its roots reach down into the soil of every nation. Its majestic trunk reaches to the very heavens. Its branches overshadow the whole earth. Its seeds are adapted to the soil of every clime. Its leaves are for the healing of the nations. Its fruits are for all the sighing sons and daughters of fallen humanity. And under its shadow, cast by the Sun of righteousness, all the denizens of the earth can find shelter and protection.

2.   A Divine principle.

(1)   Love.   Divine love.

a. The highest love of a Jew was to love his neighbor as he loved himself, and hate his enemies. This is the old commandment.

b. Jesus taught a new commandment, Love one another as I have loved you. Jesus loved them when they were his enemies, hence he says, "Love your enemies." To love our friends is human, but to love our enemies is divine. This principle was born with the introduction of Christianity into the world.

c.   Hence the Golden Rule. It is often claimed that it originated with Confucius, the great Chinese philosopher, but his rule was negative, while Christ's was positive. A stone could comply with the rule of Confucius, but it requires sanctified intelligence to comply with Christ's rule. Therefore Christ is the author of the Golden Rule. He spake as never man spake.

(2) His Divinity is the basis of his love.

a. Isa. 9 : 6 : The names of Diety are applied to Christ. He is called the Mighty God, the Father of the Everlasting Age, Wonderful, Counselor, the Prince of Peace. Paul, Rom. 9 : 5, calls him God over all. Christ is as truly God as he is man.

b. The attributes of Diety are all applied to him. The Eternal, Omniscient, Omnipresent, Omnipotent Being. He was with the Father in the beginning. He knows our very thoughts. He is every place where two or three disciples are gathered together. He has all power in heaven and on earth.

c. He conquered death, hell and the grave. He has the key of the grave. His enemies said that while they slept the disciples came and stole him away. His friends said he had risen. These witnesses were not deceived, for they were intimate with him, and were separated from him only a short time. They handled him. They were not deceivers, for they laid down their lives for their testimony. They did not expect any earthly reward. They were competent witnesses. But some say no such report of his body being stolen was ever given. Then the fact of his resurrection stands uncontradicted even by his enemies.

(3) The spirituality of his kingdom.

a. In Matt. 20 : 20-24 we learn the apostles looked upon Christ as a temporal ruler, and his kingdom as a temporal reign, in which the apostles themselves were discussing who should be the greatest.

b. In Luke 22 : 47-51 we are told that when they came out against Christ with staves and boards the apostles said, "Shall we smite with the sword?" They did not yet understand that his kingdom was to be a spiritual reign, propagated by love and not force.

c. The kingdom of Christ (John 18 : 36) is not of this world—spiritual. While in the world, not of the world. Spiritual in its origin, like the stone cut out without hands; spiritual in its nature, not of this world. Never until the apostles were endued with power from on high did they understand the nature of the reign of the Messiah.

3. Building on a divine principle.

(1) The Church, or kingdom of Christ, is built on love and not force.

a. All the great monarchs of earth built up their empires before their death, and with their death they fell. But Christ built up his kingdom after his death.

b. All the empires of earth were built upon the blood of their enemies. But the Savior of the world built up his kingdom upon his own blood and the blood of its subjects. If all the blood which has flown from the veins of Christian martyrs for nearly two thousand years could be gathered into one stream, it would make a river on whose crimson bosom the commerce of an empire could be carried!

c. Christ is the Prince of Peace, and not of war, but by peace and love a kingdom has been built up which has encircled the globe. This poor Nazarene, who had nowhere to rest his weary head, and who, when reviled, reviled not again, can command more men to-day than the queen of England, and can raise more money than the Rothschilds.

(2) Missionary work is built up and carried on by love, and not force.

a. It was love which brought Christ, the Great Missionary, to this world. He was a Missionary to a foreign land, at that. Foreign missions, then, originated, not on earth, but in heaven, a child of the skies, conceived in love and brought forth in sacrifice and blood.

b. The apostles, actuated by a love that could not be bound with chains of iron, nor imprisoned in cells, nor slain with the sword, went everywhere preaching the gospel of peace. In less than three centuries Christianity conquered the Roman empire, wrapping the robe of righteousness around it, and sat upon the throne of the Cæsars.

c. Missionaries now, as they leave their friends,

homes and native lands to carry the glad tidings to the benighted denizens of heathendom, are moved by the Spirit of Christ. When Christianity, with a message of love, knocked at the gates of the Celestial Empire, they were opened without the firing of a gun.

(3) This fundamental principle of love lies at the very foundation of all benevolent and charitable institutions.

a. There are ten churches built every day in which to adore the Redeemer of the world. If all houses of worship were placed together, they would make a city more magnificent than Paris, with its boulevards and Elysian fields.

b. If all the institutions of learning built by the influence of Christ were in one city, they would make a city larger than London. Infidelity never builds institutions of learning.

c. If all the institutions of charity, built by Christian people, were put together, they would make a city greater than New York. The influence of Christ upon the world proves his divinity. His influence only augments as the ages roll on.

Ernest Renan, the great French infidel, in his Life of Jesus, pp. 351 and 356, says: "A thousand times more alive, a thousand times more blessed, since thy death than during thy passage here below; thou shalt become the cornerstone of humanity so entirely that to tear thy name from this world would be to rend it to its foundations.

"Shall originality be born anew, or shall the world henceforth be content to follow the paths opened by the bold creatures of the ancient ages? We know not.

"But whatever may be the surprises of the future, Jesus never will be surpassed. His worship will grow young without ceasing; his legend will call forth tears without end; his sufferings will melt the noblest hearts; all ages will proclaim that among the sons of men there are none born greater than Jesus."

Christ is the greatest historic character in the annals of history. Take Christ out of the literature of the world, and there would not be a skeleton of a library left. Here is the very soul of history. In the beautiful language of another: "Ah! when the obelisk of fame shall have been erected, on which the historic characters of earth shall have their names inscribed, there on its very apex, in letters of burning light, let the name of Jesus stand, the supremest of all earth's greatness."

O, may our motto ever be expressed in these beautiful lines:

> "Reign over me, Lord Jesus,
>   O, make my heart thy throne!
> It shall be thine forever,
>   It shall be thine alone."

BIOGRAPHICAL SKETCH.

J. H. O. SMITH is the eldest son of Sarah Wilson Smith, of Warren Co., Ohio, and Edward M. Smith, of Lexington, Ky. His grandparents were among the first in Ohio to unite the Restoration Movement. Edward M. Smith is a descendant of the Trabues, French Huguenots, who were driven out of France on account of their religious convictions.

J. H. O. Smith was born in Warren Co., Ohio, Dec. 27, 1857. After teaching several terms in the country schools of his county, he began preaching at the age of twenty, in a schoolhouse at Ft. Ancient. He attended school at Lebanon, Ohio, preaching at that place and at Salem for two years. His choice of a college was made at an Ohio State Convention, while listening to the eloquent O. A. Burgess, then President of Butler University. He entered college in 1881, and graduated three years and a half later, preaching every Lord's day while in school, and holding protracted meetings during vacations. He then took charge of the church at Edinburg, Ind., from which work he was called into the field as State evangelist. As an evangelist he was very successful. He not only held large meetings in destitute or discour-

(78)

J. H. O. Smith

aged county-seats, but put fourteen district evangelists into the field, and organized the districts on a self-supporting basis. I believe that in every instance where he organized churches or held large meetings, he saw to it that the work was followed by competent pastors, and regular preaching has been sustained ever since.

During the past five years Bro. Smith has been pastor of the Church of Christ at Valparaiso, Ind., the church membership increasing in that time from eighty to twelve hundred.

During his pastorates at Edinburg and Valparaiso he has held successful meetings at Atlanta, Ga., Elkhart, Ind., Cleveland, Ohio, Boston, Mass., and Ada, Ohio.

As an evangelist and pastor Bro. Smith is not only a born general, gathering strong men about him and organizing and disposing of his forces to the best strategic advantage, but he leads in every attack, and is always found in the thickest of the fray, urging on his men by word and example, caring for the wounded, cheering the discouraged, spurring the laggard and recapturing the deserters. He is a close student both of books and of human nature, reading men as quickly as the printed page. His "methods" seem to be simply careful thought and preparation, and then tireless, enthusiastic, aggressive work.

He often quotes the words of Jennie Deene: "When sorrows come, as they will come to the rich and poor alike; when death comes, and it will come to the great and to the small, it is not that which others have done for you, but that which you have done for others that will make you happiest." He knows no such word as *fail*. If he becomes disheartened no one knows it. A favorite text is, " He that saveth his life shall lose it." In all his work he remembers his dependence upon the Lord. "Except the Lord build the house they labor in vain that build it."

Bro. Smith's work in Valparaiso has been largely evangelistic, owing to the great number of students attending the Normal School. The work must be done quickly and thoroughly, as many of our enthusiastic young converts go out into fields where primitive Christianity is untaught and unknown, and they must be equipped for pioneer and aggressive effort.

He has preached in nearly every schoolhouse within a radius of ten miles, and formed bands of Christians who support the student-preachers whom he encourages to enter this work.

Every winter he conducts a protracted meeting at home, each effort resulting in from one hundred to three hundred accessions to the church.

As a preacher, he sets the spiritual standard high, and clings close to the Word of God. He is clear, forcible and convincing, with an occasional gleam of humor and an undertone of pathos that reaches the highest and lowest chords of the human heart. As a student once remarked at the close of our church services, "Every time I come down here I feel like being a better man."

A MEMBER OF THE CHURCH AT VALPARAISO.

6

CHRIST'S METHOD OF SAVING MEN.

J. H. O. SMITH.

Faithful is the saying, and worthy of all acceptation, that Christ Jesus came into the world to save sinners, of whom I am chief: howbeit for this cause I obtained mercy, that in me as chief might Jesus Christ show forth all his long-suffering, for an example of them who should hereafter believe on him unto life eternal.—1 Tim. 1: 15, 16.

PAUL was a successful evangelist. He has been admired as the great *Apostle* to the Gentiles ; as a profound *logician;* as the greatest *teacher* of the doctrines of Christianity, Christ only excepted. But he was a winner of souls. "But though I was free from all men, I brought myself under bondage to all, that I might gain the more. And to the Jews I became a Jew, that I might gain the Jews ; to them that are under the law, as under the law, not being myself under the law, that I might gain them that are under the law; to them that are without law, as without law, not being without law to God, but under law to Christ, that I might gain them that are without law. To the weak I became weak, that I might gain the weak; I am become all things to all men, that I may by all means save some." 1 Corinthians 9: 19-22.

This was a statement to the church at Corinth of his work among them.

His great argument in the Roman letter is in defense of the proposition found in the sixteenth verse of the first chapter : " I am not ashamed of the gospel of Christ, for it is the power of God unto salvation to every one that believeth ; to the Jew first, and also to the Greek."

Paul knew that Rome had conquered the world, and had made conquest of its religions and philosophies. She had the Pantheon, where all the principal gods and religions were represented. He knew that great men had wrought out, line by line, their best philosophies for the good of the race. Paul was ready to stand in that presence and compare the Gospel with the systems of the world, having for their purpose the elevation of man.

The great difference between the Gospel and other religions is that *it has power to save*, and they have not. It was Paul's great argument for the World's "Parliament of Religions" assembled at Rome.

Paul would say : " You try your plans, and show results in men redeemed, or admit the Gospel has power that your systems have not. You teach your philosophies and offer your sacrifices to gods known and unknown. I will preach the Gospel and pursue Christ's methods, and we will see which can save."

The same test should be submitted to-day. Christ came to save *sinners*. To translate men

from darkness into light, from the power of Satan
into the kingdom of God's dear Son. This includes
all. The Gentile when he knew God, glorified him
not as God, neither gave thanks. The Jew also
committed sins while condemning them. "For
there is no difference, all have sinned."

My text might be translated into everyday language something like this: "Christ Jesus came
into the world to save sinners, and I am one of
them, one of the greatest." This is a good motto.
It should be hung up with such mottoes as "God
bless our home," "What is home without a mother?"
and "Home, sweet home." This motto is worthy
of universal adoption. It would grace the walls
of a king's palace, as well as the hovel of the poor,
or the rude wigwam of the savage.

Paul had been a Pharisee of the Pharisees. He
had doubtless tried to worship God in the spirit of
the man who thanked God he was not as other
men, but now as the publican he prays, "God, be
merciful to me, a sinner." The Pharisees were
failures as soul-winners. As evangelists they
would have reported the difficulties as insurmount-
able. They would have explained their failure
by saying that the people would not endure sound
doctrine. It never would have occurred to the
Pharisee that his methods were wrong and his
gospel no message of good news.

Let us prayerfully and thoughtfully study together,

I. The world into which Christ came.

II. His mission—to save sinners.

III. His method.

I. THE WORLD INTO WHICH CHRIST CAME.

1. *Christ came into a world of sinners.* Read Paul's description in the first and third chapters of Romans. Gentiles had refused to have God in their knowledge, being filled with unrighteousness, covetousness, maliciousness, full of envy, murder, strife, deceit, malignity; whisperers, backbiters, hateful to God, insolent, haughty, boastful, inventers of evil things, disobedient to parents, without understanding, covenant breakers, without natural affection, unmerciful.

Of the Jews it was written and sanctioned by the Apostle: "There is none righteous, no not one: there is none that understandeth, there is none that seek after God. They have all turned aside, they are together become unprofitable; there is none that doeth good, no, not so much as one: their throat is an open sepulchre; with their tongues they have used deceit; the poison of asps is under their lips: whose mouth is full of cursing and bitterness: their feet are swift to shed blood: destruction and misery are in their ways: and the way of peace they have not known: there is no fear of God before their eyes."

We are all constantly raising the question how we can *reach* the masses. We must get to them. Christ, by the way, never speaks of masses and classes. He spoke of *this* man, *that* woman, who could never be lost from him in the crowd. He put himself in *his* place, *her* place, *their* place. His earlier years on earth were spent in a home of poverty. He knew from experience how hard was the struggle sometimes in the most of the homes around him. Every laboring man can see in him a brother, who knew what toil was day after day.

Later on he was without a home. "The foxes have holes, and the birds of the air have nests; but the Son of man has not where to lay his head." Nothing in literature is more touching than his occasional utterances, which show us how lonely he sometimes was. He was a child of the common people, as well as the Son of God. We have a great High Priest who can be *touched.* "Then *drew near* all the *publicans* and *sinners* to hear him." When God spoke on Sinai's burning summit, "*the people* drew back and said, Let not God speak any more, or we will all be dead men;" and so terrible was the sight that Moses said, "I exceedingly fear and quake." When God spake by his Son, "*the people press d* upon him to hear his words." "The *common people* heard him gladly." God's gentleness made him great. "It became him in all things to be made like unto his brethren, that he might be a faithful High Priest in things pertaining to God to make propitiation for the sins of *the people.*" He is able to succor them who are tempted in that he hath suffered, being tempted. "A bruised reed he would not break, or smoking flax he would not quench."

It was only when the Pharisees came between him and *the people* that his lightning lash hissed and writhed around their hypocrisy; and his power threw open the doors of their whited sepulchres.

2. *Christ came into a world of sorrow.* The shadow of disappointment lay like a pall upon every path. How does the unbeliever account for man's restless discontent? In the world of life we see rank rising above rank in one grand series from the smallest of animalculæ up to the line which separates the creature from the uncreated. Fvery rank is full and its creatures just as happy as their capacity for enjoyment and their environment can make them. All are happy except man. Every cup of pleasure seems to have bitterness mingled with the sweet for which he is longing.

> " Ambition's temple never yet
>   Let in a well-contented guest;
>   Some spoil unwon, some deed undone,
>   Mars the sweet accents, ' Rest is won.' "

Why did God make all his creatures happy except man? The Bible explains it by stating that man was made in the image of God, and lived a life of joy. Man sinned, and by so doing he spoiled his adaptation to his environment, which is God. "In him we live and move and have our being." If the fin of the fish is broken, it cannot be content until restored. If the wing of the bird is broken, it will not fill the air with song until nature's healing agencies have made recovery of the broken wing, and its adaptation to the atmosphere, its home, be restored. Man by sin went out of harmony with God, and cannot be happy until restored to perfect conformity to God, his true environment. The Christian can say of Christ, "He is our life." "To this end Christ came, that he might reconcile us to God." "Wherefore, if any man is in Christ, he is a new creature: old things have passed away, behold, all things have become new." "But all things are of God, who reconciled us to himself through Christ, and gave unto us the ministry of reconciliation; to-wit, that God was in Christ reconciling the world unto himself." "God gave him to be head over all things to the church, which is his body, the fullness of *him that filleth all in all.*" "And you did he quicken when you were dead through your trespasses and sins." Read Ephesians 2: 1-10. Through page after page of the Bible is this truth illustrated. Sin and sorrow go hand in hand; they are joined together as cause and effect. "The wages of sin is death, but the gift of God is eternal life through Jesus Christ our Lord."

What wonder Paul would say to Timothy, a young evangelist: "It is a good motto, and worthy of universal adoption, that Christ Jesus came into the world to save sinners, and I am one

of them." The man who sins not only suffers, but
he disappoints God. "Oh, that thou hadst heark-
ened unto my commandments, then had thy peace
been like a river, and thy righteousness as the
waters of the sea." Those who sin by accom-
plishing their own desire, bring their own gray
hairs "in sorrow to the grave." Byron said
toward the close of a sinful life :

> " I've spent my summer ere 'tis June,
> Have quaffed my cup of life too soon,
> And found its dregs were wormwood."

Mrs. Browning's pure life led her into the light
of God. She said :

> " I smiled to see God's greatness
> Flow around our incompleteness,
> Round our restlessness His rest."

Oh, I think this Savior of ours, when here, went
about looking into the faces of men, longing to see
them become and live as he knew they might live!
" Come unto me and I will give you rest." " Learn
of me and you shall find rest for your souls."

II. CHRIST'S MISSION.

1. *Christ came into the world to save sinners.*
There are two ways of looking at sin. One regards man as under law, and, having violated it,
must be condemned without discrimination. No
allowance for frailty ; will not hear of temptation
nor distinguish between circumstances. The other
speaks of sin as a mistake, as human weakness.
Christ's view of guilt brought him here. Sin kills.

It's awful consequences pursue the sinner like the day of doom. For this reason the Son of God "bowed the heavens and came down."

A recent writer has said: "When a Reformer demands our support, we ask him four questions:

"1. What do you propose to accomplish?

"2. What means do you propose to employ?

"3. How can these means work out the result?

"4. On what power do you rely?"

2. *Christ proposes to save sinners.* The instrumentality is love. If love fails nothing can succeed. The power is the power of God. Government has tried punishment; society has tried exclusion and indiscriminate laxity. All have proved failures. Christ proposes sympathy, holiness and Divine help. Christ has nothing in common with hardened guilt, with malice, cruelty, oppression, hypocrisy; but he gives his life to redeem the guilty, the malicious, the cruel, the oppressor and the hypocrite.

Isaiah, looking down the centuries through the glass held by God's hand, saw Christ anointed, and heard him saying:

The spirit of the Lord is upon me.
Because he anointed me to preach good tidings to the poor;
He hath sent me to proclaim release to the captives,
And recovery of sight to the blind,
To set at liberty them that are bruised,
To proclaim the acceptable year of the Lord.
"I came not to condemn the world, but that the world through me might have life." He said, "I came not to destroy but to fulfill. My father worketh hitherto and I work."

III. CHRIST'S METHOD.

His love for men marshaled him the way that he should go. He knew man, and what would win him, if anything would. His method should be the careful study of all those who would succeed as soul-winners.

Let us briefly consider some narratives in the Gospel where he led men from sin to righteousness.

His enemies surround him, and after his arrest, hurry him away with indecent haste to the trial. They introduce bribed witnesses to testify against him. The soldiers make a holiday by putting a crown of thorns upon his brow, a mock sceptre in his hand, and a purple robe upon him; they blindfold him and spit upon him.

> " Still from his lip no curse hath come,
> His lofty eye hath looked no doom;
> No earthquake burst, no angel brand
> Curses the blaspheming band."

Upon the cross they torture this lover of men and Savior of the world. Oh! how "each gaping wound pleads like an angel trumpet tongued against the deep damnation of his taking off." This was the supreme manifestation of his unfailing love. In this very city, over which he had wept, and in which he had preached and suffered, thousands became his followers. After his resurrection, he said: "Go tell the men who sat in judgment over me, that they may reign with me,

if they will accept my love. Tell the soldiers
that they become soldiers of the Cross and followers of the Lamb. Tell Pilate that he may be
glorified with me if he is willing to suffer with
me." If such love, the highest effort of God, is
rejected, "there surely remaineth no more offering
for sin, but a fearful expectation of judgment, and
a fierceness of fire which shall devour his adver-
saries." "Father, forgive them, they know not
what they do." He believed in love, and for that
reason said to his disciples: "Fear not, I have
overcome the world." "And I, if I be lifted up,
will draw all men unto me." These exhibitions of
his love represent his method throughout.

Take the case of Zacchæus, recorded in Luke
19. Jesus was coming down toward Jerusalem,
and was passing through Jericho. Great multitudes were following him. Eager, anxious throngs
were listening to his wonderful words of life. *We*
need elegant church houses with all the beautiful
modern appointments, and even then sometimes
fail to secure a hearing. The dusty highway, a
mountain side, or the wilderness was good enough
for him.

> " Christ's sermons were the healthful talk,
>   That shorter made the mountain walk;
>   His wayside texts were flowers and birds,
>   Where mingled with his gracious words
>   The rustle of the tamarisk tree,
>   Or ripple wash of Galilee."

Men must have loved to hear him talk, and must often have said, "When I hear him I feel like being a better man. If he were near me all the time, I am sure I could live a grander life."

The crowds were coming with him. Zacchæus, a chief publican and very rich, heard of Christ's coming. He possibly left a notice on his door, "Back in half an hour," and hastened to the place that Jesus must pass. He was unable to see for the crowd, for he was short of stature. He ran before and climbed up into a sycamore tree.

Jesus came on and stopped beneath the tree, and looked up at the little rich man, who was known as a sinner. Had the Master pursued the method of some of his disciples, he would have said: "Zacchæus, come right down out of that tree. You are trying to make some one believe that you have an interest in me, and want to be religious. I know all about you. I can tell you in the presence of this crowd all the meanness you ever did." I think the shrewd man of business would have said: "Never mind about that. I do not profess to be perfect. I make no claim to be very good, but I want to say that I do claim to be just as good as some of those old Pharisees I see walking along with you. I know those men. I have done business with them, and I see them doing things every day that I would not do. *Lecture them.*"

No. He who came not to condemn but to *save*

the lost would not shut up the avenues of approach
to that heart by such a fusillade of words. He
said: "Zacchæus, I want to go down to your house
to dinner to-day." The man came down and said,
"You'll be welcome in my house." He forgot
business, doubtless saying to himself, "I didn't
suppose he would associate with such a man as I
am." The royal guest crossed the threshold, and
Zacchæus made himself busy ministering to his
comfort.

Our curiosity is not satisfied with an account of
the conversation in that elegant home, but we
know what the holy Preacher always talked
about. He would talk of the Father in heaven,
and how much he loved us all ; what men ought to
be, and what they ought to do; and how they
ought to love each other, and try to make this a
happier and better world, because they had lived
in it. All this time Zacchæus would be compar-
ing himself as he was with what he might be, as
he listened intently to this Savior of men.

Outside the multitude murmured, saying: "He
is gone to lodge with a man who is a sinner." "A
man is known by the company he keeps." "Like
seeks like." "Birds of a feather flock together."
"If Jesus is not a sinner he would not lodge with
this man." The publican must have known of the
talk outside.

After a while he said : " I have not lived as I
ought to have done, but I want to do so. When

you go out again the people will expect to see a
change in you because of your association with
me. Instead of that, they will see a *change in me.*
I hope you will never have occasion to regret having been my guest to-day, and having spoken
these kind words. I intend to try to be what *you*
want me to be, and do what you want me to do;
and will try not to disappoint you. I want to live
from this time on so that you will call me your
friend." And Jesus said unto him "To-day is
salvation come to this house;" "The Son of Man
came to seek and save that which was lost." The
angels in heaven rejoiced, and the redeemed for all
time have an example in soul-winning. A rich
man was won for the kingdom of heaven so near at
hand.

At one time Jesus was standing in the temple
teaching. The multitudes were there, as usual:
"*All the people* came unto him; and he sat down
and taught them." John 8 : 2. The scribes and
Pharisees had more regard for the technicalities of
the law than the sacredness of human life. These
men brought to him a woman charged with an
awful sin. The witnesses were there to prove her
guilt. She had been arrested while committing
the crime. They were intent on scoring a point
against our Holy Preacher; our Divine Winner of
Souls; our Savior of men. They break in upon
his teaching; they rudely bring the shrinking
woman before him, dragging her into his presence.

It was a clamorous group: "Now Moses in the law commanded us that *such* should be stoned, but what sayest thou? We will not endure this suspense longer. Are you loyal to the law or not? We can prove the charges. Answer without evasion. Here's the law."

Oh, how our language betrays us. "*Such*," "*such as she.*" She belongs to the class of the abandoned. She has been abandoned. God and society have abandoned her. There she stands in that multitude. Every eye is upon her. Her sentence may be read already on the faces of those around. Oh, woman! did you not know that the wages of sin is death? We can almost hear some one say, "Serpent! The vile creature!"

The dilemma they presented was like that in the question as to the tribute money. To advise the execution of the woman would be contrary to Roman law. To counsel against Moses would be to yield all claims of allegiance to the law; fatal to his claims of Messiahship.

We can imagine the clamorous crowd was hushed as the Savior stooped down and wrote on the ground. But still they continued asking him. There stood the woman with eternity before her. It is an awful thing to die as a sinner, unforgiven. How sacred was any life to our dear Master! Then "he lifted himself up, and said unto them, *He* that is without sin (or sinless) among *you*, let *him* cast a stone at *her*." And again he stooped down and wrote on the ground. "And they that heard it, being convicted by their own conscience, went out one by one, beginning with the elder even unto the last." What a procession that must have been! There were good men and true in the city of Jerusalem, but they were not in that company.

"Brethren, if any of you be overtaken in a fault, you who are spiritual *restore* such a one *in the spirit of meekness*, considering thyself lest thou also be tempted."

The woman remained still bound by her sin to his presence. What will he say? Will he deliver a lecture upon the terrible crime which brought her under such condemnation? Will he tell her of the inevitable doom of the impenitent? Will he preach a sermon upon the great sins of the city of Jerusalem? "He lifted himself up and saw none but the woman. He said unto her, Woman, where are thy accusers? Did no one condemn thee?" She said, "No man, *Lord*." "*She* said," and "*Jesus* said," and so the conversation went on. You might have supposed she would have been speechless in his presence. "Neither do I condemn thee; *go and sin no more*." Do you not think she said as she went out of his presence, "I hope you will never regret having saved my life to-day. I'll try to *be* what you want me to *be*, and *do* what you would have me to *do*. I will try not to disappoint you."

The good work was going on and the number of

7

His disciples was increasing daily. This very woman may have stood beneath the shadow of the cross, and may be in heaven now. " The thief cometh that he may steal and kill and destroy ; I am come that they might have life, and that they might have it more abundantly."

"I am the Good Shepherd, I lay down my life for the sheep. I leave the ninety and nine and go to the wilderness to find the one that is lost. The Father's house is waiting for the return of his prodigal children." "The gates are not shut at all by day and there is no night there. Come unto me all ye that labor and are heavy laden, and I will give you rest."

In Luke 7: 36-50, we have an account of the anointing of the Savior's feet by a woman who was a sinner. From verse 39 we judge that she was a notorious and abandoned character. An eastern house is open at the hours of meals so that it is not uncommon for strangers to enter and take part in conversation with the guests at table. The guests recline on couches, their faces toward the table, their feet turned toward the outside of the room. The sandals were removed ; the feet of each guest bare. A woman in the city, who was a sinner, heard that Jesus sat at meat in the Pharisee's house. She had doubtless heard of his gracious words, giving hope of a better life for all. She had seen the channels which linked her life to others one by one closed up. There was a desert around her lowering with gloom and covered with desolation, on whose rank ground no green thing grew, and through whose heaps of drifted bones the bleak wind sighed, while the lights of social privilege glimmered afar off. She had made the desert out of her own life, had spread abroad this desertion and scorn.

She came in and bending over kissed his feet, wet them with her tears, and wiped them with the hairs of her head, and anointed them with ointment. The Pharisee saw and spoke within himself, " If he were a prophet, he would know *what manner of woman* this is who toucheth him." Then Jesus told the story of the lender who had two debtors, one owing him five hundred pence and the other fifty, and when they had nothing to pay he forgave them both. Who would love him most? Simon answered, " He, I suppose, to whom he forgave most." " And he said, Thou hast rightly judged; and turning to the woman he said to Simon, Seest thou *this woman?* You did not extend to me the commonest courtesies when I entered your house. This woman has wetted my feet with tears and wiped them with her hair. *Her* sins which were many are forgiven; for *she loved much;* but to whom little is forgiven, the same loveth little. And he said unto her, Thy sins are forgiven. Thy faith has saved thee; go in peace." That forgiven soul must have said as she went out on that day, " I hope you will never regret having spoken in love to me to-day. I will try to be what you would have me to be and live as you want me to live. I will not disappoint you." Heaven recorded the winning of one more soul.

We are all familiar with Peter's denial of the Savior. He added to lying, cursing and swearing while forsaking his dearest friend on earth. The sweet face of the sufferer was turned toward Peter as full of love as in all those days gone by since Peter had forsaken all to follow him. Peter's heart was broken. He went out and wept bitterly, and I have no doubt sought an opportunity before the close of the awful tragedy to tell him how deeply he repented. No opportunity came. The good confession on the coasts of Cæsarea Phillipi, "Thou art the Christ, the Son of the living God," had been supplanted by a denial from the same impulsive lips, "I know not the man."

Peter said, "I'll go back to my fishing. I ought never to have left it to follow him. What use for me to try to be what he wants me to be. See what I have done!" The other disciples said, "We'll go too. Did not all of us forsake him." The morning of the third day came. The women came back from the sepulchre to tell them it was empty. Peter and John ran to the empty tomb, but John outran Peter. What was Peter thinking of as he ran expecting to meet the risen Lord? He was doubtless wondering what to say. Would the Lord forgive him for his awful sin? We have no record that Christ ever mentioned the sin. One morning, however, while preparing for the morning meal, the Savior asked him three times if he loved him, telling him to feed his sheep and lambs. When Jesus asked him the last time, Peter said, "Thou knowest all things; thou knowest that I love thee," and may have thought, "I loved you when I denied you." "Feed my sheep." That is, "Peter, you are going out to win souls and to help make them meet for the inheritance among the saints in light. Be very gentle with these men I came to save. Remember the influence my kindness has had upon you and don't make it hard for sinful men to return to me." Peter as well as Paul could say: "It is a good motto and worthy of universal adoption, that Christ Jesus came into the world to save sinners, and I am one of the greatest." When Jesus met Saul of Tarsus but little was said about the persecutions in which Saul was engaged.

Our Savior told the story of the boy who went away from home and wasted his powers in a dissolute life, and when he came back home he found a welcome waiting, and a father's open arms. The elder son said that if his father would receive the prodigal he was not the kind of man he had thought him to be, but the son had been dead and was alive, lost and was found. "There is joy in heaven over one sinner that repenteth more than over ninety and nine just persons that need no repentance.

In " Les Miserables " Victor Hugo tells the story of Jean Val Jean turned away from door after door. He had been in prison. His offense was stealing bread for his sister's starving children. When released, he was a jail-bird, and every door was closed against him and every heart was cold. One night, when even denied a dog's kennel for shelter ; when the inn-keepers had refused to receive him under any consideration, some one found him in the street and pointed to the house of the old Bishop, saying, "Knock there ; no one is ever turned away from that door." The old Bishop answered his summons and told him to come in. "This is Christ's house, and you have as much right here as I have ; come in." Jean Val Jean's heart was softened by the treatment of the kind old man. When showing him his room that night the old man said, "Everything here is yours, so feel at home." Jean Val Jean threw himself on the bed. About two o'clock he awoke; sat up; looked about him, and the old despair seized him. He rose, took the silver candlesticks, and found the door ajar between his room and the next, where the old Bishop was wrapped in undisturbed and dreamless sleep. The door between them had not been barred. Are not the angels of God all ministering spirits sent forth to minister to those who shall be heirs of salvation ? The struggle went on in the heart of the hardened man. He was tempted to kill his gentle host, but perhaps some angel led him out into the night, under the star-light, where so many fierce battles have been fought out on the battle-field of the human heart. The next day Jean Val Jean was arrested and the candlesticks were found in his possession. He was brought back to the Bishop, who said to his cap-tors, "I gave him the candlesticks," and asked him why he did not take the gold ones, too, as he gave him them also. When the officers had re-tired, the old man said, "Jean Val Jean, I've bought you to live a better life." The jail-bird was saved by the love of God which is shed abroad in human hearts by the Holy Spirit which is given unto his children.

Suppose I should bring into this room the worst man in your community, the very worst here. Get him in your mind and think about him, and I will ask this audience what the philosophers of the world propose for his improvement. Some would propose a good bath and respectable clothes. He would feel more like a gentleman and be more like one. That might be termed the "dude" theory of reformation. Some of the greatest scoundrels are clothed in the latest style. That plan will not save my notorious character. Some one suggests that he should be educated, meaning simply an intellectual training. It has been demonstrated in many instances that an education simply gives a man keener weapons with which to do his work, if he has a wicked heart. Some one else suggests giving him a position of trust. Every day the futility of this plan is demonstrated. The latest, the very latest announcements of scientific men will give my man no hope. The man of science would say, "I know the man's father and mother and his grandparents, and the circumstances under which he was brought up; in other words, 'his heredity and environment' are both bad. You can do nothing for him." "Just as I expected," my poor vagabond would say. "I did not want to come. There's no hope for me." At this moment my Savior of men speaks: "Wait, wandering prodigal, wait. You may be born again. I know your heredity is bad." The very first thing God does is to look after a man's heredity. "You must be born again." Then your pedigree will be as good as any man's on earth. "From this time on if any one asks about your father, tell them I am your Brother." Jesus says, "If they ask any thing about your family, refer them to me." His environment is provided for; he is given a place in the great family of the redeemed, and the angels of God are his servants. Many a tramp sitting by the roadside is thinking over his past life. Memory is busy with the past. He admits he is not what society wants him to be, and not what God intended he should be. He is not what he himself wants to be. "Oh, if I had a chance to begin again!" The Savior says, "Ill give you the chance, and stand by you while you make the effort."

There is a legend that God, before he made man, called Justice, Truth and Mercy, and asked, "Shall I make man?" "No," said Justice, "he will break thy law, and thou wilt have to destroy him." "No," said Truth, "he will disobey thee and thou canst not trust him." "Yes," said Mercy, with her eyes streaming tears, — she on her bended knees—"yes, and I will shield him and lead him back to the path of truth and justice." In Jesus, Mercy incarnate came.

At the battle of the Wilderness a young man fell, as was supposed, mortally wounded. His mother received a telegram announcing the sad news. Although orders had been issued forbidding any one to pass through the lines, the mother made her way down to her wounded boy. Finally she stood at his tent door. After pleading with the surgeon she was permitted to sit near his cot and watch him in his slumber. While sitting there listening to his heavy breathing, and wondering if he would awaken again to speak to her, almost unconsciously her hand stole over to his forehead, and she began to stroke the tresses that in his boyhood she had loved to caress, and without opening his eyes in his dreams he murmured, "Mother, you have come!" He knew the touch of his mother's hand. So the broken heart responds to the gentle touch of the Savior's love. He came to save sinners. I am one of them and so are you. Shall he regret having given his life for you? Will you disappoint him? Oh, say to him, " I will try to be what you would have me be, and do what you would have me do." That's all there is of Christianity.

In the presence of such love say not with the poet:

> " The rocks may rend, the earth may quake,
>   Of feelings all things show some sign,
>   But this unfeeling heart of mine."

Say rather:

> " I yield! I yield! I can hold out no more;
>   I sink by dying love constrained,
>   And own thee conqueror."

S. M. MARTIN.

BIOGRAPHICAL SKETCH.

S. M. MARTIN was born August 16, 1857, at Antioch, Ohio. His father, Enoch Martin, was a prominent teacher in Southeastern Ohio, and S. M. was enabled to enter the same profession at the early age of 15, and continued to teach for 15 consecutive years. His summer vacations were spent in attending Normal Schools, until he was 22 years of age. Much of his teaching was in Normal Schools and Colleges. He joined the church at Stafford, Ohio, in a meeting conducted by the lamented John W. Tate, and was baptized Aug. 23, 1875— just one week after his 18th birthday. He was married Dec. 23, 1876, to Mary C. Barnes of Summerfield, O. He has three daughters, Nina, Lela and Minnie Dee.

S. M. Martin moved to Missouri in the fall of 1884, and became Vice-President and Professor of English Literature, Elocution and Natural Science in Bowling Green College. It was here that he was induced to enter the ministry, through the influence of Rev. A. H. Carter and Rev. A. C. Walker, who thought they saw in him the qualifications of a successful gospel preacher. He was formally ordained on the third Lord's day in July, 1885, and preached his first discourse the next

Sunday at Frankford, Missouri, the place where Knowles Shaw made his confession many years before. For two years he combined teaching and preaching, when he abandoned his old profession for the new one, which he liked better. In a little more than two years' time from his ordination, he had gained such recognition in the church as to be selected by the Missouri Board of Missions for their State Evangelist. Here he continued to labor for three years and three months, when he resigned the State work and entered the general field as an independent evangelist, July 1st, 1891. He has been evangelizing five years, during which time over 4000 persons have been added to the churches in his meetings. The following is a list of those meetings in which there were more than 100 accessions:

Poplar Bluff, Mo., 113; Malden, Mo., 125; Kennett, Mo., 187; Louisiana, Mo., 111; Hannibal, Mo., 161; Moberly, Mo., 201; Warrensburg, Mo., 205; Columbia, Mo., 112; Oakland, Cal., 153; Plattsburg, Mo., 374; Lexington, Mo., 252; Richmond, Mo., 112; Dallas, Tex., 153; Paris, Ky., 143; Bedford, Iowa, 113; Cynthiana, Ky., 143; Jacksonville, Ill., 124; Seattle, Wash., 239; Atlanta, Ga., 105.

The above meetings were all conducted within a period of five years.

RELIGION — WHAT IS IT?

S. M. MARTIN.

"Howbeit, in vain do they worship me, teaching for doctrines the commandments of men."—Mark 7: 7.

THAT which we *want*, and that which we *need*, are often two very different things.

The heathen *need* the gospel, but they *want* to be let alone.

Barbarians *need* civilization, but they prefer their untamed savagery, and *want* to be let alone. The criminal *needs* punishment and restraint, but he also *wants* to be let alone.

The man who is wrong invariably resents any interference upon the part of those who would set him right, in either morals or religion, and yet these are the very ones that should not be let alone. If you are wrong religiously, I injure you for time and eternity by *letting you alone*—if it should be in my power to set you right. If I am wrong, then you are under the same obligation to set *me* right. Somebody *is* wrong on this subject of religion, and Henry Ward Beecher said in *The Christian Union* of Jan. 22, 1873: "Nothing so demoralizes a people as to be set for the maintenance of a creed which they do not sincerely hold; and these are the latter

(109)

days of shaking and trial when the rubbish of all creeds will surely be made manifest and cast out."

A man's creed is what he believes, and if there is any rubbish in your religious belief the sooner you discover it and *cast it out* the better.

The following are the only instances of the use of the words *religion* and *religious* in the Bible:

Acts 26: 5.—"After the most strictest sect of our *religion*, I lived a Pharisee."

Gal. 1: 13.—"For ye have heard of my conversation in times past in the Jews' *religion*."

Gal. 1: 14.—"And profited in the Jews' *religion* above many in mine own nation."

Jas. 1: 26.—"If any man among you seem to be *religious* and bridleth not his tongue, but deceiveth his own heart, this man's *religion* is vain."

Acts 13: 43.—"Now when the congregation was broken up, many of the Jews and *religious* proselytes followed Paul and Barnabas."

Jas. 1: 27.—"Pure *religion* and undefiled before God, the Father, is this."

We find the word *religion* five times and the word *religious* but twice in the Bible. No such expressions as "*getting religion*," "*losing religion*," or "*experiencing religion*" are found in the Bible, nor any teaching to warrant the use of such expressions. The following from the secular press will show the way the wind is beginning to blow:

"A STIR IN RELIGIOUS CIRCLES.

"INDIANAPOLIS, Feb. 19, 1890.—Methodist circles are badly shaken up. A paper was read last week at a ministers' convention on class meetings, some of the clergy denouncing them. A published report caused a sensation. At another meeting the proceedings created much astonishment. Dr. Goodwin declared that the Methodist creed, like that of the Presbyterians, is defective—some hymns teach erroneous doctrine, and pulpit terminology is frequently bad. Dr. Cleveland, cousin of the ex-president, recently from New York State, agreed with him, as did two or three others. Goodwin said the cant phrases, 'Have you got religion?' 'Do you enjoy religion?' and 'Are you saved?' were condemned as improper pulpit terminology."

I like to hear these men talk that way, inasmuch as they are largely responsible for the use of such language in the churches of this generation.

The derivation of the word *religion* is veiled in obscurity—its etymology is not easy to determine. I have been at some pains to look it up, and give the following as the best I can arrive at: *Latin— Religio*, from *re-li-ga-re*, to bind anew, or back, to bind fast. *Religeus*, revering the gods, pious, religious. The words "ligament," "ligature," etc., have a similar derivation. *Re*, as a prefix, means *again*, hence *re-ligion* is the process by which one

who has wandered away from God is to be bound
back to him again. But it means more than this.
It has both an objective and a subjective phase.

RELIGION OBJECTIVELY is the divinely revealed
process by which man is bound back to God, or,
as Mr. Campbell says, "It is what God does for
us."

RELIGION SUBJECTIVELY is piety, obedience, Godliness, holiness, or, as Mr. Campbell says, "It is
what we do for ourselves." It consists in adding
to our faith, courage, knowledge, temperance, pa-
tience, godliness, brotherly kindness and charity.

God's part of religion consists in his giving
Christ and the gospel, inspiring men to preach it
with power by the Holy Spirit sent down from
heaven, granting forgiveness of sins, etc. While
man's part is to preach, hear, believe, repent, confess, be baptized, and then devote himself to living
the new life in Christ Jesus, having been born
again, not of corruptible seed, but of incorruptible,
by the word of God.

The religion of an individual, or religion subjectively, is embraced in his thoughts, feelings and
actions toward God.

His thoughts toward God result from his knowledge of God. His feelings toward God result from
his esteem of that knowledge, as to whether it is
true or false, answering the question, "What think
ye of Christ? whose Son is he?" If he believes in
him he answers, "He is the Christ, the Son of the

Living God." If he disbelieves, he will not feel like trusting him, but hates and rejects him, and will not obey his commandments. His actions toward God are the manifest result of his "thoughts" and "feelings" already alluded to. If he "thinks" the knowledge true, and "feels" love for Christ, he will obey the gospel, otherwise he will not obey. "If ye love me keep my commandments."

The "mourners' bench" system of "getting religion" teaches that it is a "feeling" resulting from some supernatural influence of the Holy Spirit upon the individual, assuring him of justification or pardon, and hence he "feels" very happy, and believes in God because of these "experiences" or "feelings." If you ask him to give you "a reason for the hope that is in him," he refers you to his feeling, which is his anchor. When he loses this "feeling" he thinks he has lost his religion. Some people who try and yet fail to get this same "feeling," become discouraged and drift into infidelity. I have found a number of such. One's faith should not be based upon one's feelings. Let your own good sense answer these questions:

1. Does joy (good feeling) produce faith, or does faith produce the joy?

2. Is your faith in God built upon your good feeling, or does your good feeling result from faith in God?

3. Do you do right when you feel good, or do you feel good when you do right?

8

4. Do you think you are pardoned because you feel that you are, or do you feel you are pardoned because you think that you are?

"Now faith comes by hearing, and hearing by the word of God," yet there are those who imagine that faith is received by a sort of miraculous " hypodermic injection!" The mourners' bench system is predicated upon the bald assumption that pardon comes in answer to prayer of a penitent believer, and that it is evidenced by sensation, that is, by hearing, feeling, seeing, smelling, or tasting something!

This system repudiates Peter's answer on the Day of Pentecost—"Repent and be baptized every one of you in the name of Jesus Christ for the remission of sins, and ye shall receive the gift of the Holy Spirit. And they that gladly received his word were baptized." Their efforts at the mourners' bench seem to be to convert God, and induce him to save the sinner in "some other way," and leave baptism out. "Full well ye reject the commandment of God that ye may keep your own tradition." (Mark 7: 9).

"Feeling" is very treacherous, and those who are trusting to the evidence (?) of "feeling" for pardon may be mistaken. I do not think this witness (feeling) is at all reliable. I shall proceed to show you why:

A stranger comes up and asks you if you've "got religion." You answer him, "Oh, yes, I've got religion; I'm justified, I'm pardoned."

He asks: "How do you know?"

You answer, "I know by my feelings," and you proceed to relate your experience.

He says, "That's right! Bless the Lord! Give me your hand!" After a hearty shake, he asks: "Have you got the *Second Blessing?*"

You exclaim, "*Second* blessing! Why, what's that?"

He answers: "Ah, my brother, there is a Second Blessing, the blessing of sanctification! You have got religion and you have your witness, but you still sin sometimes, do you not? Ah, yes! Well, you must repent of such sins and pray to God and he will give you the *Second Blessing*, which is sanctification, after which you will be able to live without committing any sin at all— you will be 'holy, even as he is holy.'"

You ask: "How shall I get this blessing? and how shall I know that I have it? How do *you* know that you have it?"

He answers: "I know by my 'feelings,' and that's the way you'll know it. Come, get right down here and get to repenting and praying, and I will pray with you until the Lord blesses you the second time."

You do so, and passing through the same process you did when you first went to the "anxious seat," you finally get *the feeling* again, and jump up saying, "I've got it! I've got it!" Got what?

"O, sanctification, that's what!" How do you know? "Why, by my *feelings!*"

You are very happy, and so is the stranger, because you have gotten through so gloriously, and while you are enjoying your *new* experience, a *second stranger* comes along, and asks: "Are you *justified?*"

You answer: "O, yes!"

He asks: "How do you know?"

You answer: "By my *feelings*—my experience."

He says: "That's right! Bless the Lord!"

He then asks: "Have you experienced the Second Blessing?"

You answer: "Yes, bless His holy name! I am sanctified, wholly sanctified. Glory!"

He says: "I am so glad! glory to God! But how do you *know* you are sanctified?"

You answer: "*I know by my feelings!*"

He tells you that's the right answer and you rejoice together for a while, and then he asks: "Have you experienced the *Third Blessing?*"

You exclaim: "*Third Blessing!* What is that?"

He says: "Ah, my dear brother, there is a *Third Blessing* following the other two, and more glorious still than either of them—it is the blessing of GLORIFICATION!"

He then begins to *juggle* with all the *threes* he can call to mind, such as air, earth and water!

Animal, vegetable and mineral! Soul, body and
spirit! Sun, moon and stars! Samuel's *three*
calls! Peter's *three* denials! *Three* years' ministry of Christ! *Three* thousand conversions on
the day of Pentecost! Peter's *three* visions upon
the housetop! *Three* witnesses on earth and *three*
witnesses in heaven! Elijah prostrated himself
three times! Samson deceived Delilah *three*
times! Jonah was *three* days and *three* nights in
the great fish! Christ was *three* days and nights
in the grave! Job's *three* friends, Eliphaz, Bil-
dad and Zophar! Ham, Shem and Japheth!
Shadrach, Meshach and Abednego! Abraham,
Isaac and Jacob! Father, Son and Holy Ghost.
Amen!

Rom. 8 : 30. "And whom he called, them he
also justified; and whom he justified, them he also
glorified." And then he informs (?) you that
there are *three* blessings—justification, *sanctification* and *glorification*, corresponding to the soul,
body and spirit of man; that *justification* is for
the *soul, sanctification* is for the *body*, while *glorification* is for the *spirit!*

You ask him, "How can I get this *Third Blessing?* What is it like? And how can I *know*
when I've got it ?"

He answers : "You get it in answer to prayer,
and you will know it by your feelings! O, it is
such a glorious, heavenly feeling! You will have
trances and visions, and you cannot tell whether

you are in the body or out of the body, but the Lord knoweth!"

You then kneel and begin praying for this *Third Blessing*, and you continue until you are greatly wrought up and in an ecstasy of excitement and religious fervor you exclaim, "I've got it! I've got it!!" and fall in a swoon. When you are restored and calmed you tell your friends of this glorious experience, you tell them you are *glorified* and you *know it by your feelings!*

But, gentle reader, I hear you say: "Well, I never heard of a *Third Blessing* before!" I answer: "Neither did I, but I don't see what is to hinder some fanatic or fool from starting it, and *proving* it *too*, by this ubiquitous witness, called *Feeling!**

Mohammedans use the anxious seat, and prove that they are all right by their feelings. Did you know that? The Roman Catholic, just from the

---

* NOTE.—I almost tremble in using the above illustration, lest Satan should put it into the heart of some wretch to act upon the suggestion, and create another sect which might be appropriately called the *Glorifiers!* Feeling is such a slave to the wishes of the heart that he offers his services in vindication of even the most heinous crimes. Guiteau *felt* that he had a commission from God to "remove" Garfield! The free-lover *feels* that he has a *divine* right to any woman whom he may fancy, and *feels* that he can abandon her just as soon as his *feelings* change! Is it possible that a man can do with impunity whatever he *feels* like doing? Here is a man who *feels* like stealing, but "thou shalt not steal." Another *feels* like murdering, but "thou shalt not kill." Another does *not feel* like serving God, but "thou shalt worship the Lord, thy God, and him only shalt thou serve." S. M. M.

confessional, tells you that he *knows* the priest has power to forgive sins, for when he was absolved he *felt* the burden rolled away, and he was so happy!

Thus we *impeach* this witness called "Feeling," as *utterly unreliable*. He testifies pardon to one man, then he testifies sanctification to another, and glorification to another. He attests the truth of Mohammedanism and also the power of the priest to forgive sins!

Can you prove your *justification* (pardon) *by your feelings* and then deny *sanctification* to another who brings forth the same witness to prove it? And the same of Mohammedanism and Catholicism? Does a *reliable* witness testify in such a manner?

The following is from Rev. Kerr B. Tupper, pastor of the First Baptist Church of Denver, Col. His subject was, "KNOWING YOU ARE A CHRISTIAN," and delivered at the Capitol Hill Baptist Mission, Feb. 24, 1892. Dr. Tupper said that the question involved in his discourse was one of the fundamental questions of Christianity. He said: "All thorough Christians have absolute certainty," but he thought that many people put wrong tests to themselves in settling the matter. "Many make feeling the standard of judgment. Nowhere in the Bible is emphasis placed on emotion. In Scripture it is always principle and truth, never feeling and emotion. The only test is obedience, based on an intelligent faith. The true Christian is the man who is willing to yield heart and intellect to the service of God."

So much for Doctor Tupper. But penitents are taken to the "mourners' bench" to "get religion," just when they should be taken to their baptism for the remission of sins.

When the children of Israel came to the Red Sea they stopped and began to cry unto the Lord, (set up a "mourners' bench.") "And the Lord said unto Moses, Wherefore criest thou unto me? Speak unto the children of Israel, that they go forward." (Ex. 15 : 15.)

Yes, they were to go forward to their baptism, for they were all baptized into Moses in the cloud and in the Sea. But let me *prove* to you that the "mourners' bench" has been put in the place of baptism. Chas. G. Finney, (Congregationalist), born at Litchfield, Conn., 1792, called to Oberlin College, Ohio, as a professor in 1835, and died there as its president in 1875, (see Biographical Dictionary,) said in one of his revival lectures, in making a defense of the "anxious seat:" "The church has always felt it necessary to have something of this kind to answer this very purpose. *In the days of the apostles baptism answered this purpose.* The gospel was preached to the people, and then all those who were willing to be on the side of Christ, were called out to be baptized. *It held the place that the anxious seat does now as a public manifestation of their determination to be Christians."* (Italics mine.)

President Finney is the man who popularized the "mourners' bench" in this country, and here you have his candid confession that the system of evangelization practiced by the apostles has been *changed* by uninspired men, in that the "anxious seat" has taken the *place of baptism!* Our Lord said, "In vain do they worship me, teaching for doctrines the commandments of men."

Geo. P. Fisher, Professor of Church History in Yale Divinity School, says: "The one article of faith at the outset was that Jesus was the Messiah. Whoever acknowledged him in this character was baptized." (Page 42, Chap. 3, "Christian Life, Christian Worship, Christian Teaching.")

Neander's Church History, Vol. I., pp. 335, says: "At the beginning when it was important [is it not still important?] that the church should rapidly extend itself, those who confessed their belief in Jesus as the Messiah (among the Jews), or their belief in one God, and Jesus as the Messiah (among th Gentiles), were immediately baptized, as appears from the New Testament."

Dr. Robinson says: "Among primitive Christians there was a uniform belief that Jesus was the Christ." And again: "These churches were all composed of reputed *believers*, who had been baptized by immersion on the profession of their faith." (Benedict's History, vol. I., pp. 8, 99.)

Mosheim says: "Whoever acknowledged Christ as the Savior of mankind, and made a solemn profession of his confidence in him, was *immediately baptized* and received into the church." (Maclain's Mosheim, First Century, p. 38, Part II., Chap. 2, Sec. 7.) And again, p. 42, Chap. III., Sec. 5, he says: "In the earliest times of the church all who professed firmly to believe that Jesus was the only Redeemer of the world, and who in consequence of this profession, promised to live in a manner conformable to the purity of his holy religion, were *immediately received* among the disciples of Christ."

"He went on his way rejoicing." Who? The Ethiopian eunuch, *after* he was baptized but not *before.*

"He rejoiceth, believing in God, with all his house." Who's that? The Philippian jailer, *after* he was baptized, and not *before.*

"And now why tarriest thou? Arise and be baptized and wash away thy sins, calling on the name of the Lord." Who is that? Saul of Tarsus, who had seen Jesus on the way to Damascus, and had been praying three days and three nights, without eating or drinking; but he is commanded to be baptized, as a penitent believer, for the remission or pardon of his sins. "And [he] arose and was baptized; and when he had received meat he was strengthened." (Acts 9: 18, 19.) If the anxious seat is the Lord's way, why didn't Ananias keep Saul there until he "got through," "got religion?"

We leave the question with you. Will you follow the Lord, or will you keep your own traditions?

R. A. OMER.

THE subject of this sketch was born in Adams County, Ill., Sept. 8, 1857. His parents, who were of Pennsylvania Dutch extraction, moved to Illinois from Jefferson County, Ky., in the spring of 1855, and settled on a farm near Camp Point. It was here, amidst the privations and hardships common to the poorer classes, that Robert was born. His early educational advantages were very much limited. He attended the district school three months in the year, and worked upon the farm the remainder of the time. But the vigorous exercise of farm life had a very salutary effect upon his physical organization.

When nineteen years of age he began a course of study in the High School at Camp Point, which at that time was presided over by Prof. S. F. Hall, one of the best educators and disciplinarians in the West. After the completion of the course of study here, some time was spent in Abingdon College and Christian University.

Bro. Omer obeyed the gospel when he was seventeen years of age, during a series of meetings held by D. R. Lucas at Pleasant View Church, in Adams County. From this time he manifested a deep desire to become a preacher of the gospel,

R. A. OMER.

and at once began preparation for the work. At the age of twenty-three he began to exercise his talents in some of the neighborhood school houses. December 29, 1882, he led to the matrimonial altar Miss Jessie B. Dewey, of Camp Point. To them have been born three children, two boys and one girl; the oldest, a boy, died when only four months old.

Bro. Omer has always made Camp Point his home and preached for surrounding churches. He served the church at Camp Point as pastor for four years, and during the time, without any outside help, succeeded in adding over three hundred to the membership. He entered the evangelistic field three years ago, in which he has been very successful, having added over fifteen hundred to the various churches where he has labored.

He is a fine specimen of physical manhood, standing five feet and eleven inches tall, and weighs two hundred and twenty pounds. He possesses a clear strong voice and a robust constitution capable of much hard work.

As a preacher, one of his brethren thus describes him: "Bro. Omer now occupies the front rank among our people as an evangelist, and hundreds are being converted under his ministry. His sermons are scholarly, logical, and pre-eminently scriptural. He is bold in the denunciation of sin and tender in appeal to the sinner. He never fails to entertain, but commands the attention of earnest, thoughtful hearers from night to night. Does not resort to any of the modern ' clap-trap' or sensational methods so frequently employed, but combines eloquence, argument and exhortation in such a way as to reach the head as well as the heart, and hold his audiences in rapt attention during every service. He never writes a sermon or commits one to memory, and seldom uses notes, but speaks altogether extemporaneously. He makes no pretensions to being a writer and must be heard to be appreciated. Is a fine judge of human nature, which is very helpful to him in his work."

Bro. Omer is now in the field, where he expects to continue, and is being assisted in his work by the singing evangelist, Prof. C. C. Maxwell, of Lincoln, Ill.

CHRISTIANITY VERSUS MORALITY.

R. A. OMER.

(Mark 16: 15, 16; 2 Cor. 5: 17.)

JESUS gave his disciples two commissions. The first contained geographical and national boundary lines. " Go not into the way of the Gentiles, and into any city of the Samaritans enter ye not. But go rather to the lost sheep of the house of Israel." (Matt. 10 : 5, 6). But in the last commission, which was given them from Mount Olivet just before his ascension, geographical and national boundary lines were forever discarded, and in the proclamation were included every nation, kindred, tongue and tribe. "And he said unto them, Go ye into all the world and preach the gospel to every creature. He that believeth and is baptized shall be saved; but he that believeth not shall be condemned." (Mark 16 : 15, 16). In this proclamation he did not except any nationality or class of persons. Did not so much as intimate there were those who were sufficiently good without obeying the gospel, or who needed no regeneration. Their mission was not restricted to the grossly immoral, or outbroken sinner, "but every creature," regardless of past life or character. This is the truth

(127)

which is so plainly taught in the parable of the marriage of the king's son. "Go ye therefore into the highways, and as many as ye shall find, bid to the marriage. So those servants went out into the highways and gathered *all*, as many as they found, both *bad* and *good*, and the wedding was furnished with guests." (Matt. 22: 9, 10). This part of the parable evidently has reference to the preaching of the apostles, and the faithful men who were to take up the work after them, under the last commission. And among the number who accepted the invitation were the *good* as well as the *bad*. This Scripture, of itself, should forever silence the supporters of the *good-enough theory*.

A DIFFICULT TASK.

It is a most difficult task to convince many people that it is their duty to become Christians or members of the body of Christ. Some of them will reason like this: I pay my honest debts and attend to my own business. I have never wronged anyone, but try in a general way to observe the *Golden Rule*. I give to the church, and to the poor and needy. I have no bad habits, such as swearing or drinking, and try to live and do as nearly right as possible.

The difficulty with the majority of this class of persons is this: They look upon the church as a reformatory institution, designed for the benefit of the disreputable and exceedingly wicked classes; and in no way intended to benefit or help them. If they were as vile and godless as some people, it would be all right for them to become church members; but as it is they are good enough as they are, and a profession of Christianity is not necessary in their case. And they fully expect to share in the welcome plaudit, "Come, ye blessed of my Father, inherit the kingdom prepared for you from the foundation of the world."

There are still others who excuse themselves for not becoming Christians upon the ground that there is no difference between the church and the world. In their estimation the average man of the world is as good as the average man of the church. Some of this same class take a still more unreasonable position. They reason like this: The church does not change any one's moral character, consequently the church does not save any one. If a man is by nature a liar, the church can never make him truthful; if he is by nature a thief, the church can never make him honest. And upon the other hand, the man who belongs to the church and is strictly honest, truthful and sober, would have been just as much so out of the church as in it.

The difficulty with this class of persons is plainly apparent. They regard man as making his moral character just what it is, regardless of any outside influence; that our surroundings and

9

associations have nothing whatever to do with us. In other words, that we stand or fall by our own efforts alone in life, and that whatever we are we owe to self alone; which is unreasonable, contrary to the facts in the case, and above everything else, unscriptural.

WHAT WE PROPOSE DOING.

In this discourse we wish to examine very critically the positions taken by these different classes of persons, and show how unreasonable and untenable they are in the light of God's word and the facts in the case. We do not for a moment question the honesty or sincerity of many persons represented in these classes; but it should be remembered that it is not a question of honesty or sincerity, but, What saith the word of the Lord? And what are the facts in the case? " Let God be true though every man a liar." On all questions relating to life and salvation there should be a direct appeal made to the Scriptures. I like the spirit which manifested itself in one of God's true noblemen in the following language: "To the law and the testimony; if they speak not according to this word, it is because there is no light in them." (Isa. 8 : 20.) Let us then in this investigation make the Bible the man of our counsel and from its truth and the facts in the case we trust there shall be no appeal made.

THE FIRST CLASS EXAMINED.

Let us examine the position occupied by the first class of moralists enumerated in this discourse, those who are *already good enough*, and who are depending wholly upon the morality-alone theory to save them. It would be highly satisfactory to know how this class of persons meet the issue contained in the Savior's language to Nicodemus, "Except a man be born again he cannot see the kingdom of God." (John 3 : 3.) Nicodemus, like many good moralists of to-day, was slow to understand, and Christ further explained to him, "Except a man be born of *water* and of the *Spirit*, he cannot enter into the kingdom of God." (Verse 5.) What may we learn from this interview? What important lessons did the Savior intend to teach Nicodemus and all the world of mankind? (1) That man in his unconverted or unregenerated state is not in the kingdom of God. (2) That in order to get into the kingdom of God he must be born again. (3) That the new birth is of a twofold nature, consisting of *water* and the *Spirit*. But the moralist may inquire : Does it necessarily follow, because I am not in the kingdom of God, that I am going to be lost? We reply, Under the reign of Jesus Christ the church, or kingdom of God, is the only appointed institution in which man can be saved. And that there may be no misunderstanding in the use of terms we take

occasion to explain the signification of the following expressions : Kingdom of God, Kingdom of
Heaven, Church of God, Church of Christ, Church
of the First Born and Body of Christ, are synony-
mous terms and represent one and the same institution, and are used interchangeably in the Scriptures ; except that the terms " Church of Christ "
and " Church of God " are sometimes used in a
limited sense, that is, with reference to some particular congregation of believers, as the Church of
God at Corinth, or the Church of Christ at Rome.
While the terms, Kingdom of God, Kingdom of
Heaven, Church of the First Born, and Body of
Christ are used in an unlimited sense and include
the whole family of God.   We use all these terms
in this broad, unlimited sense, representing the
entire body of Christ on earth.

NO HOPE OUT OF THE CHURCH.

That no person has any hope or assurance of
salvation out of this institution, we offer in testimony the following Scripture facts as truths for
consideration.   All the promises of God are in the
church. (2 Cor. 1: 20); these promises include the
following: (1) Remission of sins. "Who hath delivered us from the power of darkness, and hath
translated us into the kingdom of his dear Son, in
whom we have redemption through his blood, even
the forgiveness of sins." (Col. 1: 13, 14).   (2) The

gift of the Holy Spirit. "Then Peter said unto them, Repent and be baptized every one of you, in the name of Jesus Christ for the remission of sins, and ye shall receive the gift of the Holy Spirit, (Ac. 2: 38). "In whom ye also trusted, after that ye heard the word of truth, the gospel of your salvation, in whom also after that ye believed, ye were sealed with that Holy Spirit of promise." (Eph. 1: 13). (3) Eternal life. "And I heard a voice from heaven saying unto me, write, Blessed are the dead which die in the Lord from hence forth; yea, saith the Spirit, that they may rest from their labors, and their works do follow them." (Rev. 14: 13). And there can be left no possible room for controversy or quibbling over the expressions, "in whom" and "in the Lord," found in these Scripture references, since they refer to the church or spiritual body of Christ. "And hath put all things under his feet and gave him to be the head over all things to the church, which is his body, the fullness of him that filleth all in all." (Eph. 1: 22, 23). Considering the great blessings and benefits to be derived from membership in the Church of Christ, well may we say with the poet,

> "I love thy church, oh, God,
>   Her walls before thee stand,
> Dear as the apple of thine eye,
>   And graven in thy hand."

MORALITY ALONE WILL NOT SAVE.

Of this we have some very forcible Scripture examples. Returning to Christ's language to Nicodemus, the Savior says: "Verily, verily I say unto thee, Ye must be born again." This to Nicodemus was strange and startling language. And while he failed to grasp the meaning of the Savior, as is apparent in the answers made him, "How can a man be born when he is old?" "How can these things be?" It would doubtless have proven equally strange and startling had he fully understood it, for the simple reason that Nicodemus must have been, to say the least of it, a very good, moral man. He was a ruler of the Jews, and in religion a Pharisee, the straitest sect of the religious orders of the Jews. Under these circumstances it would be but natural for him to regard himself as being good enough. But Jesus did not so recognize him; without the *new birth* he was an unsaved man. A few reflections upon this case. If Nicodemus, without the *new birth*, was an unsaved man, every other accountable person is in an unsaved state without the *new birth*. And if in Nicodemus' case a two-fold birth was necessary, a birth of "water and the Spirit," a two-fold birth is necessary in every other case. These conclusions are logical and scriptural and therefore irrefutable. Let us take another Scripture example. Turn to the tenth chapter of the book of Acts. In this chapter we have an ac-

count of the conversion of Cornelius, the captain
of a Roman military band, and his household,
also a description of the character of Cornelius.
Let us give attention to the character of Cornelius.
What kind of a man was he? The inspired historian describes him in the following language:
"A *devout* man and one that *feared God* with all
his house, which gave *much alms* to the people,
and *prayed to God* always." (v. 2). Luke, in this
passage, ascribes to Cornelius four as noble traits
of character as are to be found in any man; traits
which, as a whole, are not possessed by one man
in five thousand outside of the Church of Christ.
And yet with all these noble and commendable
traits of character, Cornelius was an unsaved man,
for the angel gave him the following instruction:
"And now send men to Joppa, and call for one
Simon, whose surname is Peter; he lodgeth with
one Simon, a tanner, whose house is by the sea-
side; he shall tell thee what *thou auuhtest to do.*"
(v. 5, 6). Cornelius' example upon the receipt of
the angel's instruction is very commendable and
worthy of special emphasis. Had some of our
modern moralists been there, instead of obeying the
instruction of the angel, they would have protested
and offered a hundred and one objections to such a
procedure. But not so of Cornelius; for as soon as
the angel departed he at once proceeded to follow
out the instruction given. "And when the angel
which spake unto Cornelius was departed, he called

two of his household servants, and a devout soldier of them that waited on him continually. And when he had declared all these things unto them, he sent them to Joppa." (v. 7, 8). With this reflection we dismiss the case. If it was necessary for Cornelius to submit to the authority of Christ and obey the gospel, it is absolutely necessary for all other persons to submit to the authority of Christ and obey the gospel, no matter how good their moral standing.

MORALITY ALONE WILL NOT SAVE, BECAUSE IT DOES NOT RECOGNIZE THE AUTHORITY OF CHRIST.

We do not deny that there are many good people outside of the church. Cornelius, as we have learned, was an exceptionally good man. And we are willing and free to admit that so far as this world is concerned there are people out of the church—just as good and many of them much better than some who are in the church. By this we mean that there are those who are just as honest, as honorable and upright in their dealings with their fellow-man, as good neighbors, fathers, mothers, husbands and wives out of the church as many who are in it, and some of them much better. But we may be honorable and upright in our dealings with our fellow-man, be kind and affectionate fathers and mothers, husbands and wives, and at the same time not recognize Christ as our Savior. It requires a pretty good man to live up to the teachings of Odd Fellowship, Free Masonry, and many other man-made institutions. But you may become a highly honored member of any of these orders without becoming a Christian, for to become a Christian is to recognize Christ as a personal Savior by obeying him in all his commandments. And the Scriptures plainly teach that Jesus alone can save. Jesus himself declared: "I am the way, the truth and the life; no man cometh to the Father but by me." (Jno. 14: 6). Peter, in vindicating himself and John before the Jewish council for teaching and healing in the name of Christ, used the following impressive language: "Neither is there salvation in any other; for there is none other name under heaven given among men, whereby we must be saved." (Ac. 4: 12). Paul, speaking of Jesus, says: "And being made perfect, he became the author of eternal salvation unto all them that obey him." (Heb. 5: 9). The force of these passages cannot be evaded. Jesus is the "way," the "truth" and the "life;" the only one through whom salvation can be attained and eternal life enjoyed. This same Jesus says, "Ye must be born again," or you "cannot see the kingdom of God;" and "Except a man be born of water and of the Spirit he cannot enter into the kingdom of God." Christ has all authority; we cannot ignore him, we cannot leave him out. Then let us say with the poet,

" All hail the power of Jesus' name,
　Let angels prostrate fall;
　Bring forth the royal diadem
　And crown him Lord of all."

OBJECTIONS REFUTED.

Let us give attention to some of the objections
which naturally follow the above Scriptural conclusions, such as the following: "I am just as good
as many of your church members, and much
better than some of them. In fact there are people
in the church who do things I would not be guilty
of doing under any consideration. I know people
who profess to be church members, who drink, go
to the theatre, dance and do many other things
of like nature, I would not think of doing." Granting the truthfulness of the above objections, which
I do not pretend to deny, what does that have to
do with you? Does it amount to any argument
in favor of your salvation? Most assuredly not.
Simply because some people in the church are
acting the hypocrite is no reason why the Lord is
going to save you in neglect of duty. The difficulty with this class of objectors is this: They
seem to take it for granted because persons have
their names in the church book they are going to
be saved, which is not necessarily true. We may
be lost in the church as well as out of it if we are
unfaithful. And because we have our names on
the church book is not of itself an assurance of
our salvation. The Savior had this same thought

in view when he spake "the parable of the ten
virgins" (Matt. 25: 1, 13), and "the parable of the
draw net" (Matt. 13: 47, 49).   Every parable contains a central thought or truth as well as a leading lesson.   The central thought or truth contained
in both of these parables is the possibility of unfaithfulness in the church.   The lessons are those
of warning to them who may be trusting to a nom-
inal church membership to save them.   Paul had
in mind the possibility of unfaithfulness and loss
of the soul in the church when he spoke thus of
himself: "But I keep under my body and bring it
into subjection, lest that by any means, when I
have preached to others, I myself should be cast-
away." (1 Cor. 9: 27).   Dear sinner, do not rely
upon the lack of steadfastness upon the part of
some in the church as an excuse for neglecting
your duty; or take it for granted because some
one else is unfaithful that the Lord is going to save
you in your sins, but come to Christ, obey him
and live.   Hear the sayings of Jesus and do them,
regardless of how others may treat him, and you
will have a foundation which all the storms and
tempests of time can never undermine or sweep
away.

THE SECOND CLASS OF MORAL OBJECTORS.

Those who contend there is no particular difference between the church and the world; that the
average man of the world is as good as the aver-

age man of the church.   Of this class of persons
one of two things is absolutely true, they are either
dishonest or inexcusably ignorant.   If there is in
reality no difference between the church and the
world, then the world would be just as well off
without the church as with it, a conclusion to which
honesty and intelligence combined could never
lead anyone.   And yet if there is no difference
between the church and the world this is the logical conclusion to which all must come, a conclusion which is wholly foreign to the light in which
Jesus regarded the relation of his disciples to the
world.   "Ye are the salt of the earth;" "Ye are
the light of the world.   A city set on a hill cannot
be hid." (Matt. 5: 13, 14).   Here Jesus positively
declares his disciples to be the "salt" of the earth
and the "light" of the world.   And I would rather
have the authority of Jesus on any subject than
the combined testimony of men and angels.   Inasmuch, then, as the disciples are the salt of the earth
and the light of the world there must of necessity
be some difference between the church and the
world.   But this affirmation does not, of course, pre-
clude the possibility of the salt losing its savor
or of the light going out; for in the same connection in which the Savior speaks of the disciples'
being the salt of the earth and the light of the
world, he grants the possibility of such a misfortune.   "Ye are the salt of the earth; but if the salt
have *lost its savor*, wherewith shall it be salted?

it is thenceforth good for nothing, but to be cast out and to be trodden under foot of men;" "Neither do men light a candle, and put it under a bushel, but on a candlestick, and it giveth light unto all that are in the house. Let your light so shine before men that they may see your good works and glorify your Father which is in heaven." (Matt. 5: 13, 15, 16). But while the salt may lose its saltness, and the light go out in the lives of many, certainly no fair-minded person would have the audacity to affirm this to be true of all the professed followers of Christ; or, in other words, that all the vast army of Jesus Christ are simply an assembly of hypocrites. None would dare make a charge of this kind, for the time has never been in the history of the church, notwithstanding the reverses and mighty conflicts through which it has passed, that it was wholly void of "light" and "salt." Look at the darkness and superstition which reigned and ruled in an apostate church during the fifteenth century, and yet the church of that century furnished a Luther who dared assail the Vatican at Rome and face the Diet of Worms. And while to-day the percentage of unfaithfulness in the church may be very large, yet there is "light" and "salt" enough in it to save the world from wreck and ruin. We should also remember that it does not require any large number of faithful disciples to become the light of the community or city in which they live. This

is the view which was held by Paul in his epistle
to the church at Philippi: "Do all things without murmurings and disputings, that ye may be
blameless and harmless, the sons of God, without
rebuke, in the midst of a crooked and perverse
nation, among whom ye shine as lights in the
world." (Phil. 2: 14, 15). This comparatively small
and struggling congregation of disciples were recognized by Paul as being the light of all Europe,
for it was the only church at this time in Europe.
And if one congregation can become the light of a
great nation, certainly one faithful disciple may
become the light of a whole city. Only about
one person out of six in this country is a Christian, and yet the leaven is sufficiently powerful to
lighten the whole lump. And the influence of
Christianity permeates the whole country from
center to circumference.

THE RELATION OF THE CHURCH TO THE WORLD.

The church sustains the same relation to the
moral and spiritual world, that the sun does to the
physical world. As the sun gives light and heat
to the physical world, so the church gives light and
warmth to the moral or spiritual world. While on
earth Jesus was the light of the world. "Then
spake Jesus again unto them, saying, I am the
light of the world, he that followeth me shall not
walk in darkness, but shall have the light of life."

(Jno. 8: 12). In the absence of Jesus the disciples became the light of the world. Their light, like that of the moon, is a reflected light. The moon has no light within itself, but simply reflects the light of the sun; so the disciples have no light within themselves, but they reflect the life and image of the Christ-likeness which is in them. This is the sense in which the disciples are the light of the world. And in preaching the gospel of Christ, and living it out in their lives, they become the salt of the earth. Take away the physical sun and the natural world would be left in darkness, and in a very short time become as cold and sterile as Greenland upon a wintry morning. And so if you were to remove the spiritual light bearers, the spiritual world would become dark, cold and cheerless. Who would desire such darkness to settle down upon us as to-day envelopes China, India, the South Sea Islands and many other portions of the earth? Those who talk about there being no difference between the church and the world would not, under any consideration, live in a country where they have no Christian churches. Remove all the churches from this country for ten years and how many of these people who assert that there is no difference between the church and the world would want to remain here ten years longer without them! With all the organized forces of the people of God working for the overthrow of the works of the devil, in many places he holds high carnival and sin goes unrestrained. The Lord only knows what the results would be if the agencies and instrumentalities of the church for good were entirely withdrawn. And yet you say there is no particular difference between the church and the world. This class of people, to say the least of it, must be morally blind.

GOOD INFLUENCES OUTSIDE OF THE CHURCH.

But, says one, did you not admit that there were good people outside of the church, and this being true, would not they wield their influence for good and save the world from going to the bad without the influence of the church? We would ask, How came these good people outside of the church? The answer is very apparent to every intelligent mind. They are walking by the light others are carrying. To illustrate: One very dark night two brethren walked home together from the meeting. They succeeded in getting along without difficulty, for one of them carried a lantern, which gave a very bright light. The one without the lantern succeeded in getting along fully as well as the one who carried it, for he enjoyed the benefit of its light. And so of these good, moral people outside of the church; they have no light of their own to guide them through this sinful world, but they are walking by the light the people of God are carrying. What a grand thing it is for some people to have the light and influence of Christian people by which to pilot their lives, and then, in a semi-pharisaical way, parade themselves before the world as being as good as the people whose lives and examples have made them what they are.

> " Lives of great men all remind us
> We can make our lives sublime,
> And departing, leave behind us
> Foot-prints on the sands of time."

It is Christian life and influence which produce the difference in the morals of the people outside of the church in different places. Go into a community or town where they have strong, influential churches and a good, healthy Christian life, and there you will find the moral condition of the people, in general, outside of the church, far superior to those communities or towns where the churches are weak and not so well represented. This certainly proves beyond all doubt that there must be some difference between the church and the world. And Jesus understood himself when he said of his disciples, "Ye are the salt of the earth," " Ye are the light of the world." There may be little difference between some people in the church and some people of the world, but to say there is no difference between the church and the world is a falsehood too glaring to need any further refutation. But suppose—

10

for the sake of argument—we grant, what is not true, that there is *little* difference between the church and the world.   A little difference in the beginning sometimes makes a very great difference in the end. To illustrate: There is a courthouse in the state of Ohio where the water falling upon the western slope of the roof runs into the Ohio river, then into the Mississippi and finally empties into the Gulf of Mexico.   While that which falls upon the eastern slope runs into the Atlantic basin and empties into the Atlantic Ocean.   What a little difference in the beginning, and yet how great the difference in the end!   So sinner, there may be little difference between you and some weak disciple, but in the final winding up of human affairs that difference may be sufficiently great to place the weak disciple upon the right hand of Jesus and you upon his left.   But once more, for the sake of argument, suppose we admit, what is not true, that there is *no* difference between the church and the world. Please tell me how that would in any wise help the case of the unconverted or unregenerate? Would not all share alike the same condemnation? " Depart from me, ye that work iniquity."

GROUNDS OF ACCEPTANCE WITH GOD.

Our acceptance with God does not depend upon what others are doing.   We cannot go riding into heaven on the bad record some one else is making.

The church may be full of hypocrisy, and there may be little difference between the church and the world, but that will not save the unconverted. Our salvation rests upon two points. First, we must be born again. "Marvel not that I said unto thee, Ye must be born again." (Jno. 3: 7). "Therefore if any man be in Christ he is a new creature; old things have passed away, behold all things are become new." (2 Cor. 5: 17). Second, "We must develop in Christian life." (2 Pet. 1: 5, 11). Then let us all, both saint and sinner, come to a knowledge of the truth, obey the commandments and live. So that when time and timely things have passed away and the day of judgment appears we may hear the welcome plaudit, "Come, ye blessed of my Father, inherit the kingdom prepared for you from the foundation of the world."

BIOGRAPHICAL SKETCH OF GEO. F. HALL.

GEO. F. HALL was born at Clarksville, Butler County, Iowa, September 23, 1864. He is the eldest child of John and Mary Hall, who were brought up in McLean county, Ill., and emigrated to Iowa at an early day, thus experiencing the hardships incident to pioneer life.

George's early days were spent on a farm, working hard in the summer-time, and attending the district school in the winter. In 1880 he attended the Clarksville Graded School, where he was distinguished by close application to study, and stood highest in his classes on final examination.

Desiring to attend this school another year, and being short of funds, he applied for the position of janitor of the school-building, which paid the munificent salary of $8.00 per month, but was unsuccessful in securing the prize.

Nothing daunted, however, George secured the agency for the "Life of Garfield," and being a good talker, he was so successful in selling the book that he was able to enter Drake University in January, 1882, the second term in the history of this now well-known and highly successful institution.

He attended the University " off and on," as he characteristically expresses it, for four years, but did not graduate, the call being too strong for him in the ministerial field.

Bro. Hall made the " good confession " when he was 13 years old in a meeting held by N. A. McConnell and J. W. Moore, two of Iowa's noble pioneer preachers. Practically he was born and reared a Disciple, and loves " our plea " with a passionate devotion. He early thought of entering the ministry, but at one time came very nearly giving it up for journalism, for which profession he has many good qualifications.

After the death of his mother in December, 1884, he could not think of any other profession than the ministry. So in January, 1885, he entered Drake University again, and placed himself under the instruction of that noble teacher, Prof. D. R. Dungan. He preached his first sermon in February following.

In April, 1886, he accepted a call to become pastor of the church at Manhattan, Kansas, where he labored successfully for one year and a half.

While at Manhattan July 14, 1886, he was married to Miss Laura Woods, a quiet and true woman, and a most worthy help-meet in every respect. She is earnest, but modest in the Lord's work. Two boys have been born to them, Paul, born in June, 1887, and Barton, born in January, 1891. Theirs is a happy home, indeed, filled with books, flowers, music and sunshine, but above all with the love of Christ.

On leaving Manhattan, Bro. Hall became pastor of the church in Lincoln, Kansas, where he labored very successfully one year. He reluctantly gave up the charge there to enter the evangelistic field; but in February, 1889, he accepted a call to the pastorate of the First Christian Church at Emporia, where he spent two and a half years, and where his enthusiastic labors were highly appreciated and crowned with marvelous success. Under his *regime* over 440 were added to the church, a large debt paid off, and a missionary spirit quickened, the results of which eternity alone can fully measure.

In the fall of '91, Bro. Hall resigned at Emporia to gratify an ardent ambition to enter the general evangelistic field. Engaging his brother-in-law, Prof. E. M. Hutto, of St. George, Kan., as soloist and musical director, a young man of many rare, good qualities, he launched upon his work at Chariton, Iowa, and soon gained national fame as a revivalist.

Following is a list of his larger meetings in the order of their size: Eureka, Ill., 36 days, 187 accessions; Chariton, Ia., 36 days, 156 accessions; Sterling, Ill., 29 days, 143 accessions; Griswold, Ia., 35 days, 126 accessions; Cameron, Mo., 36 days, 101 accessions; Emporia, Kan., (first meeting) 51 days, 81 accessions; Emporia, Kan., (second meeting) 51 days, 63 accessions; Hartford, Kan., 22 days, 75 accessions; Griswold, Ia., (second meeting) 16 days, 54 accessions; Fairfield, Iowa, 32 days, 54 accessions; Louisiana, Mo., 31 days, 53 accessions; Johnstown, Pa., 29 days, 59 accessions; Carthage, Ill., 29 days, 55 accessions; Toronto, Canada, 23 days, 40 accessions.

His health becoming impaired from the effects of la grippe and over-work together, he cut off all engagements in the autumn of '92, and located with the North Side Church, Chicago, Ill., where he labored 14 months under many disadvantages, but succeeded in adding 110 names to the church roll, and purchased a valuable building site. January 1st, 1894, he removed so Decatur, Ill., and took charge of the First Christian Church, where he is now actively engaged in what promises to be the greatest work of his life thus far.

Bro. Hall is an untiring worker, and knows no such thing as fail, although he plans everything on a large scale. He is cheerful in disposition; sees the ludicrous and turns it to many a good purpose; courageous, daring to say boldly what he believes to be right, without sugar-coating his statements. He is a man of methods, and believes thoroughly in printer's ink. Few preachers give so much attention as he to the organization and management of forces. He is not only an earnest and eloquent speaker, but a fluent writer, and has already copyrighted several works,—"Some American Evils and Their Remedies," "The Lord's Exchequer," and "Plain Points on Personal Purity," all of which have received much favorable comment, and are having a splendid sale among all the leading religious books. He is enthusiastic in the work of missions, as well as in every other good work. He is a great reader and keeps abreast with the important events of the times; indeed, constant growth seems to be one of his chief characteristics.

GEO. F. HALL.

THE ROMAN GOVERNOR'S QUESTION.*

GEO. F. HALL.

"Pilate saith unto them, What shall I do then with Jesus, which is called Christ? They all say unto him, Let him be crucified."—Matt. 27: 22.

L ET us for a few moments imagine ourselves a hundred miles above the earth, and that everything we see beneath us is a sea. Now we are just where I want us to be for a little while at the beginning of this sermon—a great, broad sea stretching out before us. Away yonder on the left we see land; away yonder on the other hand also land; land on the left and land on the right. As the earth appears rounding, so also the sea appears rounding. Sailing out from yonder land, the dim outlines of which we can just perceive, is a little boat, and as it comes nearer and nearer we can observe it more closely. It passes on and is soon out of sight.

We will call this imaginary sea the *ocean of life*, and that land on the left *eternity*, and that on the right *eternity*. The ocean of life lies between two mighty extremes!

*This sermon, delivered in Chicago, Ill., April 3, 1892, was stenographically reported by Miss Jessie Williams, from whose notes it is here presented, as revised by the author.

(153)

Now if you will notice that little boat as it puts out from the land on the left you will observe that it is in good trim.   The paint is fresh; the sails are bright; the ropes are new and strong.   Everything is fair and promising, full of hope and life.   But as the boat advances across the sea we notice that it comes in contact with storms and tempests, and sometimes they are wrecked on the rocks, and go down in the sea.   Even if a boat sails on safely we see that it becomes in time much dilapidated, and must finally be taken from its course.

So we start out on the voyage of life, full of hope and enthusiasm.   You can't discourage a young man or woman.   They are full of life and health and strength, and have all the delights of anticipation which only the young can know.   But as they pass on many go down in mid sea, and fail to reach the golden harbor of a good old age.   In due time all pass out of sight, and the place that once knew them knows them no more.

The question to-night is, when a soul has run its course on the ocean of life, is there any place beyond where it can anchor in safety?   Is there a life beyond the sea of time?   Is there a harbor beyond this sea which we commonly call earthly existence?   Is there *hope beyond?*   This is the question, and it is the greatest question with which we have to do.

Men talk a great deal now-a-days about the tariff question—high tariff and low tariff, protec-

tion and free trade, (and about all common mortals
can get out of it after all is *tweedledee* and *tweedle-
dum*.) Then there is the race question, and it is a
great question. The saloon question is a great
question. And to a young man just starting out
in life there are some great personal questions:—
What am I going to be? a doctor, merchant, lawyer, or what? (and too many of them become
"what," and are failures in life). And where shall
I live? in country or city, in Europe or America?
Young men and young women sometimes say,
Whom shall we marry? and that is a great question. But great as these questions are they sink
into insignificance beside this one, *Is there life beyond?* Beyond what we can see with these earthly eyes, and experience with these mortal senses,
is there joy? is there safety? is there life? *What
is beyond?* It is the old question. When the father
and mother take the babe from its little crib and
lay it away in the cold grave, they naturally inquire, Shall we see our darling beyond? When we
mournfully smooth back a mother's gray hair and
lay her cold form in the tomb, we anxiously inquire, Shall we see mother again?

I once preached the funeral sermon of a railroad
man, who had fallen from his train and been killed;
nineteen cars had passed over his body, and he
was carried home crushed and bleeding. His fel-
low-workmen sent for me to come down and preach
a sermon at his funeral. I asked them, What do

you want me to talk about? and they said, "Is death the end?" That's what they wanted to hear, a discussion of that same old question Job asked so long ago. Railroad men often do not think much about such subjects when they are well and strong and healthy; but when one of their companions is snatched away they begin to think.

Is there hope beyond? We see them going one by one, now the children, now the middle-aged, now the old. During the past year thousands of old people have gone with the dreadful disease known as la grippe, or Russian influenza. During the spring of each year we have scarlet fever and diphtheria carrying away thousands and thousands of little folks. And at all times we have accidents, dangerous alike to both old and young. So it seems to me that people ought to stop and think about these things. And yet men go on with their swearing and drinking, with their lying and cheating. They go on with their wickedness and meanness in its various forms, acting as though the present would continue forever with its freedom from judgment and retribution.

A man said to me once in Emporia, Kan., "I have not been to church but two or three times in five years." Said I, "This thing is going to stop after awhile." He looked up inquiringly. "This thing is not going on just as it is now," I continued. "After awhile you will *come up a-standing*, as the expression is; you will have to give an ac-

count of the deeds done in the body." It made
him think.

After awhile there will be no more sixteen-story
buildings; there won't be any more railroads or
telephones; and it will not matter then whether
you put your electric wires on poles or down in the
ground; whether you have cable trains or horse
cars. After awhile *all this is going to stop*, I repeat! The pertinent question is, Am I ready for
it? Changes are coming on continually. Loved
ones and friends are passing away. The successes
to which we had hoped to attain and which, perhaps, we may have gained to some extent, are passing away. The present is continually shifting. To-
day luxury, to-morrow poverty. *Everything goes,
goes continually*. Earthly success goes. Worldly
prospects go. Our sweetest cups of pleasure are
soon quaffed to the bottom. Like blades of grass
which come forth and soon wither away, and to-
morrow are cast into the oven; like the tender
rose, now blooming in its beauty, but which in a
few days will be gone forever. Leaves drop one by
one, fade away, and are gone. The great question
is, Will it be so with man?

> "Flitting, flitting away—
>   All that to me is most dear;
> There's nothing on earth that can stay,
>   The roses must die with the year."

Will it be so with man? we ask. Must you and

I thus pass away after we have spent our three
score years and ten? Must we literally die and be no
more? Die like the roses, or like the morning glory
which charms for a little season and then is gone
forever? or will there be an abiding place beyond?
and shall we enter another and brighter life?

There will be an abiding place beyond. You believe it, and I believe it, for we are Christians, and
this hope is the backbone of our philosophy. The
majority of my audience to-night is Christian, and
the thought of a happy future strikes a sympathetic chord in your heart. But there are persons
who say there is no beyond. There are many who
pride themselves on being skeptics, agnostics and
infidels, and the various other names by which unbelievers are known. They say there is no future
life; that there is nothing in the promises of Christianity, and that there is no hope beyond. But we
say there is. Why do we say it? Because Jesus
Christ has said it; because the word of God teaches
it; and because a deep-rooted human instinct the
world over has in all ages and under all circumstances declared its faith in a life beyond. We
can not, of course, say it because we have seen it
with our physical eyes, or known it from a personal experience; but we can say it because we believe on the Lord Jesus Christ, the truest friend the
race ever had. He has promised it, and we know
he will not fail us.

But the skeptic says, "I cannot reason it out;

and I cannot accept what I do not understand."
This is a common subterfuge among skeptics.
This is an amusing dodge. Why, friend Skeptic,
you don't understand why the grass is green and
not red; you cannot reason this out for your life,
and yet you accept it. You cannot understand
why it is that a dun or spotted cow should always
give snow-white milk; and yet you accept it. You
cannot understand the various mysteries of creation; and yet you accept the fact of creation. You
cannot understand the mysteries of plant life, much
less of human life; and yet you accept the fact that
life is. You marvel at a future life; but with Joseph Cook I would ask you, *Is it any more wonderful that we should live again than that we
began to live?*

It is child's twaddle to say you will not accept
anything you can't understand. You do it every
hour you live, every breath you breathe. You
say the grass is green, but why it is that color instead of any other you do not know. Perhaps you
suggest that it is nature's law. But, my friend,
nature has no laws. The laws of the universe are
God's laws, the laws of the Great First Cause. It
is ridiculous for men to talk thus about nature's
laws, as if nature were God of all creation. Nature itself is only one law among perhaps millions
of the laws the Divine Creator has in his vast universe. So I repeat, we accept the philosophy of a
life beyond, not because we understand it fully,

but because Christ taught it, and the Bible is full of its promises.

In our text we read that on the memorable day on which our Lord was tried and condemned to die, Pontius Pilate appealed to the Jews, saying, " What shall I do with Jesus which is called Christ ?" The circumstances are as follows : Judas had betrayed the Master the evening before, and they had taken him before Annas, the father-in-law of the high priest, a rich and powerful Jew, whose enmity toward the Nazarene was one of his most prominent characteristics. He was tried before Annas, and then before his son-in-law, Caiaphas, the high priest. On the morning of the crucifixion he was taken before the Sanhedrim, the most august assembly among the Jews, the supreme court of their nation. When declared by that body worthy of death, he was taken before Pontius Pilate, the Roman governor, who asked him, " Are you King of the Jews ?" and he said, " I am." The governor put other questions to him, some of which the Lord did not heed, whereupon the exasperated civil dignitary said, " Why do you not answer me ? Do you not know who I am ? Do you not know that I can take your life or spare it, just as I choose ?" Jesus was not at all frightened at this, but said, mildly, " My kingdom is not of this earth. You could have no power at all, oh, Pilate, except my Father gave it you." Learning that the prisoner was a Galilean, the governor then

sent him to Herod, who was at that time residing
in the city, probably in the old palace of the As-
moneans. Herod and his courtiers received him
with delight, for he was bound. They mocked
him awhile, and then sent him back to Pilate,
agreeing with the latter that there was no cause
for death in the case. So the Roman governor
stepped out before the mob and cried, " I find no
fault in the prisoner; no, nor Herod. Hence I will
simply chastise him and let him go." But the
chief priests said, " That will never do." And
moving about hastily among the assembled masses
a few ring-leaders soon succeeded in creating a
general demand for the Nazarene's blood. So
Pilate sat down upon the judgment block and was
just about to pronounce sentence of death, when
he received an unexpected message from his wife,
saying, " Have nothing to do with that just man,
for I have suffered many things in a dream because of him." Looking into the face of the Nazarene he evidently saw the stamp of divinity. He
was seized with fear, and did not know what to do.
Finally a happy thought came to him, and he said,
" I will propose to release unto them Barrabas or
Christ, and they will certainly choose Christ in
preference to that terrible villain." And so turning to the leaders of the mob he said, " You know
that it is my custom to release unto you a favorite
prisoner at the Passover, and I have accordingly
11

made up my mind to release unto you Barrabas
or Christ; which do you choose?" He supposed
of course they would say, "We will take Christ
every time," for Barrabas was not only a robber,
but he was guilty of the foulest deed in the whole
category of crime, that of *murder*.

But the old chief priests went among the crowd
and told the people to cry out "Barrabas!" Possibly they hesitated at first, but presently some
fellow in front said "Barrabas!" And then another
behind him said "Barrabas!!" And then others
took up the cry, and soon thousands and tens of
thousands were shouting that shameful request,
"Barrabas!!!" So Pilate again took his position
on the judgment block, but not until he had pro-
pounded to that surging, seething multitude the
question I want to put to you to-night, "What shall
I do with Jesus which is called Christ?"

There stood the gentle Nazarene, the Man of sorrow, the only begotten Son of the Eternal God.
"What shall I do with him?" repeated the govern-
or. The old chief priests again nudged the
masses—gave their dupes the cue. Probably the
same old fellow who had first cried "Barrabas"
now said, "Let him be crucified!". And then the
man behind him repeated the cry, "Let him be
crucified!!" And following him others, until soon
the streets of Jerusalem were ringing with that
fearful death-knell, "Let him be crucified!!!"
Men shudder to-day when they think of that awful

scene. They say, How could those people have treated an innocent being so? And yet there are greater multitudes to-day, who, in answer to Pilate's question, which has come rolling down the ages, say practically the same hard, cruel thing as did those wicked Jews 1800 years ago,—"Away with him!" Perhaps not in words, but in actions, and you know that "actions speak louder than words."

And now I want to put the question to-night, not to the people of New York, or Philadelphia, nor of Kansas, or Iowa, but to those right here in Chicago,—to those right here before me in the West Side Church. And will you please make it a personal question? Don't say, "What will you do with Jesus, Bro. Hall?" or "What will you do with him, Bro. Allen?" Don't try to shift the responsibility, but face the matter fairly and squarely to-night,—face it individually. Young men and women, husbands and wives, fathers and mothers, ask of yourselves each this question of tremendous import, "What shall I do with Christ?" Make it even more personal and emphatic, if possible. By changing the tense, say, "What *am I doing* with Jesus which is called Christ? What am I doing with him to-night? What have I been doing with him the last five years? the last ten years? What will I do with him to-night when the invitation song is sung? When I go home and pillow my head to rest as the night shades close about me, what will I be doing with Jesus—receiving or rejecting ? "

There are just three classes which answer this question differently (barring consideration of those of course who have never yet heard the Gospel,— we will just waive the heathen question to-night.) Class number one says, " What will we do with Jesus which is called Christ ? Why, we will ignore him; we will scoff at him; we will ridicule him; we will laugh to scorn all the claims of his friends as to the divinity of his religion." A rough reply, isn't it ? What shall be done about it ? I suggest that we submit this class to a scrutinization, just as we do political classes, for instance. Here we have Democrats, and Republicans, and Prohibitionists, and the People's party. There are a few pertinent questions which every citizen should consider with reference to each. Who are their leaders, and what are their platforms ? How strong are they ? What have they done ? What are they doing ? What do they hope to do ? etc. If I should ask, How many of you gentlemen are Democrats ? a lot of you would raise your hands, I presume. And then if I should inquire, Who are your leaders ? you would say, " Grover Cleveland, Thomas Jefferson, Andrew Jackson." If I should ask the Republicans present to raise their hands a lot more would respond. And if I should inquire of them, Who are the leaders of the Republican party ? they would say,

"James G. Blaine, Abraham Lincoln, James A. Garfield." Americans are always proud of their political leaders, and always ready to talk hopefully of their party.

If I should ask yonder Democrat, Why are you a follower of Jefferson and Jackson? he would probably say, "Because I am in favor of free-trade, or tariff for revenue only," or something of that sort. And if I should ask yonder Republican, Why are you a follower of Lincoln and Blaine? he would probably say, "Because I am in favor of protection." (Between protection as advanced by one party, and free-trade as advocated by the other, it is difficult for the average voter to tell the difference, and if I were to ask my male auditors to-night, they would probably begin scratching their heads and blinking the wisdom of ignorance, and we would have to go home without solving the problem; yet there are multitudes of men in this Christian land who give the comparatively unimportant questions of politics ten times as much attention as they do the questions relating to the soul.)

Well, now, if it is fair for us to question political classes sharply, why not all other classes also? It is common sense so to do, and we ought to use a little common sense in getting the gospel into the hearts of the people. It is certainly fair for we ministers to use 19th century tactics in defending the truth; to use methods similar to those used in politics and business. So let me inquire, who are the leaders of that class which says, We will ignore Jesus? In answering we must go away back, for it is an old class. We must go back to Pilate. Before he pronounced judgment on the Nazarene he took a basin of water and dipped his hands in it, saying, "His blood be on your hands."

Why, Pilate, is he innocent? "Don't know."

Don't you think you ought not to condemn him? "Not going to answer that question."

Do you think he is an impostor? "No, for I have found in him no fault at all. However, I have decided to simply ignore his claims." And Pilate lived only to lose the position he thought to hold by slaying Jesus, and died in shame and sorrow.

Herod also belonged to this class. Jesus being sent to him for judgment, he robed him in scarlet, placed a staff in his hand, and bade his soldiers pass before him and mock him, crying, "Hail, king!" Herod lived only to die in exile and infamy.

The chief priests also mocked him; others spat upon him, and smote him, and laughed him to scorn. They all belong to this cruel class. They said, "Let his blood be upon our heads," and sure enough it was. Many of those present on that sad occasion lived to endure the siege of Jerusalem, when they were starved, captured by their enemies, and trampled under the iron foot of

Roman contempt. The words of the old prophets were fulfilled, and the Jews were scattered to the far quarters of the earth, and became a by-word and a hissing among the nations. Even to this day it is practically a sin in many places to be a descendant of Jacob. How often in our own land do we see people point at this rejected race and say derisively, "There goes a Jew!" Ah! They were once God's chosen people, but they fell from grace when they rejected all warning and cast off the Son of David. And yet, bless God, there's salvation for the penitent Jew!

Coming down through the centuries we find men like Voltaire, Rosseau, Tom Paine, and that celebrated "Colonel" from Illinois, (whose brief war record is said to have wound up in a hog-pen, where he was chased and captured by a boy.) In reply to the question, "What shall we do with Jesus, which is called Christ?" these notorious characters, with all their ilk, say, "Why, we will reject him. We deny his divinity, and scorn his service."

In his room in Paris Voltaire wrote, "One hundred years from now the Bible will not be read any more than a last year's almanac." Yet that room has since been used as a Bible Repository, and the very presses Voltaire used in printing his blasphemous books have been more wisely employed in printing "leaves for the healing of the nations."

Mr. Ingersoll would take away from us the Bible, Christ, and all that is cherished as divine. He belongs to this class. He thinks there is nothing in it. Oh, no. Nothing in it! Yet when he stood over the dead form of his brother, he said, "Hope sees a star, and faith hears the rustle of an angel's wing." The flinty-hearted "Colonel" weakens once in a while. Some years ago, when riding on an Illinois railway train one day, he was blaspheming in his usual way and talking about upsetting what he is pleased to call the superstition of Christianity. It seems that no one in the car dared to venture a reply to his keen thrusts, until a good old lady arose and pointing her finger at him, said: " You are privileged to hold those opinions if you choose, Mr. Ingersoll, but I want to remind you of one thing : it was that kind of talk that justly lost you the governorship of Illinois." This was an unexpected bomb-shell, and effectually silenced the vain boaster. The people of Illinois are bad enough, but I rejoice to know that they are a little too good to elect an infidel to the highest office in their noble State.

A few years ago Prof. Hutto and myself were in Wichita, Kan., attending a Sunday-school convention. One day we dropped into a restaurant to get dinner. We had to wait awhile for our bill of fare to be served, for good things come slow, you know, in this world, especially at restaurants. While we sat there a young man came in and sat down beside us; then shortly another came in and seated himself at the same table. They were elegantly dressed young men who evidently would have nothing but the latest cut of coat and trousers, with neckties of the latest style, and everything up to date, — in short, what common parlance designates as *bon ton* young fellows.

" How d'ye do, Chawly."

" How d'ye do, Gawge."

" Have you seen the North American Review— the last number ?"

" No, I haven't."

" Then you have not read Gladstone's reply to Col. Ingersoll ?"

" I hope Gladstone does not attempt to reply to Col. Ingersoll !"

The idea of Gladstone's successfully replying to Ingersoll's imagined logic was preposterous to these young bloods. They thought it utterly impossible for the great statesman to do it. But if I dared suggest a criticism of " the grand old man," it would be that he stooped to reply to Ingersoll at all. It was certainly unnecessary, and it seems to me that the great Englishman should not have thus exalted the flippant American skeptic at the expense of a dignified faith. And I think things are coming to a pretty pass when certain of our great magazines give so much space to the rantings of unbelievers, devoting page after page to such matter, but comparatively little space to representative Christian pens. These journals attempt to create a public demand which, to say the least, is not germane to the general welfare of any nation. It is a mistake to say that the public desires such intellectual trash, for it does not, as is clearly attested by the infinitely greater popularity of periodicals that honor things sacred and divine.

Discussing religious matters one day with a college chum, who sat with his chair tilted back and a cigar in his mouth, I asked him if he believed the Bible. With sophomoric presumption he replied, "Part of it I do, and part of it I don't." But what must we say of that young man's opinion when Gladstone, the greatest living statesman, believes the old Book from back to back; when Garfield, the most cultured scholar and polished Christian who ever occupied the president's chair, believed it through and through,—not only believed it, but *preached it;* when Lincoln believed it from Genesis to Revelation,—not himself a professing Christian, but the son of Christian parents, and an earnest believer in their religion! But this young upstart, hardly out of his Freshman year, said, "Part of it I believe, and part of it I don't."

What has this class done? It has become a familiar assertion, and I think a true one, that Tom Paine died regretting that he ever wrote the Age of Reason. Yet men will say, "Have you read the

Age of Reason?" or, "Have you read Voltaire's books?" or "Have you read Ingersoll's works?" as if Ingersoll had ever *worked* on the great subject of religion. "Ingersoll's works!" That always strikes me as a joke. Often on railway trains I have been offered "Ingersoll's Complete Works." His own testimony puts the length of time he ever devoted to the study of the Word of God at three months, I believe, and as to his general education, if he ever attended a first-class institution anywhere I have yet to learn the fact. The distinguished debater, Clark Braden, has proven in a pamphlet entitled "Ingersoll Unmasked" that one of his most famous speeches was stolen from one of old Dr. Gunn's medical works. Having a gift of oratory, probably inherited from his preacher-father, he has gained prominence and fortune. He defended D. M. Bennett in the publication of obscene literature, and plead for the Star Route thieves. And yet he is often paid several hundred dollars a night for his rare blasphemies, for certain bloods, young and old, must have an escape valve for their guilty consciences. Infidelity is often an apology for secret sin!

Do you belong to that class that says, "We will laugh at the claims of Jesus?" Do you deny the divinity of Christianity? If so, you must be classed with the vilest thugs that ever infested modern generations. There are about two hundred thousand saloon-keepers, many of whom be-

long to the same class. Nearly all anarchists
are atheists. Gamblers, thieves and dwellers in
the various dens of infamy to be found in every
great city usually belong to that class. Such
characters are glad to say there is no God, because
they would fear the judgment of a just God. The
motives of this class are all summed up in one
word, *selfishness*. It accepts Ingersoll's creed,
"No God, no Christ, no Bible, no Religion, no
Hope, no Hell, no Heaven. Grab all you can get,
but be careful that you don't get grabbed. Amen."
Will you lower your manhood and degrade every
fiber of your being by casting in your lot with such
a class? Beware! Beware!

But we turn to class number two. In answer to
the question, "What shall we do with Jesus?" this
class says, "We will neglect him." Who are the
leaders of this class, and what is their platform?
Let us see:

"Do you believe in Christ?"

"I don't know whether I do or not. Sometimes
I think I do, and then again I think I do not. There
are pretty good reasons on both sides."

"Do you believe the Bible?"

"It is hard to say. Parts of it are easy to believe, and other parts are not. There are good arguments on both sides."

Oh, when will this poor, dying world learn that
there are *no two sides* to the question? A man
said to me out in the Western part of this State,

"I would like to hear the other side." I said, "There is no other side." And I wish to-night to declare to the young men who may be thinking that there are two sides to the question of the Bible's inspiration that they are laboring under a delusion. There are no two sides to it; there is only one side. Jesus Christ is divine, and the Bible is true. There are no *may be sos* and *may be nots* about it.

But the class to which I have just referred don't know whether the Bible is true or not; whether there is a heaven or not; and whether they are saved or lost. They just drift on through life, carelessly, undeterminedly, fatally. We find them in high life, and in low. Some live in gilded mansions, and drive their coach and four; others live in hovels and struggle with poverty. Some may be found in stores, and shops, and offices; others on the streets in idleness. Ah! there are millions who belong to the class that says, "We will neglect him for the present." It is by far the largest of the three classes, and very dangerous to the soul.

In conducting meetings everywhere I find my greatest impediment in the indifference of the people. In answer to our appeals the majority seem to say, "I don't know whether or not Christ is Divine, and I haven't time to investigate it now; I am so busy." It seems to me a very foolish thing to do. Oh, why not be either *for* or *against* Christ? Have a positive conviction! Stand up for

Jesus, or else array yourself against him! Don't sit on the fence! Don't be driftwood floating down the stream of time! Be an individual of *principle.* This is the great need of the age— men and women of *decision.* If, after a thorough investigation, you find the Bible is not true, then go out and fight against Christ and Christianity. But if you find the Bible to be true (as every honest, consistent, and scholarly student must find it), then, I beg of you, come out and testify before the world to this effect, and by a consecrated life prove your devotion to the religion of your Lord.

Again, there are some who say, "We will wait; we will see what others do." Or, "We are not quite ready yet; we wish a little more time. We want to see what Tom and Dick and Harry are going to do; if they join, we will." In one of my revivals in a western city a gentleman listened for 29 days without obeying the gospel. He said, "I am going to hear him through. I want to see what he is going to do before I come in." Scores accepted the Savior's sweet message, but the meetings closed with that man still sitting on the stool of do-nothing; still drifting down the stream of time, and breaking in pieces on the shoals of curiosity. Let me plead with you who have never taken a stand for or against Christ to do so to-night. Oh, decide! And decide quickly! As Lowell says:

" Once to every man and nation comes the moment to decide,
In the strife of Truth and Falsehood, for the good or evil side."

That moment comes to you to-night. What do you decide about Jesus?

It is with pleasure that I now turn to class number three. In answer to the Roman governor's question, "What shall I do with Jesus who is called Christ?" this class says, "*We will accept him with all our hearts.*" Who are the leaders? The Apostle Peter was the first. Two different times he said, "Thou art the Christ, the Son of the living God." And greatly was he blessed for it. Jesus gave him the keys of his kingdom, which to-day has its four hundred millions of members, and which has done more to uplift humanity than all other agencies combined in the history of the world.

To this class belonged also the Apostle Paul, one of the greatest scholars of his age, and among the most devout of the Jews. He gave his long and eventful life to the preaching of the Gospel; "in journeying often; in perils of waters; in perils of robbers; in perils by his own countrymen; in perils by the heathen; in perils in the city; in perils in the wilderness; in perils in the sea; in perils among false brethren; in weariness and painfulness; in watchings often; in hunger and thirst; in fastings often; in cold and nakedness,"—what a checkered career! Yet the Great Apostle to the Gentiles never wavered in his faith, nor shunned to "endure hardness as a good soldier of Jesus Christ." And as Paul passed up and down the

streets of those ancient cities he was comparatively
unknown; but here and there he gathered together
a little handful of believers in whose hearts he
planted the "seed of the kingdom." His work has
gone on, and on, and on, until now in all the books
of the world there is probably no name, with the
exception of "that name which is above every
name," which stands higher than the name of
Paul. No one ever surrendered self more completely to Christ.

Glancing over the pages of history we find that
John the beloved, Polycarp, Wyckliff, the Wes-
leys, Martin Luther, and our own Beechers and
Spurgeons and Campbells, have all said in answer
to this question, "I will accept him, believe him,
receive him, love him, give my life for him. I am
willing to lay my all at his feet." The men who are
moving the world to-day are men of this stamp.
I want to urge it upon the young men with whose
attention I am honored to-night that the grandest
thing for you to do is to take your stand with
these men,—to take your stand with Christ.

In concluding allow me to emphasize the fact
that Jesus Christ is either what he claimed to be,
or he is not. If he is not the Son of God, if he was
not Divine, if he was not the only-begotten of
the Eternal Father, if he was not the Messiah of
prophecy, and therefore not all he claimed to be,
then he was the worst impostor, the biggest de-
ceiver and the most terrible character that ever

drew the breath of life! We have a little, narrow sect in our country to-day which is becoming somewhat prominent, boasting as it does of its elegance, its learning, its refinement, its culture. It is quite numerous in Boston. Yet this self-same church teaches that *Christ was a good man, but was not Divine.* What shocking inconsistency! Why, Jesus said, "I am the way; I am the truth; I am the life." And Paul said, "He thought it not robbery to be equal with God." There are hundreds of similar references. And in view of all this I must repeat that if he was not what he claimed to be, then he was the worst character the world ever saw. There is no half-way ground; we must either accept his divinity, or reject him altogether.

What are you going to do about it?

Will you not do what the best and wisest men in the world are doing? Why not fall into line with those who are living under Immanuel's banner? With those who are trying to redeem lost souls in the power and gloy of his name?

Infidelity is doing nothing for the world. Christianity is doing all that is being done toward uplifting humanity. The skeptic says, " Christianity is a good thing for women and children, but for strong-minded men it will not do. We would *educate* the masses—have libraries, and schools, and everything to give them a better chance." It

12

sounds very nice to hear infidels talk that way. But how many schools have they ever built? How many halls have they constructed? How many asylums have they founded? It is Christian money that supports the benevolence of the world. It is Christian money that disseminates learning, and fosters intellectual and moral growth. Talk about educating the masses! Why, you can count the infidel schools of America on the fingers of one hand—all the schools infidelity has ever founded. Indeed, you can count them on the thumbs of one hand! And that is allowing them Girard College, and I am not sure that we should grant them that much. Stephen Girard was evidently soured on preachers rather than Christianity. From some cause he did not like ministers. And when he came to die he seems to have apportioned out his wealth, giving some to his cousins, and some to his nephews, and some to his nieces, etc. And still he had quite a snug little sum left, with which he decided to found a college and put in a condition that no clegyman should be permitted to pass over its threshold. Well, if you are familiar with the history of Girard College, will you kindly tell me of a single great statesman who ever came from the walls of the institution? Or of a single poet, or a writer of prose, or an orator, or anyone who ever attained to great distinction and honor in any department of human activity. I have asked this question many times in different States and I have yet to see a person who has the courage to stand up and mention any names. An infidel school is not a good place to "teach young ideas how to shoot," nor to quicken aspirations, and fan into flame a noble ambition.

Speaking of Girard College reminds me of a good story I once heard an old professor of mine relate. One day a couple of gentlemen came to look over the beautiful grounds of the famous institution. The gateman saw them approaching, but stood there stolidly, as had been his custom for years.

"We would like to enter and look over the grounds," said one of the visitors.

"You can't go in."

"Why?"

"No clergymen allowed." The gentlemen had on fine silk hats, and posed with much dignity, just like we preachers always pose, you know!. Hence the watchman naturally mistook them for clergymen.

"But I am not a minister," said the spokesman of the two.

"What are you then? You are dressed like one."

"I am a saloon-keeper, sir!"

"Ah! I beg pardon. Pass right in. Pass right in."

Whether the incident be true or not, this is a good illustration of the spirit of infidelity.

No, infidelity has done nothing for the world. It is and ever has been a curse upon humanity, a frightful excrescence. It would take away all that is dear to us in this life, as well as in the life to come, and feed us on the dregs of passion, appetite and lust. Yet the fatal fallacy is ever boasting of what great things it would do if it had a chance! It has been proven over and over again, and there is nothing in it. So I would to God that every young man would say, " I will cut loose from it."

Would you be ashamed to stand with Napoleon Bonaparte? He was once walking on the deck of his ship, plowing through the waters of the Mediterranean. It was night. In the cabin some of his officers were discussing religion. The controversy waxed warm, but without conclusion. It was finally agreed upon that the matter should be presented to the great warrior, and upon his opinion the case should rest. So one of the disputants approached him and said, " General, do you believe there is a God?" The great hero stopped, and pointing toward the moon and the stars in all their silvery beauty, calmly asked, " Who made those?" There was silence for a few moments, when the young skeptic went back to his friends, and there was no more discussion.

Washington, the father of his country,

> " The first, the last, the best,
> The Cincinnatus of the West,"

was an earnest, baptized believer. Benjamin
Franklin, in an ever-memorable speech before the
Colonial Congress, moved that the sessions of
Congress should be introduced with prayer. All
truly great men are men who reverence God.
Daniel Webster said the greatest thought he ever
had was as to his responsibility to God. If
you want to be true and great, if you want to do
something for yourself and humanity, be a Christian. Gladstone says that during the long years of
his connection with the government he came in contact with sixty master minds, and all but five of
them were Christians.

What shall I do with Jesus? Accept him. What
are you doing with him to-night? You know, and
God knows. Oh, do not be indifferent to the appeals of Heaven! I beg of you to get right with
God now. The time is speedily coming when the
opportunity will not be given you. Jesus has done
his part; the Church has done its part. All through
the centuries evidence upon evidence has been
piling up in favor of Christianity. Then why not
embrace it promptly? There is no time to be lost.
If you do not answer the Roman governor's question quickly and rightly, a terrible future awaits
you,—a future of banishment from the presence of
God and his holy angels. The question will be
reversed at judgment. It will not be, " What shall
I do with Jesus?" but, " What will Jesus do with
me?" " *After death, the judgment*," the Book says.

In crossing the ocean of life shall we be stranded on the shoals of unbelief, or wrecked on the reefs of procrastination ?

Oh, what will Jesus do with me ? If I refuse him here, he will say, " Depart from me, I never knew you.   Go from my presence, you who tried me, and condemned me to die.   You who in your health and lifetime and strength said, ' Away with him for the present.'   You who said, ' Let him be cruci-fied.'   Begone now, begone forever !"

Dear, unsaved friend, do not tarry longer away from the arms of redeeming love.   Come to-night ! In answer to this burning question, " What shall I do with Jesus ?" say, " By the grace of God I will accept him,—I will serve him."   Heaven help you !

> " To-day the Savior calls,
>   For refuge fly—
>   The storm of vengeance falls,
>   And death is nigh! "

A. MARTIN.

FEW men in the Christian brotherhood have had a wider or more varied experience than the subject of this sketch. Though comparatively a young man, he has been before the public so long that those who do not know him personally often believe him to be an elderly man. He was born July 22, 1851, in Sullivan county, Indiana, and consequently is now 42 years old—just in the prime of a vigorous manhood. He is light-complexioned, five feet and eight inches tall, and weighs 150 pounds. His paternal ancestors were Scotch-Irish, and his maternal ancestors, English. He belongs, on his father's side, to a family of preachers, but they are all Presbyterians but himself, many of them occupying places of the highest honor in that church. When 15 years old Bro. Martin confessed the Savior and was baptized into Christ at Liberty, in the north part of Sullivan county.

At 17 he began to preach, and for a long time was known in Western Indiana and Eastern Illinois as the "boy preacher." He held many good meetings and brought a goodly number to Christ while yet in his "teens." At 18 he baptized M.

D. Adams, who is now our missionary at Bilaspur, India.

While very young he was married to S. Florence Adams—sister to Martin D.—and to them have been born seven children, one of whom has gone to the better land. His oldest daughter, Miss Rose, is the author of "Feodora," a story of Northern England, and is already a writer of ability and bright promise. The second daughter, Miss Maynie, is a fine singer and accompanies her father in many of his meetings, as his organist and soloist.

Bro. Martin's first regular pastorate was at Centralia, Ill., from May, 1876, to October, 1878. During this time the membership of that church was nearly doubled. In 1878 he was called to New Lisbon, Ohio. Here the young preacher had his hands full in succeeding such men as Isaac Errett, Joseph King, and William Baxter, but he succeeded, and he looks upon his work in New Lisbon as a turning-point in his life.

In May, 1880, he moved to Portland, Maine, and assumed the duties of evangelist for the New England States. His first meeting here was in Boston, and May 23, 1880, he organized our present church in Boston with thirteen members. He remained in New England two and a half years, where his work was crowned with a good measure of success. During this time he and F. N. Calvin edited the first paper ever published by the Disciples in New England. It was called *The New England Evangelist*, and was a bright little paper which continued several years.

In October, 1882, he accepted a call to the " Old Bedford " church, near Blandinsville, Ill., and it was during his work there that he formed the acquaintance of H. C. Patterson, and the two have continued in unbroken and loving friendship since that date.

In answer to a call from our Foreign Board, in April, 1884, Bro. Martin went to England as one of our evangelists in that country, where he remained with his family for four years. He was one year in Birkenhead, founding our church there, and three years in Liverpool, succeeding the lamented M. D. Todd. In England his work was very successful. He baptized 125 people and did much work that cannot be put upon paper.

In the spring of 1888 he returned to this country and became pastor of the First Christian Church in Omaha, Neb. Here he continued two years, adding 125 to the church and giving the work in that city an impetus that it feels to this day. In 1890 he returned to Indiana, and much of the time since has been in the general field. At some time in his life he has held meetings in Portland, Me., and in Boston, Cincinnati, and New Orleans, and during the last year in Ohio, Indiana, Illinois, Missouri, Iowa, North Dakota and Texas. He has not held as great meetings as some of our evangelists, but he never makes a failure, and many of his meetings have been large ones.

Bro. Martin has a forcible and pleasing style, and never fails to interest an audience. His preaching has been characterized as sound, forcible, scholarly, witty, pathetic, eloquent and entertaining. He is considered as a good evangelist and a first-class pastor combined. His fund of anecdotes is large and his illustrations are many and copious. During the past four years he has been much upon the lecture platform, and his "Life in England," and other lectures never fail to please the people. But in order to be with his family and his books, he has for the present retired from the general field and become pastor of the church at Marshalltown, Iowa.

A. MARTIN.

THE WORLD'S DEBT TO CHRISTIANITY.

A. MARTIN.

"How much owest thou unto my Lord?"—Luke 16: 5.

THIS is the question of the wise but unjust
steward unto his lord's debtors, and with
more wisdom and a feeling of triumph may be
asked by the Christian to the world to-day, "How
much owest thou unto *my* Lord?" What effect
has the religion of Jesus had upon the history of
the nations, or what would be our condition without it? Time and space and our ability are insuf-
ficent to tell the whole story, but it is the purpose
of this sermon to point out some of the blessings
of Christianity to the world, and these will
doubtless suggest many others to the thoughful
reader. In a Christian spirit the unbeliever is
challenged to show that *any ill* has come to the
world through the propagation and reception of
the Christian religion. Is any man or any country
worse off for having believed in Jesus Christ and
observed his teaching? Not only must this question always be answered with an emphatic negative, but it shall be our privilege to show upon the

(187)

other hand the infinite benefits and blessings that always accompany the Christ life.

I. *The world is indebted to the Christian religion for its present state of civilization.* We have only to note a few historic facts here to demonstrate this great truth:

1. In the highest and best civilization of the ancient "classic" world the people were not only warlike, drunken and licentious, but these things were a part of their religion. Mars, the God of war, Bacchus, the God of wine, Terpsichore, the goddess of revelry, and Venus, the goddess of love and licentiousness, were all worshiped by the old classic Greeks. And every well-informed man knows that the history of the world in *ante Christum* days was a history of barbarism and blood. When our blessed Savior made his advent here the whole world was shrouded in pagan darkness except the little narrow strip of Palestine, and even there God's own people had so far forsaken him that they had made his holy temple a den of thieves. It is written of them in the Holy Oracles: "There is none righteous, no, not one: there is none that understandeth, there is none that seeketh after God. They are all gone out of the way, they are together become unprofitable; there is none that doeth good, no, not one. Their throat is an open sepulchre; with their tongues they have used deceit; the poison of asps is under their lips; whose mouth is full of cursing and bit-

terness; their feet are swift to shed blood; destruction and misery are in their ways; and the way
of peace have they not known; there is no fear of
God before their eyes." (Rom. 3: 10-18). What
an awful picture of human depravity! And this
was true of both Jews and Gentiles when Jesus
came into the world.

2. The history of the Anglo-Saxon race is an
unbroken record of the triumphs of the religion of
the Nazarene. Before the reception of Christianity by this noble people, they were semi-barbar-
ous and half-civilized; but after they heard the
story of Jesus they not only improved themselves
and their own "Isle of Beauty," but they have
gone everywhere, carrying with them education
and culture and good government. If you will but
look carefully into the reason of the difference between England and Spain, Scotland and Italy, and
the United States and Mexico, you will find that
the different people and their *religion* have much
more to do with it than either soil or climate.

"Righteousness exalteth the nations, but sin is
a reproach to any people." This is the history of
all countries and peoples. Egypt, Greece and
Rome are now chiefly interesting for what they
have been; for they have gone down in their
wickedness and shame, and have been superseded
by the strong and glorious nations whose God is
the Lord.

3. There is now no civilization that is worthy

the name where the Christian religion is not dominant. Spread out a map of the world before you, and you will find that all the free and enlightened and happy countries are where Christianity is the prevailing religion, and all the dark and uncultivated and unhappy countries are where the Bible has not gone. *And there is not a single exception to this statement.* This can not be simply *accidental.* First to the individual, and then to the nation, the reception of the gospel is elevating and ennobling. The word of God is within us "a well of water springing up into everlasting life."

II. *We are indebted to the Bible for the basic principles of the world's jurisprudence.* The common laws of all civilized countries are based upon the law that God gave Moses from Mount Sinai. The moral principles of the Ten Commandments and the Pentateuchal laws respecting the rights of property are recognized in the courts of all enlightened countries, and in their civil aspects have never been improved upon. We owe the protection of our property and the safety of our lives to the practical triumph of the Christian religion, for it includes all of the *moral* principles of the law of Moses, united with the higher law of a universal love for mankind and the spiritual laws and ordinances of the Church of Christ. What are life and property worth where the Bible has not gone?

1. The Bible laws against theft build our jails and penitentiaries, placing stone walls and iron bars between the thief and our property.

2. The laws against unbridled lust remove the libertine from our homes, and save the purity and honor of our families.

3. Its statute against murder erects the gallows or sends the electric fluid to remove the murderer to that land where he can not kill. In fine, all the laws regulating human life and conduct, punishing the wicked and rewarding the righteous, are found in the Bible. What if these were taken away! Why, our knowledge of *sin* comes from a comparison of our lives with the law of God, and ourselves with the Bible character of Jehovah. The ancients had no conception of a *moral sin*, and no word in their language to express it. All sin with them was either legal or ceremonial. But God's law brings the knowledge of our weakness and sin. Rom. 7: 7. It is the mirror revealing the soil upon our souls. The reason why some men don't like the Bible is that it shows to them how black and mean they are, and the picture is not complimentary.

Along with the basic principles of law contained in the Bible, we find the true direction of *conscience*. There was little thought of the rights of the individual conscience in addition or as opposed to any outward authority until Christ came. Now legal restraint is good, but moral restraint is better. External authority must be used upon people who have not sufficient moral principles to do right from within; but how much stronger and better is that man who does right at the dictation of love and manhood within him! DUTY is a marvelous little word. Let the man who can find it outside the teaching or influence of Christianity! A world without Christianity is a world without *duty, conscience,* or *moral restraint*—a world of selfish passions and hopeless suffering.

III. *We are indebted to Christianity for the* FATHERHOOD OF GOD *and the* BROTHERHOOD OF MAN.

This is a day when men everywhere are trying to get equal rights. All the "unions" are so many declarations of equality. "Union carpenters," "union brick-layers," "union tailors," "union barbers," "union dairymen," etc., are upon every hand. Where did men get this idea of equality, or equal rights "to life, liberty and the pursuit of happiness?" Let us go on a search after this principle and see where we can first discover it.

1. Ancient Egypt, the mother of "classic" civilization, was not only ruled by her tyrannical Pharaohs, but had all grades of people in her subjects. The great pyramids could be built because the labor and life of the common people were of little value.

2. To the Greeks the word "humanity" as a term for the brotherhood of all men was unknown.

Socrates daily thanked the gods, (1) For being a *man* and not a *beast;* (2) Because he was a *male* and not a *female;* (3) Because he was a *Greek* and not a *barbarian.* He called all other people barbarians, and considered the Greeks as much their superiors.

3. The Romans considered all other people as their inferiors and enemies, and knew no law save physical strength. The dwellers on the opposite side of a river from the Romans were their *rivals.* And with the Greeks and the Romans, as with the Egyptians, there were many grades and classes among themselves, and anything like equal rights was unknown. Speaking of the Christian religion Celsus says: "The man who can believe it possible for Greeks and barbarians in Asia, Europe, and Libya to agree in one code of religious laws, must be utterly devoid of sense." Antiquity had no conception of a religion that would be common to the aristocratic and the vulgar, where the rich and the poor could sit down together, regarding the Lord as being equally the maker of them all.

4. Even the Jews regarded themselves as being much better than other people. They were the elect of God, and others were strangers and for-eigners—Gentile dogs, who might be thankful to eat of the crumbs that fell from their table. The Rabbis taught that "a single Israelite is of more worth in the sight of God than all the nations of

13

the world." This is far worse than any national, or sectional, or race feeling to-day, and still we are not altogether rid of this kind of prejudice. Americans often wonder how anybody can live in any other country, and Englishmen have been wont to teach their children that *one* Englishman was equal to *five* men of any other nation. National *pride* may be pardonable, but either individual or national *bigotry* is un-Christian.

5. It is *Christ* that teaches the equality of all men in privilege—the Fatherhood of God and the Brotherhood of man.

(1) He had equal sympathy with the beggar and the rich man, the slave and the ruler.

(2) He ate and drank with publicans and sinners, and offered salvation to the woman of Samaria as well as to Nicodemus.

(3) He died for all alike—by the grace of God he tasted death for every man.

(4) He sent his gospel to "all nations" and "every creature," and offered salvation to all on precisely the same conditions.

(5) And in the Church of Christ, "we, being many, are one body in Christ, and every one members one of another." (Rom. 12: 5). " Where there is neither Jew nor Greek, circumcision nor uncircumcision, Barbarian, Scythian, bond nor free: but Christ is all, and in all." (Col. 3: 11). God's distinctions are distinctions of character, and that depends upon *us.* Our own government, where all

have equal political and religious rights, is the out-growth of the Christian religion. Thus we are in-debted to Christianity for the abolition of human slavery, the royal dignity of every man, and the real and right independence and individuality of the soul.

IV. *We are indebted to the Bible for* THE BIND-ING FORCE OF THE MARRIAGE RELATION, AND THE SACREDNESS OF THE HOME.

It is the Bible that gives us the exclusive love of our husbands and wives. This, I believe, is so nowhere else and with no other religion. And the elevation of woman is due to Bible influence. Let us hear from President Angell, of Michigan Uni-versity, on the condition of woman and the "home" in non-Christian lands: "The attention of the traveler is strikingly arrested by the sur-prising contrast in the position accorded to woman in the Christian and non-Christian countries. Often as I contemplated the wretched lot of women in Asia did the pathetic words in which Goethe makes Ephigenia pour forth her pathetic plaint spring to my lips: 'The condition of woman is lamentable.' Those words might be scribbled as an appropriate inscription on the gates of the cities and on the door-posts of the houses in the eastern world. Woman is doomed to ignorance. She is the slave and drudge of man. Her mind is not deemed worthy of cultivation. I know of nothing in all the east so painful to the view of men from a Christian land as the condition of women. It is only where the gospel has shed its light that woman is recognized as the companion of man, with faculties susceptible and deserving of as careful training as his, with a soul touched to finer issues than his, with duties, if in some respects different, yet every whit as important and as responsible as his, because her primal duty and responsibility to God are the same as his."

In India the following things are true concerning females:

(1) The birth of a daughter is regarded as a calamity, and parents receive visits of condolence at such times. If one man wishes to insult another, he doesn't say, "You liar," or, "You thief," but, "*You father of a daughter!*"

(2) The girl is betrothed at two years old, and married at twelve, and if between these ages her intended husband dies, she is regarded as the object of the wrath of the gods, and as a "child widow" is doomed to a life of the most horrible slavery.

(3) In one of the sacred books of the Hindoos this passage is found: "Women's sin is greater than that of a man; women are they who have an aversion to good works; women have hunger twofold more than men, cunning fourfold, violence sixfold, and evil design eightfold. Let a wife who wishes to perform sacred ablution, wash the feet of her lord [husband], and drink the water; for

her lord to a wife is greater than Vishnu: her
husband is her god, priest and religion."

In view of her elevation by the Christian religion there is nothing more unnatural or ungrateful
than an unbelieving *woman.* Let such an one go
and perform *her* " sacred ablution," and then blas-
pheme the name of Jesus and ridicule the Bible if
she can !

V. *We are indebted to Christian influence for
the chief part of* THE INTELLECTUAL LIFE OF THE
WORLD.

It is an infidel mistake to suppose that educated
men are generally unbelievers. The opposite is
true.

1. Most of the world's educated men are believers in Christ, and this has always been true.
Even in the Dark Ages, when religion was so
corrupt, there were few educated men outside of
" the Church." The monks were almost the only
scholars.

2. The schools of the world to-day are the results of Christian influence. " Of the 300 institutions in America, called colleges and universities,
270 are supported by Christian churches ; and of
their 45,000 students the Church teaches all but
6,000. These are instructed at the expense of the
State." And a majority of the State instructors
are Christians ! How inconsistent to banish the
Bible from the public schools when its influence

has made them! It is worse than turning a man out of his own house.

3. Without Christian influence the best of everything would be taken away.

(1) Raphael, Dore and Munkacsy would be taken away from painting, and the world would never have seen "Christ on Calvary," or "The Vale of Tears."

(2) And the world's sweetest music would never have been heard. Instead of the harmonies of Mozart, Beethoven, Handel and Haydn, we would have had the wail of the wilderness, the wild cry of despair and the hopeless murmurings of hell's unutterable lament!

(3) And from literature would be eliminated the writings of the Christian "fathers," nearly all the world's historians and poets, and a majority of its scientists. Did you ever seriously think of what would be left of literature if all the Christian teaching and Christian influence were taken out?

VI. *We are indebted to Christianity for* ALL ORGANIZED CARE FOR THE POOR.

A special peculiarity of the gospel is that the poor have equal access to it with the rich.

(1) It first came to them.

(2) The common people heard Christ gladly.

(3) This regard for the poor was so *uncommon* as to be one evidence of Christ's divinity. Matt. 11 : 1-5.

(4) In nearly all human blessings distribution

is made largely according to what you *pay*. This is true in all business and secular affairs. But things that come *first hand* from God are alike to all. See air, sunshine, water, etc., *and the gospel.* If according to their ability, the man who pays five dollars and the one who pays five cents have precisely the same privileges. Here the rich and poor sit down together, and the Lord is the Maker of them all.

(5) And Christianity is the only religion that provides for its poor. That orphans' home standing majestically on the hill, surrounded by waving trees, blooming flowers, sparkling fountains, flowing streams and silvery lakes, was built by Christian people. Hear President Angell again : " The traveler in non-Christian lands is struck with the lack of those great organized charities, whether private or public, which are found so abundantly in all Christian lands. These are wanting not because there is no need of them; the poor and the suffering are everywhere; beggars line the streets and crowd the gates of temples and cities, and swarm upon your path; the blind, the deaf, the insane, the diseased, are unhappily to be found in all lands. Homes for orphans, asylums for the blind, for deaf mutes, for the insane, thoroughly appointed hospitals for the sick, nay, even humanely conducted prisons for the criminals—these all are the outgrowth of Christianity. These all belt the earth with beauty, and fill it with sun-

shine.   Smite out the Bible, and these go with it."

VII.   *We are indebted to Christian influence for* THE GENERALLY PREVAILING SPIRIT OF PEACE AMONG THE NATIONS.

Concerning the gospel age the inspired Isaiah has said: "And it shall come to pass in the last days that the mountain of the Lord's house shall be established in the top of the mountains, and shall be exalted above the hills; and all nations shall flow unto it. And many people shall go and say, Come ye, and let us go up to the mountain of the Lord, to the house of the God of Jacob; and he will teach us his ways, and we will walk in his paths: for out of Zion shall go forth the law, and the word of the Lord from Jerusalem. And he shall judge among the nations, and shall rebuke many people; and they shall beat their swords into plowshares, and their spears into pruning hooks: nation shall not lift up sword against nation, neither shall they learn war any more." Isa. 2: 2-4.   Now, let us ask a question or two:

(1)   Did you ever read of either ancient or modern heathen nations settling difficulties by *arbitration?*   Did Nebuchadnezzar, Pharaoh, Darius, Alexander or Cæsar ever so settle theirs?

(2)   If the principles of the gospel were practiced would there be any war?   All wars have been because one or both parties were wrong *and would not be corrected by moral considerations.*

Where Christianity prevails on both sides *men cannot fight.*

VIII. The blessings bestowed upon the world by Christianity are without number, but our space will only admit of the mention of one more. *We are indebted to the Christian religion for* OUR HOPE OF LIFE BEYOND THE GRAVE.

Everything else is subordinate to this. Our fathers, where are they? Gone. Where is the long line of our predecessors? Gone. Where are all the believers and unbelievers, the great and small, the happy and unhappy of former ages? Gone. Where will *we* all be in a few more years? *Gone!* The shadow-land is ruled by an arbitrary monarch called the King of Terrors. This monarch is essentially a war king, for he is never at peace. His hand is against every man, and every man's hand is against him; and yet he always conquers. It is said that he loves a "shining mark," because he lays tribute upon so many of earth's gifted children; but mayhap he is not so partial as we are wont to think, for do not *all* finally follow in his wake? He may seem to delay his coming for the sorely afflicted and destitute, but he consults his own convenience, and unless people rush unbidden into his presence, or make strong efforts in resisting him, he takes them captive at his will. He attacks people in many ways. He lays siege to their lives and seeks to destroy them by the munitions of his fierce warfare. He wraps their bodies in the flames of scorching fevers, and pierces their souls with the poisoned arrows of pain. He is especially fond of *children,* and throws intricate networks of disease around them to entangle their feet, for they stoutly resist him; but he always conquers at last. 'Tis true that his victims often so skillfully resist him as to gain a temporary victory, but he immediately renews the attack. He puts a slow poison in the water that they drink, the food they eat, and the air they breathe; he gradually removes the fuel that enkindles the fires within them, and slowly dries up the fountain whence flows the grace of life, and completes his victory by throwing upon them the burden of *time,* so that weary with contending against such odds, they give up the strife, and he carries them away in triumph. Will they ever break off his yoke and return? Is there life and victory for man beyond the grave? Here there is nothing so dear to us as life, and to live again is the fondest longing of the human soul; and anything that gives eternal life will meet the infinite want of our dying world. There are three leading departments of human knowledge, happiness and hope; let us ask them all in their turn what they can tell us as to the life beyond the grave.

SCIENCE.

1. *Pagan philosophy.*—Take an example: The Hindoos believe, (1) That the earth is flat, or the

shape of a *water lily ;* (2) That there is a mountain on the globe higher than the sun, moon and
stars, and that night is caused by the sun getting
behind this mountain ; (3) That there are seven
concentric oceans on the face of the globe : one of
salt water, one of fresh water, one of sugar cane
juice, one of milk, etc. This is but a sample of
the boasted " science " of the heathen; and if they
know so little of *this world*, what enlightened
man will trust them for his knowledge and hope
of the future ?

2. *Evolution*. According to this, man has developed from the lowest order of living creatures to
his present lofty height in the scale of existence;
but after he reaches the summit of human eminence he must *descend* again into the grave that
opens for him—and nothing is known beyond !
Whatever may be true about evolution in *material*
things, it is silent about the future life. The only
evolution that will avail us upon this question is
the *Christ-life* within us that will surely grow into
evelasting life !

3. *True science itself*, whatever that may include, can only deal with the established order of
things in *this world*. It does not reach to either the
creation or *destruction* of anything, and tells us
nothing of the *beginning of life* here, or its *con-
tinuation beyond the grave*. These things tran-
scend its limits. We must ascend to another department of knowledge, and to another and differ-

ent kind of teacher, if we would solve the great problem of the hereafter.

POETRY.

The heart of man longs for immortality, and his highest imagination has been called into requisition to find it. Has he succeeded? Perhaps no poet, of himself, has seen further across the river than Shakespeare:

> " To be, or not to be,—that is the question:—
> Whether 'tis nobler in the mind to suffer
> The slings and arrows of outrageous fortune;
> Or to take arms against a sea of troubles,
> And, by opposing, end them? To die,—to sleep;—
> No more; and, by a sleep; to say we end
> The heartache, and the thousand natural shocks
> That flesh is heir to,—'tis a consummation
> Devoutedly to be wished. To die,—to sleep;—
> To sleep! perchance to dream;—ay, there's the rub;
> For in that sleep of death what dreams may come,
> When we have shuffled off this mortal coil,
> Must give us pause."

Everything here is doubt and uncertainty, and this has been the discordant refrain of all "classic" poetry. We turn to our last and only hope,

THE BIBLE.

If it brings to us life and immortality—and it does—then it meets the last and greatest want of the human soul. A thousand passages might be given, but two or three will suffice: "I am the resurrection, and the life; he that believeth in me, though he were dead, yet shall he live." John 11: 25. "For we know that if our earthly house of this tabernacle were dissolved we have a building of God, a house not made with hands, eternal in the heavens." 2 Cor. 5: 1. "It [the body] is sown in corruption, it is raised in incorruption; it is sown in dishonor, it is raised in glory; it is sown in weakness, it is raised in power; it is sown a natural body, it is raised a spiritual body." 1 Cor. 15: 42-44. Here we may rest. Here tired, longing humanity may lie down in the bosom of the Great Father. We not only have the precious promises of the life beyond the grave, but we are shown those who have actually entered upon their reward." Rev. 14: 1-3.

> " Blessed Bible, I will hide thee,
>   Hide thee richly in this heart,
> Thou through all this life will guide me,
>   And in death we will not part;—
> Part in death—no, never, never.
>   Through death's vale I'll lean on thee,
> Then in world's above forever,
>   Sweeter still thy truths shall be!"

W. A. FOSTER.

W. A. FOSTER is just closing his term (a year and a half) as General Evangelist for California, with the best record, all in all, ever made on this coast. He began his work at Winters with 85 accessions. Then followed Woodland with 183, Santa Rosa, 116, and other places with equal success. During this time he has held but one meeting outside the State—Boone, Iowa, 156 accessions.

This is his first regular evangelistic work. Before coming to this State he was for four years pastor of the church at St. Paul, Minnesota, and before that he had preached at Brookville, Indiana.

He was graduated at Hanover College, Indiana, in 1878, with the first honors of his class. He studied law and practiced a while before entering the ministry, being at one time prosecuting attorney in the Forty-fourth Judicial Circuit of Indiana. He was born in 1857, at Scipio, Jennings County, Indiana, and his mother still lives at North Vernon, in that county.

He has a wife and four interesting and promising children; their home at present is Santa Cruz,

W. A. FOSTER.

California. The picture which accompanies this sketch is not over-true. Bro. Foster wears no shadow or frown on his face, as this cut might suggest, but has a smile and a kind word always. His complexion is light, and it is impossible to reproduce his bright and cheerful expression with printers' ink. He is over six feet tall, well-proportioned, well-dressed, and a perfect gentleman under all circumstances. His environments have left their marks upon his character. The son of a laboring man, he has sympathy and kindness for the poor that make the humblest at ease in his presence. He has something of the dignity and precision of one educated at a Presbyterian University, with the logic and directness of the lawyer. The character of his illustrations, and his scholarly and original way of presenting his subjects distinguish him at once from the evangelist who has only a set of protracted meeting sermons.

A good judge would know from any one of his sermons that he was not only educated but had held long city pastorates where he had been compelled to study and gather new material. His loyalty to the Word of God gives evidence to his connection with the Church of Christ, that he could be nothing else than a Christian.

The truth is presented lovingly and yet with power. His delivery is very impressive. Every word commands attention. He combines learning, logic, Scripture and sympathy in about the right proportions to be a success in any intelligent community, and I should say the more intelligent the people the more he would be appreciated. I have heard many of our great evangelists, and I hold Bro. Foster second to none, in ability, spirit and tact. In conducting Bible readings he surpasses any one I have heard. In fact, in all the services he is emphatically a Bible teacher.

One great feature of his meetings is the *Question Box*. He answers so briefly, kindly and correctly, that the people take a great interest in it and fill the box every night. Bro. Foster's career is full of promise. In the words of an editorial in the *Vacaville Reporter*, " We predict for him that in the near future he will be classed among the foremost pulpit orators in the country. No one who may be fortunate enough to hear Bro. Foster preach one of his best sermons will come away from church without feeling much impressed with the sacred truths that he presents."—J. E. DENTON, *Pastor Church of Christ, Vacaville, Cal., in Our Young Folks.*

THE OLD PATHS.*

W. A. FOSTER.

WHAT a grand song is this we have just been singing! And it would be a time of great rejoicing with us and in the presence of the angels, if every one here who has never named the name of the Lord would come to-night, making the sentiment of the song the pledge of his heart—

" Everywhere He leads me I will follow, follow on,
Walking in his footsteps till the crown be won."

In keeping with this is the text, Jeremiah sixth chapter, sixteenth verse. It is easy to forget God. We like to go in ways of our own devising, and sometimes we almost lose sight of the ancient landmarks. But now let me read you this passage in Jeremiah. " Thus saith the Lord, Stand ye in the ways, and see, and ask for the old paths, where is the good way, and walk therein, and ye shall find rest for your souls. But they said, We will not walk therein."

---

*NOTE.—At the California State Meeting, Santa Cruz, July 26–Aug. 6, 1893, on invitation of the committee, W. A. Foster conducted evangelistic services every evening. "The Old Paths" is one of the sermons used, and is here given substantially as spoken by Bro. Foster. Reported expressly for this work.　　　　　　　　　J. E. D.

The old is often arrayed against the new, the new against the old. You have all witnessed this conflict time and again. There are two parties in politics, the conservative and the radical. The one clings to the old, the other advocates the new. Elsewhere, too, may we see this same jealousy. The old thinks the new an upstart, an unwarranted innovation, while the new counts the old an old fogy. I suppose, though, the question ought really to be, not whether a thing is old or new, but whether it is right.

For the most part the world is now seeking the new. We are trying to improve upon the past. What we had yesterday isn't good enough for to-day. We are not willing to do as our fathers did. Between St. Paul and Minneapolis, in Minnesota, they have what they call the Interurban Line, with trains every few minutes. Suppose I should gather together the people of those cities and say to them, "You must abandon this electric railway. You must return to the old modes of travel and put on again the stage-coaches that used to run between St. Paul and St. Anthony." Would they do it? No, indeed. Instead of listening to my suggestion they would appoint a committee to inquire into the state of my mind. They would send me down to St. Peter, to the asylum for the insane. I go into a store to buy a book, and first of all I notice the date it bears. If I find that it was printed back in the sixties or seventies, say, the chances are I won't take it. I want the very latest on my subject—the new, not the old. My grandfather had a farm in Jennings county, in southern Indiana—eighty acres. That was a pretty good farm there in that day. You smile at this. Eighty acres wouldn't make much of a ranch in California. Many of my boyhood's memories are anchored about grandfather's farm. The corn-field and the meadow and the woods-pasture and the cider-press and the larkspur in the garden, and old Trailer, the dog! At the right season grandfather would go out and shear the sheep. Then grandmother would have a wool-picking. That was always a high day. All the neighbor women would be invited in, far and near, and they would pick, pick away the whole day long, and they *did* say (though I don't know how this was, and I wouldn't tell if I did,) that sometimes on such occasions they would mix in a little gossip to lighten the labor. Be that as it may, the hill of cleaned wool would grow larger and larger over in the corner, and the dish in the center of the circle would become heaping full of sticks and burs. After this the wool would be carded with the odd little hand-cards, which went this way. See? How many of you ever saw these hand-cards I am speaking of? Well, a good many have. Next thing, grandmother would spin it into yarn. She would give the wheel a good, brisk turn and then walk back—so. As if by magic, the thread would be all nicely twisted. Grandfather and grandmother have both been laid in the little church-yard at Queensville, and it is most thirty years, I think, since I saw the old spinning-wheel, but to-night I seem to hear the music of its hum as plainly as if I had heard it only yesterday. In a little out-room near the house was the loom. With its cumbrous beams, it was a wonderful machine in my child fancy. Day after day the big shuttle was pushed to and fro, and out of this marvelous loom there would come the jeans for the men and the linsey-woolsey for the women. If to-day I go to a woolen-factory, I observe that they are not doing as they did. They do not work now in that way. The wool, hundreds of pounds at once, is lifted in a moment to the top floor of the mill, where a boy at a machine, the picking-machine, takes from it all its burs and dirt as well as our grandmothers could, and there's no telling how many times more rapidly. Down on the next floor are the cards. The wool is spread in them, and it hurries through as if instinct with life. The carded wool is put in the spinning-jennies, a single one of which in a day will spin maybe a thousand times as much as could any pair of hands, no matter how deft. Another floor below we find the looms. I have seen one young woman in charge of three looms, the shuttles going this way and that so swiftly the eye could not follow them. Shall we in the making of woolen fabrics go back to the old ways? You say, No. Shall we do away with our railroads, and cross the plains with ox-teams, as our fathers did? Again you answer, No. And so it is with all of man's work. We are learning by experience, and are leaving the old for something better.

Curious advice of the old Hebrew prophet this, in the text, "Ask for the old paths." This is the difference, however. We have been talking of man's ways; in the text the prophet is speaking of God's ways. If the old paths were of man's making, we should improve on them as the years go by. But they are God's. God is not a man, that what he has done may be better done. He makes no mistakes. So far as anything is concerned that man has contributed to the belief and practice of the church, it should be considered precisely as other of man's attempts. Not long ago at Saratoga, New York, some good and great men met and, taking their dissecting knives, went down into the time-honored Westminster Confession and made some changes. They saw that it needed pruning. A work of man, the world had outgrown it. The knife is the right instrument in that kind of surgery. Their diagnosis was not quite correct; the operation, I take it, should have been decapitation. When men's creeds are out of our road we shall have little difficulty in getting back to the good ways of the Lord. "Ye should earnestly contend for the faith which was once delivered unto the saints." This is a part of Jude third. *Once* in this sentence is a strong word, and means *once for all.* No other revelations are to be looked for. There are to be no changes, for the faith is once for all delivered to the world.

Many calamities had come upon Israel. Jeremiah exhorts them to return to the Lord and walk in his ways, that their calamities might have an end. "But they said, We will not walk therein." So it is now, twenty-five hundred years later. A return now would make the people of God one in heart and hand, and enable us to present a solid front against the enemy of souls. But many will not walk by the Book. We want to go in our own ways. Sin is in the world, and it exercises a ruthless dominion. "All have sinned." Rom. 3 : 23. "The wages of sin is death." Rom. 6 : 23. Isn't this a dreadful showing? O my soul, the surprises of sin in the judgment! Now you all understand what is meant by wages. What a man earns is his wages. Whoever goes down into death will do so because he has earned this in his service of sin. The rest of that verse is, "But the gift of God is eternal life through Jesus Christ our Lord." What a work might be done this very day in pulling down the strongholds of Satan if only with singleness of purpose the people of the churches would move forward. *The old paths*—we can all walk in them.

We should return to the old paths,

1. Because they are God's, and therefore right. No man ever made a mistake when following the Word. I do not see why the good Father should have given us the Bible unless he meant for us to believe it and live it out before the world. I like the note sounded so long ago, " Where the Scriptures speak, we speak," and " where the Scriptures are silent, we are silent." Some people talk of essentials and non-essentials; of commands which it is necessary to obey in order to be saved, and commands obedience to which is not necessary. I have often wondered where they learned which commands of our Lord Jesus Christ it was essential to observe, and which not. Jesus said, " He that believeth and is baptized shall be saved." Mark 16: 16. Some say belief is essential, but baptism is non-essential. Do you know how they found that out? Friends, it is dangerous to say of *any* command of the Savior or his apostles that it is non-essential. If it was necessary for them to speak the word, it surely is necessary for us to heed it. No man in the world ought to ask other reason for his obedience than that the Lord commands it. Had the Lord said in the New Testament that whoever will hold up his right hand shall be saved, I don't believe it would be long until some people would be holding up the left instead. They'd say, "It doesn't make any difference; one is as good as the other. Do you

think the Lord cares whether it is the right hand or the left?" Or they'd say, "Of course the Bible says right hand, but then I'll hold up my left, as it is nearer my heart." Or, "I am left-handed, and the Lord knows it." Nonsense! This is child's play. Let us obey our Divine Master in everything, as those who must shortly render an accounting. "If ye love me," said Christ, "keep my commandments." But we should walk in the old paths,

2. Because we need something by which to measure—something that is certain and that does not present a new face with every change of the moon. God alone is the same yesterday, to-day and forever; all else is ever changing. In him is "no variableness, neither shadow of turning," says James (one, seventeen). His word is unchanging. Peter, in his first letter, (one, twenty-three) speaks of "the word of God which liveth and abideth forever." Two verses farther along he again assures us that "the word of the Lord endureth forever." We need some standard, and the old paths are such a standard as we need. Jesus says, "In vain do they worship me, teaching for doctrines the commandments of men." Jeremiah says, "The prophet that hath a dream, let him tell a dream; but he that hath my word, let him speak my word faithfully." Isaiah says, "To the law and to the testimony: if they speak not according to this word, it is because there is no light in them." Peter

says, "If any man speak, let him speak as the oracles of God." Now, for the illustration, I say that from the floor to the ceiling in this tabernacle is forty feet. Bro. Truax says, "No; it is fifty feet." I answer, "It isn't; it's only forty. Can't I see?" But Bro. Truax says again, "Yes, Bro. Foster; you are guessing by your eye. I was here when this tabernacle was built, and I measured the timbers with my rule. *I know.*" So some are going by the Word, the rule, while others are risking their supposition or notion or wish. Brethren, the older I grow the more do I bless God for the Bible—a message of love, an infallible guide.

> Holy Bible, book divine,
> Precious treasure, thou art mine;
> Mine to chide me when I rove,
> Mine to show a Savior's love.
>
> Mine to comfort in distress,
> Traveling thro' this wilderness;
> Mine to show by living faith,
> Man can triumph over death.

When Luther began his work, the order was Priest, Church, Bible; now the order is reversed and we have the Bible in the first place. Yes, the Bible is our measuring-reed. And, too, I might say in passing that if we could only return to the Christianity of the Bible, the infidel objections, or many of them, would be met, for if I do not mistake, these objections are not against the real religion of Christ, but rather against something else that passes current for it. Did you ever think that a vote cannot settle anything? Why, a vote never expresses anything except the idea or opinion of the voter. Here I am, standing before you. Imagine now that you are to decide how old I am. A ballot is taken. One-third of you vote that I am thirty-six, one-third that I am thirty-eight, one-third that I am forty. Says one, "This will never do; we must come to a decision, as we want to know Bro. Foster's age." Another ballot is taken. Two-thirds now vote thirty-eight and one-third forty. But on the third ballot everybody votes that I am thirty-nine. What has been determined? Nothing whatever, except the estimate of the congregation, and that is wrong, for I am not thirty-nine. And you see plainly that we could not decide questions of faith and duty in this way at all. God knew this, and so he gave us the Bible to decide them for us.

3. Walking in the way of the Lord we find rest. "Ye shall find rest for your souls," says the text. "Come unto me, all ye that labor and are heavy laden, and I will give you rest," says Jesus. In our lesson to-night Isaiah tells us that there shall be a highway, the way of holiness, for the ransomed of the Lord. In fulfillment of this prophecy, in John 14: 6, we have Jesus saying, "I am the way." Jesus our Lord came to lead us in the new and living way, that in our day of

toil and disappointment we might not despair of the rest that is ours. As in Rome in other days one must pass through the temple of virtue to reach the temple of honor, so now one must pursue this way, the way of holiness, if he would reach heaven and see the King in his beauty. They tell us that rest is harmony; rest for the soul means being at one with God. His blessings are for those who love and obey him. "Not everyone that saith unto me, Lord, Lord, shall enter into the kingdom of heaven, but he that doeth the will of my Father which is in heaven." We must be doers of the will. If you believe in Christ, that he is the Son of God, we ask you now and here to say so, before this mighty throng. As it is written in Romans 10 : 10, "With the heart man believeth unto righteousness, and with the mouth confession is made unto salvation." We would have you do no other things than those that are laid down in the Word of God. Men, women, be wise to-night. Hear the call of the Gospel and set out this very hour for the Father's house. He *is* our Father. In his matchless love he is waiting to welcome you. Will you come?

AMBROSE B. MOORE.

THE work of enlisting soldiers and planting churches is the primary function of the evangelist. It requires special powers and qualifications. These may be briefly enumerated:

1. The evangelist must be genuinely philanthropic in his impulses and sympathetic and loving in his nature.

2. He must understand human nature in all its complex forms and be able to adapt himself to it.

3. He must possess the power of presenting truth analytically and synthetically in such a manner that the people can understand.

These characteristics, I conceive, are very fully possessed by the subject of this sketch.

Ambrose B. Moore, son of Eld. Adam Moore, was born November 4, 1861, in Holmes county, Ohio. Three years later the family was moved to New Philadelphia, Ohio, where his father had been called to the pastorate of the church. In the spring of 1866 the family was again moved to near Mansfield, Ohio, on a farm. His father preached in different parts of the State, doing much evangel-

A. B. MOORE.

istic work. Here Ambrose spent his boyhood days, learning how to work, enjoying the pure air and sunshine as he roamed over hills and through the woods, which he always enjoyed. His home was a Christian one and the stopping place of many of the best preachers of the Restoration.

With such influences it is not surprising that at the age of 12 Ambrose arose one Lord's day morning at regular service, went forward and made the good confession, and was baptized by his father. Few people at that time realized the power wrapped up in that little boy. His parents desired their son to have a good education, a desire which they saw fulfilled. His education was secured in the country school, the public schools of Mansfield, and finally in the Mansfield Normal College, then under the charge of the writer of this sketch. During the last four years of his school life he made remarkable progress, always standing at the front rank in his classes. At the age of 17 he taught his first term of school, which was a successful one.

In November, 1879, his Christian mother died. This was a great blow to him, as he was devotedly attached to her.

In 1881 his father, having again married, sold the farm and moved to Canton, Ohio. Ambrose chose to remain at Mansfield. Instead of entering the ministry as his father had hoped he would do, he took a thorough business course, and with teaching and business transactions he profitably employed his time. During 1884 and 1885 we find him a successful business man, traveling in several States. In May, 1885, he was married to Miss Mary Terman. He continued in business and teaching until 1887, when a desire to enter a broader field, where he could accomplish more good, changed his whole life.

While visiting his father during the holidays he was asked to fill an appointment for him, which he did on New Year's day, 1888, and so acceptably that he was invited to fill the pulpit regularly. This church was located near Orrville, Ohio. He finished the term of school which he was teaching, only to receive the offer of a principalship in the Canton Public Schools at a good salary. This he refused. Having decided to enter the ministry, he would do nothing else.

In July, 1888, he was called to the pastorate of the Church of Christ in Findlay, Ohio. He entered vigorously into the work, greatly strengthening the church both in numbers and influence. Both himself and wife were greatly beloved by the congregation. At the end of one year he was compelled to resign, owing to failing eyesight, and undergo a long course of medical treatment.

Six months later he was called to the pastorate of the Eleventh Street Church of Christ, in Toledo, Ohio, and remained with great acceptance until

July, 1890, when the illness of his wife compelled him to resign.

In January, 1891, he went with her, for her recovery, to California. As usual we find him busy, preaching nearly every Sunday, and holding one very successful meeting. While here the Southern California Board desired to employ him as State Evangelist. In November, 1891, he began evangelistic work, and has been thus engaged ever since. His labors have blessed congregations in Ohio, Iowa, Illinois, Missouri and elsewhere. His preaching is instructive, and arouses a vigorous and healthy enthusiasm and activity.

Physically Bro. Moore is small, being only five feet six inches tall, slender, and weighs 125 pounds. He stands erect, has a bright, piercing eye, and his presence before an audience at once makes them feel that he is master of the situation. His appearance in the pulpit is manly and dignified; his diction is pure, and his ideal of Christian life exalted. He speaks entirely extempore, and in discourse his words flow like a torrent; he seldom opens the Bible to read a quotation, yet he is emphatically a Bible preacher, frequently quoting fifty or more passages in a single sermon, giving chapter and verse.

He has unbounded confidence in the gospel as God's power to save; he knows the Bible and he knows men. He is not emotional, yet he sways an audience from smiles to tears at will. His powers of endurance are wonderful; will preach and sing every night for months, and come out well and strong. His presentation of truth is clear and fearless; his appeals direct both to head and heart. He makes everything plain. To use his own words, "If I can make the children understand me, I am sure the older ones will."

His convictions are strong, and not to be tampered with. Though but a young man his fame has spread throughout the land as an uncompromising and successful expounder of God's Word, and a popular evangelist.

He loves home life, but is willing to forego its pleasures to do good. His wife has always accompanied him in his work, and greatly assists him. Their present home is at Mansfield, Ohio. It is always open to preachers, and many will testify as to the genuine hospitality enjoyed while there.

Bro. Moore is the author of several tracts, and of a volume entitled "Helpful Bible Readings," the only work of the kind ever prepared by a Disciple. This latter work has been very useful in arousing interest in the study of the Divine Oracles. It is having quite an extensive sale, and a second edition will soon be issued.

May the Lord continue to bless his labors.

J. FRAISE RICHARD,
Pres. Modern Normal College, Washington, D. C.

SOUL-WINNING.

A. B. MOORE.

He that winneth souls is wise.—Prov. 11: 30.

DID you ever win a soul to Christ? The grandest work God ever committed to man is soul-winning. God gave the motive power: "The gospel is the power of God unto salvation to every one that believeth." Rom. 1:16. The application of this power is committed to man. Hence, "It pleased God by the foolishness of preaching to save them that believe." 1 Cor. 1:25.

The gospel, then, is the mighty moral lever which we use to overturn the strongholds of sin, and by which the world will be brought to Christ. Man wields this power upon man; there is an influence exerted by the speaking of the truth which is produced by no other means. The heart filled with love for souls and earnestness to save them moves men and women to action. A thrill is sent to the hearts of listeners, carrying with it the word of truth.

God employs preachers to spread the glad tidings of salvation. Who are the *preachers*, and

15 (225)

how may they preach? I shall notice the WHO and HOW.

First, those who stand before the public assembly.

This is a time of unrest; many whose names are written high on the world's roll of fame are switching off from the Bible, feeding their congregations on doubt and criticism. Heed the words of Paul to Timothy, "Preach the word," and let speculations and criticisms alone; neither ever saved a soul. Stick close to the Word, the old Book which has come through the centuries of the past unharmed, and will stand the most rigid examination now. "The word of our God shall stand forever." Isa. 40 : 8.

Let others pursue that way if they will, but "Search the Scriptures," "Study to show thyself approved unto God." Do not advertise some error or false doctrine, which is unthought of in the community, by preaching about it. Preach Christ and fill the minds of your hearers with such exalted ideas of his love and goodness that they will be drawn to him, and want to obey his commands. Never allow yourself to settle into a rut by using certain expressions or forms, or a particular manner of speaking. Keep abreast of progress, but do not, like some, go beyond the teachings of our Leader, Christ.

In preparing sermons always keep souls before you, and in every sermon say something that will win persons to the Savior. Do not try to preach big sermons ; they are like a World's Fair, only to be had occasionally, and then for exhibition. Sermons abounding in sympathy, full of Christ and the Bible, are the best, and reach the people.

Common illustrations are much more effective than those far-fetched. Bible truths are often best illustrated by examples drawn from the Word.

The gospel is for the masses. But why is it not received by them ? Certainly not because they do not believe it is true. My experience and observation among men lead me to say that they do believe the Bible.

One reason why it is not eagerly sought after, undoubtedly, is that much so-called gospel preaching is utterly devoid of Christ and sympathy, and contains so much about old, musty creeds and dogmas that the hungry soul longing for a crumb of the bread of life, goes away as starved as before, and returneth not.

But let a man begin preaching the plain truths of the gospel, reaching down to the everyday life of the people, lovingly bringing to them sympathy for which the heart yearns, and quickly the people are aroused and accept the Savior.

While preaching a gospel of love, do not "neglect to declare the whole counsel of God." This embraces the commands of Christ as well as other things. Willingness to obey the commands is a test of loyalty. "If ye love me, keep my commandments."

Preach the Word with all the energies of your being, and as though you believed it. The message is true, and from God; let no "shakiness" ever appear in your words.

Always tell inquiring souls in the words of Scripture what to do to be saved. Peter said, "Repent and be baptized every one of you in the name of Jesus Christ, for the remission of sins, and ye shall receive the gift of the Holy Spirit." Acts 2: 38. Do the same. Common people can understand that.

A good way to close a discourse is to quote the commission.

The world longs for sympathy; let us give it. Let us be so Christ-like that every sermon and handshake shall impress Christ upon men. The world will respond to genuine Christian sympathy.

But the privilege of preaching the gospel is by no means confined to those who publicly proclaim it. Every Christian should be publishing the good news of the kingdom. A few ways by which this may be accomplished, some of which have had no prominence, are as follows:

Keep the Bible at hand. I know a merchant who always keeps the Bible in his store. When not engaged with customers it was no uncommon occurrence to see him and his clerks talking over

matters pertaining to their souls. The result was
he led a number of them to Christ.

The home is the fountain-head of society; society forms the State, States make up the nation.
Then the proper training of individuals in the
home insures good society, and this in turn a good
nation. An excellent way to preach the gospel in
the home is by means of Bible readings. By using
a concordance any family can learn a great deal
from the Bible on any subject selected. The writer
has prepared a volume of such readings, covering
a wide range of subjects especially adapted to home
study.

Almost every one writes letters. Envelopes,
with Scripture texts printed on them, afford a
means of bearing truth to those with whom you
may correspond.

Keep a supply of good tracts, and enclose one
or more with your letter. This is a quiet but
effective way of preaching, which has been much
neglected. Persons have been led to become
Christians by this humble means. Nor should
this be the only method of distribution. Place
them in the hands of your unconverted neighbors,
requesting that they be read.

One religious body has a supply of tracts in
every family of their communion which I have
visited; these they distribute as opportunity offers.
The same people energetically push the sale of
their literature until it is probably in more homes

than that of any other people. Every Christian can do work of this kind.

Take away bad influences from the young. Nude paintings and statuary should be banished. Every great art exhibition and many small ones are a disgrace. Should a man or boy be found carrying a copy of such paintings or statuary as are publicly exhibited, he would be arrested and fined. Drive out the evil with good. Surround the boys and girls with elevating influences.

Preach the gospel personally; individual attention may win when other means fail. The Savior preached to the one woman at the well, and continued to preach until the light dawned upon her. Philip preached Jesus to the one man until the truth reached his understanding and turned his heart to the Savior. Personal work by every Christian would result in the conversion of thousands.

Can you sing? Then use that voice to the glory of God and good of men. A gospel hymn sweetly sung may touch a chord which will respond in loyal obedience to Christ. In all righteous ways bear the gospel to sinful men as the power that will transform them into the image of the glorious Redeemer.

Reader, what are you doing to carry out the command to "preach the gospel to every creature?" The gospel must be borne to the masses, by a godly life, words of truth, and every ligitimate

means. Go forth, then, bearing precious seeds of
truth, sow bountifully, and God will abundantly
bless your work. Do something for the Master,
and at the end we shall come rejoicing, bearing at
least some sheaves we have gleaned from the great
harvest field of life, and lay them down at the
feet of Jesus.

Trust in God, win souls to Christ, be faithful
unto death, and "An entrance shall be ministered
unto you abundantly into the everlasting kingdom
of our Lord and Savior Jesus Christ."

B. B. SANDERS.

BLENFORD BRADFORD SANDERS was born near Carrollton, Pickens County, Alabama, Sept. 19, A. D. 1840, and was married to Miss Tinie Prestridge, August 10, 1859, nine children being the issue of their marriage, two sons and seven daughters, seven of whom are living, a son and daughter being dead. In 1867 he was converted, and immediately connected himself with the Missionary Baptist Church, but not being satisfied with their doctrine, "final perseverance of the saints," "hereditary total depravity," and "close communion," and learning of the doctrine and worship of the Disciples, two years thereafter he united with them.

In 1883 he removed to Texas and settled in Bryan, Brazos county, and two years thereafter his brethren, believing he had the ability to preach the gospel, persuaded him to retire from business that he might devote his entire time to preaching, which he hesitatingly and with some misgivings agreed to do, and the work as State Evangelist, under the auspices of the Texas State Board of Missions, being tendered him, he accept-

(232)

B. B. SANDERS.

ed, in which work he has since been engaged, with the exception of two years, during which he served the church at Bastrop, Texas, as its pastor.

During the short time he has been preaching—about eight years—he has been eminently successful both as pastor and evangelist, and as a protracted meeting man he has made himself a wide reputation, having, for the time engaged, established more churches and made more converts than, perhaps, any other man among the Disciples in the State of Texas. Bro. Sanders has not the advantages of a collegiate education, yet his education is fair. Being what is usually called a " self-made man," backed up by a good supply of that indispensable commodity, common sense, and a fine knowledge of human nature ; being agreeable in his manners, pleasant in address, and combining the logical, the scriptural, the humorous and the pathetical in his sermons, he seldom fails in holding very fine meetings. But few men among the Disciples are making a better record, and but few men, if any in his State, address larger congregations. His home at present is Austin, Texas, whither he removed two years since.

THE CONVERSION OF CORNELIUS.

B. B. SANDERS.

Can any man forbid water, that these should not be baptized, which have received the Holy Spirit as well as we?—Acts 10: 47.

IN the investigation of the subject of conversion it must be remembered that no conversion, or any case of forgiveness of sins, can be taken as a model where the person or persons were converted or forgiven before the giving of the commission by our Savior after his resurrection from among the dead. For this commission we quote Matt. 28: 19, 20: "Go ye, therefore, and teach all nations, baptizing them into the name of the Father, and the Son, and the Holy Spirit; teaching them to observe all things whatsoever I have commanded you: and lo, I am with you alway, *even* unto the end of the world." Mark 16: 15, 16: "And he said unto them, Go ye into all the world and preach the gospel to every creature. He that believeth and is baptized shall be saved; but he that believeth not shall be damned." And Luke 24: 46, 47: "And he said unto them, Thus it is written and thus it behooved Christ to suffer, and to rise from the dead the third day; and that repentance and remission of sins should be preached in his name among all nations, beginning at Jerusalem." From this commission we see that in order to become disciples of Jesus we must believe that he is the Christ, the Son of God, repent of our sins, and be baptized into the name of the Father, Son and Holy Spirit, for this is the law of induction into the kingdom of God; therefore we cannot be saved like the palsied man, to whom Jesus said, "Thy sins be forgiven thee," Matt. 9 : 2 ; nor like the rich young ruler, to whom it was said, "Go thy way, sell whatsoever thou hast and give to the poor, and thou shalt have treasure in heaven : and come, take up the cross and follow me," Mark 10 : 21 ; nor, indeed, like the thief on the cross, to whom the Savior said, "To-day shalt thou be with me in paradise," Luke 23 : 43 ; for all these cases of forgiveness occurred before the *facts* of the gospel, or the *commands* were given. Therefore to teach that we could be saved like any of those persons to whom reference has been made would be to teach salvation or justification by an *ex post facto* law, which would be contrary to every principle of justice. But to take the cases of conversions recorded in the New Testament after the giving of the commission as models for us, and to teach that we must be converted like them, we teach the law of pardon as given by the Holy Spirit through the apostles of our Savior ; and hence let us inquire whether Cornelius was converted in accordance with this "law of the Spirit of life in Christ Jesus," and is his conversion a model to us? Did he believe the *facts*—the death, burial and resurrection of the Savior—and obey the *commands* of the gospel, which are faith, repentance and baptism? But before answering these questions let us note:

1. *The character of this man.* He was a good man, a moral man, and one that prayed to God continually, and one that gave much alms to the people, who doubtless was serving God in accordance with the best light he had, yet he *must* be converted by and through the preaching of the gospel, because it is now the "power of God unto salvation." His prayers and his alms had come up for a memorial before God, but his prayers were answered through the means of the gospel. Christ having died upon the cross, he is now the "author of eternal salvation to all them that *obey him.*" Heb. 5: 9. He could make no exception of Cornelius, however good, however moral, however charitable he may have been, without an intervention of his own will. His goodness, aside from the belief of the *facts* and obedience to the *commands* of the gospel, could not now save him. But it may be argued that the principles of divine law would not condemn a man who has not the ability to render obedience to the gospel of Christ, and this is granted; for the parable of the talents and the principles of justice teach that man's

accountability shall be commensurate with his ability, be that what it may; yet the character of Cornelius and his obedience to the gospel certainly teach us that morality alone will not save us.

2. *The appearance of the angel.* Why did the angel of the Lord appear to him? Was it for the purpose of forgiving him of his sins, and thus making him an adopted child of the Lord? This could not be. If so, why send for Peter? The gospel being *the power of God* unto salvation, and the gospel having been committed to men, it must now be preached by men, for "It pleased God by the foolishness of preaching to save them that believe" (1 Cor. 1 : 21), and the Savior had said, "Go teach all nations," Matt. 28 : 19; "Go ye into all the world and preach the gospel to every creature," Mark 16 : 15; therefore this gospel must be preached to the prayerful and charitable Cornelius.

3. *Peter the particular man.* Why was Peter the particular man? Why not send for any of the other apostles or evangelists? Did they not understand the gospel, and were they not also guided by the Holy Spirit? Yes, surely, but Peter having been chosen by our Savior when he said, "I will give unto thee the keys of the kingdom of heaven; and whatsoever thou shalt bind on earth shall be bound in heaven, and whatsoever thou shalt loose on earth shall be loosed in heaven" (Matt 16 : 19), it was he who should proclaim the glad tidings of

salvation to all the world—Jew and Gentile—and
having unlocked the treasures of heaven to the
Jews on the day of Pentecost, he must now do likewise to the Gentiles.   The angel had said to Cornelius, "Send men to Joppa and call hither Simon
Peter, who shall tell thee *words* whereby thou and
all thy house shall be saved." Acts 11 : 13, 14.   It
was then the words of *Peter* that should save this
man according to the divine arrangement.

4.   *What did Peter preach?*   Luke, in record-
ing the sermon Peter preached upon this occasion,
says : " Then Peter opened his mouth and said, Of
a truth I perceive that God is no respecter of persons : but in every nation he that feareth him, and
worketh righteousness is accepted with him.   The
word which God sent unto the children of Israel,
(*on the day of Pentecost*) preaching peace by Jesus
Christ (he is Lord of all), that word, I say, ye
know, which was published throughout all Judea,
and began from Galilee after the baptism which
John preached ; how God anointed Jesus of Nazareth with the Holy Spirit and with power ; who
went about doing good, and healing all that were
oppressed of the devil ; for God was with him.
And we are witnesses of all things which he did,
both in the land of the Jews and in Jerusalem ;
whom they slew, hanging him on a tree ; him God
raised up the third day, and showed him openly,
not to all the people, but unto witnesses chosen
before of God, even unto us, who did eat and drink

with him after he rose from the dead, and he commanded us to preach unto the people, and to
testify that it is he which was ordained of God
to be the Judge of quick and dead; to him give
all the prophets witness, that through his name
whosoever believeth in him *shall receive remission* of sins." Acts 10: 34-43. Now from this
sermon we see that Peter preached the *facts* of the
gospel, and that it was *through* the name of Jesus
Cornelius should receive remission of sins, for
"Neither is there salvation in any other; for there
is none other name under heaven given among
men whereby we must be saved." Acts 4: 12.
Therefore we conclude that the gospel was preached to Cornelius, and by it he was saved.

5. *What, then, is the gospel?* Paul answers
this question in these words: "Moreover, brethren,
I declare unto you the gospel which I preached
unto you, which also ye have received and wherein ye stand; by which also ye are saved, if ye
keep in memory what I preached unto you, unless
ye have believed in vain; for I delivered unto you
first of all that which I also received, how that
Christ died for our sins according to the Scriptures; and that he was buried, and that he rose
again the third day according to the Scriptures."
1 Cor. 15: 1-4.

This being preached to Cornelius, as already
shown, and he having been convinced that his
salvation was in and through Christ, it only now

remains for him to obey the commands, according to the great amnesty proclamation of our Savior, that he might thereby become an adopted child of God. But why must he do this? Because God is no respecter of persons; the Jews having been required to render this obedience on the day of Pentecost, to whom, after they were convinced that they had crucified the Christ, Peter said: "Repent, and be baptized every one of you in the name of Jesus Christ for the remission of sins, and ye shall receive the gift of the Holy Spirit." Acts 2: 38. Cornelius must do likewise; he, too, must *believe*, *repent* and be *baptized*. But did he obey these commands of our Savior? Let us see. By reference to Acts 15:7 we learn that the apostles and elders at Jerusalem had been called together to settle a dissension and dispute among the brethren about circumcision. "Peter rose up and said unto them, Men and brethren, ye know that a good while ago God made choice among us that the Gentiles by my mouth should hear the word of the gospel and *believe*." Peter, then, being a good witness, the question of Cornelius' believing is settled. He *must* believe that Jesus is the Christ in order to have the privilege of becoming a child of God, for John says, "To as many as received him (Christ) to them gave he power to become the sons of God." John 1: 12. It being clearly shown that he believed, the next question that presents itself for an answer is, Did he repent?

When Peter returned to Jerusalem the Jews contended with him that the Gentiles were not in covenant relationship with God, and therefore he had no right to preach the gospel unto them. "But Peter rehearsed the matter from the beginning and expounded it by order unto them," and "when they heard these things they held their peace and glorified God, saying, Then hath God also to the Gentiles granted repentance unto life." Acts 11 : 4 and 18. Thus we see that Cornelius repented, and it only now remains to show that he was baptized, and then we shall have proved that his conversion was like all others, a record of which is found in the book of Acts. "Can any man forbid water, that these should not be baptized, which have received the Holy Spirit as well as we? And he commanded them to be baptized in the name of the Lord." Acts 10 : 47, 48. In this conversion we find that he *believed*, *repented* and was *baptized*, and we do perceive of a truth that God is no respecter of persons.

OBJECTIONS ANSWERED.

It is claimed that, since Cornelius was baptized with the Holy Spirit before his water baptism, water baptism is not necessary. It is a rule in logic that anything that proves too much does not prove anything; therefore let us look both logically and scripturally at this objection, and

16

see if it be true. If it be argued that water baptism is not necessary because Cornelius was baptized with the Holy Spirit before he was baptized in water, then by the same course of reasoning we may prove that *faith in the Lord Jesus Christ* is not necessary, and surely no one who believes the Bible to be man's infallible guide will take the position that we can be saved without faith in Jesus Christ! Listen. Peter, in rehearsing the conversion of the Gentiles to his Jewish brethren when he had returned to Jerusalem, says: "*As I began to speak* the Holy Spirit fell on them as on us in the beginning." Acts 11: 15. Thus showing that in the very introduction of his discourse, which we have already quoted, Cornelius was baptized with the Holy Spirit. Peter was a Jew by blood and education, and with the illustrious history of his fathers before him, and the teaching of the Savior that he came only to the lost sheep of the house of Israel, it is not surprising that it required a miracle—the letting down of a great sheet in which were all manner of fourfooted beasts, and fowls of the air, and creeping things, and the voice of the Spirit—to conduct him into a worshiping Gentile assembly ; nor is it surprising that God should perform another miracle in his presence to convince him that "he is no respecter of persons : but in every nation he that feareth him, and worketh righteousness, is accepted with him." Here there is another witness to Peter, and a witness to his Jewish brethren who had accompanied him, that the Gentiles were gospel subjects, and that he had the sanction of all heaven in preaching the gospel unto them.

But it is sometimes said that this baptism of the Holy Spirit was for the purpose of giving the Gentiles faith. That cannot be, for Peter himself says that "A good while ago God made choice among us that the Gentiles by *my mouth* should hear the word of the gospel and *believe*" (Acts 15: 7); and Paul says, "Which in other ages was not made known unto the sons of men, as it is now revealed unto his holy apostles and prophets by the Spirit; that the Gentiles should be fellowheirs, and of the same body, and partakers of his promise in Christ *by the gospel.*" Eph. 3: 5, 6. And again Paul says, "So then faith cometh by hearing the Word of God." Rom. 10: 17. Now from these passages it is evident that faith was not given by a baptism of the Holy Spirit, but by *preaching the gospel.* In refutation of the argument that the baptism of the Holy Spirit was for the purpose of giving Cornelius faith it may be sufficient to remark that with all due deference to our heavenly Father, he has not faith to give any one, only in the sense that he gives us *eating* and *drinking.* He has given us the food and the appetite, and we do the *eating;* he has given us the water and so made us that we thirst, but we do the *drinking;* he has given us the testimony and the faculty of believing, and we do the *believing*. So then it could not be for the purpose of giving him faith.

But again, we are told that this baptism of the Holy Spirit was for the purpose of *purifying the heart*. The Scriptures again make this plain when it is said, " And put no difference between us (the Jews) and them (the Gentiles), purifying their hearts by *faith*." Acts 15: 9. If, then, Peter understood this conversion, Cornelius' heart was made pure by faith in the Lord Jesus Christ; and this accords with Paul, when he says, " Therefore being justified by faith, we have peace with God through our Lord Jesus Christ." Rom. 5: 1. It could not, then, have been for the purpose of purifying the heart.

But again, we are asked if this Holy Spirit baptism was not for the purpose of converting the soul? In answer we again quote from the Oracles of God. Psa. 19: 7, David says, " The law of the Lord is perfect, converting the soul," and Paul says, " The law of the spirit of life in Christ Jesus hath made me free from the law of sin and death." Rom. 8: 2. This " law of the spirit of life " is but a complex name for the gospel of Christ, hence he was made free from sin, or his soul was converted, by believing the facts and obeying the commands of the gospel. In further proof that Cornelius was not baptized with the Holy Spirit for the purpose of converting him I quote from 1 Pet. 1: 23: "Being begotten again, not of corruptible seed, but of incorruptible, by the word of God, which liveth and abideth forever." Once more: "Of his own will begat he us with the word of truth." James 1 : 18.

Thus it appears that David, Paul, Peter and James all teach that conversion is a process, and that process, according to the Scriptures of inspired truth, is *hearing, believing, repenting,* and being *baptized.* But there is still another objection that is sometimes stated, and that is, that the baptism of the Holy Spirit upon Cornelius was a confirmation to him that God had forgiven him, and that he was now a child of God. But was it for this purpose? The angel which God sent to Cornelius told him to "send men to Joppa, and call hither Simon Peter, who shall tell thee *words* whereby thou and thy house shall be saved." If then it were *words* by which he was to be saved, were not the *words* preached by Peter to him the confirmation of his acceptance with God, accompanied with a consciousness on his part that he had obeyed the commands given him by Peter, the Lord's servant? Thus it is, and thus it appears.

If, then, the baptism of the Holy Spirit was not for the purpose of giving Cornelius faith, or of purifying his heart, or of converting his soul, or a confirmation of his salvation, what, then, was it for? We answer that it was a witness to the Jews and Gentiles—the whole world—that God was no respecter of persons; that every nation, tongue, kindred and tribe had now an access to the throne of grace, and that all were now invited to the gospel feast. See Acts 15 : 8 and Acts 10 : 34, 35.

Again, there is still another reason for saying that the baptism of the Holy Spirit was not for the purpose of forgiving sins, or a confirmation that their sins had been forgiven, and that is, that the baptism of the Holy Spirit was not of common occurrence. About eight years had passed between the day of Pentecost, when God baptized the apostles with the Holy Spirit, and the baptism of Cornelius. During these eight years Peter and the other apostles and the evangelists had been engaged in preaching the gospel of Christ, and hundreds and thousands of people had been converted to the Lord, and yet we do not read of a single baptism of the Holy Spirit between Pentecost and the conversion of Cornelius! And is it not passingly strange that if a baptism of the Holy Spirit was necessary, or in order to a genuine scriptural conversion, or a confirmation that persons had been converted, that Peter, to whom the keys of the kingdom of heaven had been given, would absolutely forget it? He says, when he saw that Cornelius was baptized with the Holy Spirit, "And as I began to speak, the Holy Spirit fell on them, as on us at the beginning. *Then remembered* I the word of the Lord, how that he said, John indeed baptized with water; but ye shall be baptized with the Holy Spirit." Acts 11 : 15, 16. It had been so long since he had seen anything of the kind that it had passed from his mind, and now, perhaps, for the first time in all his preaching experience did he realize the full import of the gospel, and that all nations and peoples were invited.

We are aware that Paul says, "For by one Spirit are we all baptized into one body" (1 Cor. 12 : 13), but conversion is not his subject. His teaching in this verse is that by one Spirit—that is by and through the teaching of the Holy Spirit— we are all baptized into one body, which is Christ our Lord, whether we be Jew or Gentile.

Again, there is still another reason for believing that we are not now baptized with the Holy Spirit, and that is, that we do not see the effect it had upon the day of Pentecost and the household of Cornelius. *They spake with tongues.* We do not now see this effect. The days of miracles have ceased, and no one nowadays speaks in any language except that in which he has been taught. That God had a design in the outpouring of the Holy Spirit on the day of Pentecost and the household of Cornelius, has already been shown; but it must be remembered that while we are not baptized with the Holy Spirit, the Holy Spirit is an agent or factor in every conversion. The work of conversion is begun, carried on and ended by and through the Holy Spirit, for "No man can say

that Jesus is Lord but by the Holy Spirit." 1 Cor.
12 : 3. The Scriptures make a distinction between
the baptism of the Holy Spirit, and the work, min-
istration, or operation of the Holy Spirit. And a
proper division of the Word of Truth will assist us
very greatly in understanding that all the conversions recorded in the New Testament after the
giving of the commission by our Savior are alike—
all did the same things ; they all *believed*, *repented*
and were *baptized*, thus teaching us that sinners
must now be converted in the same way.

Sinner, would you be converted like Cornelius?
Then you must believe with all your heart that
Jesus is the Christ, the Son of God ; repent of your
sins, and be baptized into the name of the Father,
Son and Holy Spirit, and arising to walk in new-
ness of life, give yourself to the service of him who
so loved you as to give his life for you. Oh, way-
worn traveler o'er the rugged roads of earth, would
you reach the city of light, walk its golden streets,
listen to its heavenly music and dwell with God
forever? Storm-tossed mariner on life's tempestu-
ous sea, would you safely anchor your frail bark
in the haven of endless rest, where no storm will
ever burst, and no wave of trouble ever roll? Then
come to Jesus and find rest for your grief-laden
and sin-burdened soul. Give him your heart,
your life, your all, and be at peace with God and
man. God loves you ; can you doubt it when you

look upon the cross and its bleeding victim?
Christ loves you; can you doubt it when for you

> " He left his starry crown,
>   And laid his robes aside;
>   On wings of love came down,
>   And wept, and bled, and died?"

H. C. PATTERSON.

In the fall of 1875, while the writer was a student in Butler University, Irvington, Ind., an awkward boy, *fresh from the farm*, entered my study-room. He told me he came to study for the ministry. I looked him all over, and said to myself, "Young man, if you have any of the elements of a minister in you, they surely are *within*, for all your outward appearances are against you." When it was noised about that this unripe Rush county boy had entered the Bible Department, the risibility of the entire school, faculty included, could not be suppressed. Students treated it as a joke. He was poor, and I was poor. We were soon good friends, and became room-mates, *batching* together. I soon learned to love him, and found there was a man wrapped up in this inexperience. Yet I believed he had missed his calling. One night after we had finished our lessons four of us were in one room, talking and joking. Bro. Patterson changed the theme of conversation and said: "Brothers, all of us claim to be Christians, and some are preparing for the Lord's vineyard. Can we separate to-night and go to rest without going to God in prayer? Boys, let us all

H. C. PATTERSON.

get down here and pray." We kneeled down and tried to pray, and when I arose I was fully persuaded that Bro. Patterson would be a great power to save souls. With great interest I have watched his career, and as I saw his horizon widening, my mind would go back to that little room where I heard him pray on bended knees, "Lord, if you can use a poor, weak creature like me, here I give myself to thee."

Bro. Patterson was born in Rush county, Ind., July 3d, 1856, and moved to Missouri in 1870. He united with the church when 13 years of age. He was reared under the best of Christian influences. His mother, father, brothers and sisters were all Christians. When he entered Butler University, in 1875, his friends bitterly opposed his entering the ministry, thinking that failure would follow him. He entered the University with only $75, and lived on $4.50 a month for three months. Remaining here two years, he returned to Missouri and taught school and preached occasionally for five years, receiving only $50 for all this preaching. Bro. Patterson says that the preaching was high at $50. In 1879 he entered Kentucky University. He was married in 1880 to Miss Kittie Veach, of Augusta, Ky. God has blessed them with two dear children, Ethel, who is now a Christian, and Keene, a dear little girl. He attended college three years after his marriage. Sister Patterson has always been a great support to her husband.

In her lonely home she has gathered her dear ones around her and asked God to give her husband strength to do the work God has called him to do. She has traveled much with her husband, and all who meet her are high in her praise. If there is one prettier crown in heaven than another, I say, "Dear Lord, give this prettiest, brightest and best crown to the wife of the evangelist." She makes more sacrifice than he, and has fought and won battles in the home greater than ever won by Napoleon, Grant, or Lee.

Bro. Patterson has been pastor of the following congregations: In Illinois—Versailles and La Harpe. In Missouri—Neosho, Appleton City, and Higginsville. He was engaged one year as State Evangelist in Missouri. In 1889 he made a journey through Europe, Egypt and Asia. He visited the Holy Land and made a careful study of the country and people. His lecture on Palestine has given him national recognition as a platform lecturer, and he has more calls than he can answer. But his greatest victories have been won in the field as an evangelist. Since he entered the field thousands have confessed under his preaching. Bro. Patterson does not hunt for easy fields. He goes to those places that cry for help, often refusing flattering offers in order to help the needy places.

In October last he became the pastor of Higginsville church. Since that time over one hundred persons have united with the congregation. He is an indefatigable worker, and his house is always crowded with anxious listeners. He will enter the field again next year as an evangelist.

In conclusion, let me say that the awkward country boy now stands at the head of the list of successful evangelists. May the dear Lord give him greater victories than even his best friends anticipate !   J. V. COOMBS.

THE UNPARDONABLE SIN.

H. C. PATTERSON.

Wherefore I say unto you, All manner of sin and blasphemy shall be forgiven unto men; but the blasphemy against the Spirit shall not be forgiven unto men. And whosoever speaketh a word against the Son of man, it shall be forgiven: but whosoever speaketh against the Spirit, it shall not be forgiven him, neither in this age nor in that which is to come.—Matt. 12: 31, 32.

THUS spoke Jesus of Nazareth over eighteen hundred years ago; and from that time down to the present, humanity has been curious to know just what he meant by that expression. I am sure that my audience will be perfectly willing to accept the declaration that there is no utterance which our Savior ever made that has remained enshouded in greater mystery. Athanasius, Origen, Chrysostom, Augustine—in fact all the greatest theologians of past ages have grappled with and tried to solve this (to them) difficult question, and their views differ as widely as possible. Modern expounders of the Scriptures have spoken and written on this subject, but have failed in elucidating it. It is almost a daily occurrence that I am confronted by the question, "What is the unpardonable sin?" I once heard a preacher (now

president of a female college) exhort his hearers
to obedience upon the ground that God had hid
away a sin somewhere, and in a moment when
they least expected, some of them might commit it
and their destiny would be sealed for time and
eternity. This set me thinking, if it were indeed
true, after all I had heard of the goodness of God,
that he was dealing treacherously with humanity.
Has God, like the elephant hunters, actually dug
dead-falls along the line of human march, so
nicely concealed that the most wary are taken
therein only to awake, perchance when too late,
to a realization of their awful doom? And after
my reflections I am forced to cry out, No! A
thousand times, *No!* The Bible, which I believe
from lid to lid, declares that " God is not willing
that any should perish; but that all should come
unto repentance." I, therefore, am forced to the
conclusion that everything pertaining to our eternal weal or woe has been clearly set forth in God's
Holy Word, and if in anything we are unen-
lightened, the fault lies in *us*, or in our blind
leaders; each of which is equally inexcusable.
We have been informed by Paul that " The Scripture given by inspiration of God is profitable for
doctrine, for reproof, for correction, for instruction
in righteousness; that the man of God may be
perfect, thoroughly furnished unto all good work."
Therefore, we have been commanded to " search
the Scriptures," and to study the Word, since

therein the will of God concerning us is made known. He who seeks to know the truth, and has an earnest desire to come into the light, will as certainly find his pathway glow as that God himself is light. That is to say, there will be no hidden snares nor pits of sin of which he will have no previous knowledge. So, I conclude, that if you and I are ever lost, it will be our fault and not God's, which could not be true if we cannot know to a certainty what the Unpardonable Sin *is*. Away, therefore, with that preconceived idea that we can never understand just what the Savior meant when he uttered that warning cry. For convenience and in order to simplify I divide my discourse into three heads:

I. THE UNPARDONABLE SIN WAS NOT POSSIBLE UNDER THE JEWISH DISPENSATION.

II. IT WAS NOT AND IS NOT AN OVERT ACT.

III. IT HAS ALWAYS BEEN POSSIBLE UNDER THE CHRISTIAN DISPENSATION.

I.

THE UNPARDONABLE SIN WAS NOT POSSIBLE UNDER THE JEWISH DISPENSATION.

I make the above declaration upon inferential grounds (one of the ways in which God speaks to us through His Holy Word). The Old Bible is silent concerning such a sin, and if its commission had been possible in that age it would have been but the duty of a merciful God to have apprised man of that fact, and warned him of the danger, since he was not willing that any perish. From the very fact, therefore, that the law and the prophecies are as silent as the grave in which Moses and the prophets sleep, we conclude that no such thing was ever known to them, or at that time. The first mention ever made of this unpardonable offense is found in the Gospel of Matthew, from which we have taken our text to-night. In view of what I have already said I am now prepared to declare that nothing was known of this terrible sin until after Jesus came into the world; and all we know or can know about it is to be found in the New Testament Scriptures.

II.

IT WAS NOT AND IS NOT AN OVERT ACT.

I have, not unfrequently, met persons who entertained and advocated the theory that this sin was an overt act, such as murder, adultery, drunkenness, idolatry, or the like. No one ever made a greater mistake than when he adopted such a false theory. We may take the catalogue of crime, beginning with the most heinous and running down to the least offensive known in our civil code, and then turning to the Bible we can read of some who have been guilty of the commis-

17

sion of one or more of these crimes; but who, upon a genuine repentance thereof, were pardoned, and were afterwards taken into divine favor and declared to be men after God's own heart. Further, that it cannot be any one of these crimes is clearly seen from Paul's language (1 Cor. 6: 9, 10), "Know ye not that the unrighteous shall not inherit the kingdom of God? Be not deceived; neither fornicators, nor idolaters, nor adulterers, nor effeminate, nor abusers of themselves with mankind, nor thieves, nor covetous, nor drunkards, nor revelers, nor extortioners shall inherit the kingdom of God." The apostle here speaks figuratively, naming only a few of the numberless crimes as including the whole list, and it is as though he had specified *every* overt act. But, we hear him continuing in the same connection, "And such were some of you; but ye are washed, but ye are sanctified, but ye are justified in the name of the Lord Jesus and by the Spirit of our God." Away, therefore, with the idea that in the commission of any overt act we are guilty of the unpardonable sin.

In discussing this subject I desire to begin at the very foundation, and this I do by inquiring, "What is sin?" We have not been left without a clear-cut and definite definition, for John (1 John 3: 4) declares that "sin is the transgression of the law." Now, John speaks in a *general* way; but Paul, being more explicit, gives us to understand that there are *two* (and I add, *but* two) ways possible whereby man can sin. In his letter to the Hebrews (Heb. 2 : 1-4) he says : "Therefore we ought to give the more earnest heed to the things which we have heard, lest at any time we should let them slip. For if the word spoken by angels was steadfast, and every *transgression* and *disobedience* received a just recompense of reward ; how shall we escape, if we *neglect* so great salvation; which at the first began to be spoken by the Lord, and was confirmed unto us by them who heard him ; God also bearing them witness, both with signs and wonders, and with divers miracles, and gifts of the Holy Spirit according to his will ?" From these two apostles we learn that before there can be any sin, three conditions are essentially necessary, and these are :

1. There must be law *enacted.*

2. That law must be *simplified*, or brought within the comprehension of every one of whom the Lord would take account.

3. That law must be *revealed*, since Paul (Rom. 4 : 15) declares, "For where no law is, there is no transgression."

As an illustration of the above facts we consider the case of Adam and Eve. When God had finished all his creation he placed Adam and Eve in Eden's lovely bowers, he saw fit, in the chamber of his own council, to place them under law. Consequently these three conditions were complied

with. Then, and not till then, did he require obedience of them.

Another illustration of the same is found in the
case of Israel. The law was *enacted, simplified*
and made known, so that Moses could say: "For
this commandment which I command thee this
day, it is *not hidden* from thee, neither is it far
off. It is not in heaven, that thou shouldst say,
who shall go up for us to heaven and bring it unto
us, that we may *hear* it and do it? Neither is it
beyond the sea, that thou shouldst say, who shall
go over the sea for us and bring it unto us, that we
may hear it and do it? But the word is very nigh
unto thee, in thy mouth, and in thy heart, that
thou mayest do it." Not until after that law had
been read and all the people had had an opportunity of understanding it did God require obedience to its precepts. So that if any were found
disobedient to its precepts they should not be held
guiltless, but punished the same as though they
had *transgressed* the law by performing an overt
act. *Transgression* and *disobedience* are, therefore, the only two ways possible for us to sin. The
word *transgression* is a compound derivation from
the Latin, and means a going over, trampling under, or *breaking* the law. Hence all overt acts,
such as murder, idolatry and adultery are *transgressions*, and are pardonable sins; but not so
with *disobedience*, which simply means a knowledge of the law, and a recognition of one's obliga-

tion to render obedience thereto, but a stubborn and willful refusal to yield. There is nothing more clearly revealed in the Scriptures than that *disobedience* to known duty is as great a sin, before God, as the most heinous crime that one can possibly commit. From some cause the world has failed to grasp this truth, consequently the majority of people seem to think that the good moral (but disobedient) man stands about, or quite, as good a chance to enter heaven as he who makes an effort to keep all the commandments of our God. My hearers are hardly ready to receive it, but I am ready to make the statement that the moralist, who has never obeyed the Savior in his commandments and ordinances is no more certain of heaven than the vilest murderer who languishes in a felon's cell. I know no such thing as gradation of sins with God; but rather understand the Bible to teach that *all* who *refuse* to render obedience to a known law or command are classed among those who commit the most atrocious overt acts, or transgressions. James says (James 4: 17), "Therefore, to him who knoweth to do good and *doeth it not,* to him it is *sin.*" All *disobedience,* therefore, is sin, and can only be remedied by rendering *obedience,* which, if not done, forever precludes the idea of *pardon* and *salvation.* The Savior himself says: "Whosoever heareth these sayings of mine and doeth them not, shall be likened unto a foolish man, who built his house upon the sand; and the rain descended, and the floods came, and the winds blew, and beat upon that house; and it fell, and great was the fall of it." Again in his description of the general judgment he says: "Inasmuch as you have *not* done it unto one of the least of these my brethren, you have not done it unto me." And these shall go away into everlasting punishment. "He who knoweth his Master's will and doeth it not shall be beaten with many stripes." From these and many other passages that we might quote we learn that we will stand or fall as we *have* or *have not* done the will of God. Cornelius was a devout and praying man, and one whose prayers and alms came up before God as a memorial, and yet he was in an unsaved condition, and was told that he *must* obey the Savior before he could be saved. Think not my hearers to-night that thou shalt escape because of thy *morality*. "To *obey* is better than *sacrifice*, and to hearken than the fat of rams." Therefore *obey*, and be sure thou wilt never commit the unpardonable sin; but if you do not you certainly will commit it sooner or later. From all that we have said on the second division of our subject we conclude that the unpardonable sin cannot be an overt act, since all such are pardonable, but *disobedience* is not excusable or pardonable; and persisted in too long must carry one beyond even the *inclination* to obey, without which his destiny is sealed, though he may live a score of years.

III.

Jesus Christ came into the world to show God's hatred for sin and his love for man, and the miracles which he wrought were for the purpose of demonstrating the fact that he was the Son of God, and therefore the Savior of men. Consequently the first proposition the Savior ever made to the world was: "If I do not the works of my Father, believe me not." "The works that I do they bear testimony of me." "If I had not come and done among you works which no other man ever had done then you would not had sin, but now you have hated both me and my Father, and you have no cloak (excuse) for your sins." All of this was spoken in connection with the miracles which he had and was working in attestation of his divinity. Now, to apply this to the case in hand. Jesus had performed a wonderful cure on one who was possessed of a devil, and was blind and dumb. The Pharisees, beholding it, and being unable to deny that the wonderful cure had been effected, at once undertook to justify themselves in their opposition to him on the grounds that he was performing these things by Beelzebub, the prince of demons. Jesus, perceiving that they were of that class to whom Isaiah made allusion, now quotes their own Scriptures as against them (Matt. 13 : 15), "For this people's heart is waxed gross, and their ears are dull of hearing, and their eyes they have closed; lest at any time they should see with their eyes, and hear with their ears, and should understand with their heart, and should be converted, and I should heal them." This Scripture shows that they *believed* him but would not receive and obey him from pure stubbornness. Now, Jesus perceiving that they were indisposed to receive him and his word, *admonishes* them in the following language: "Whosoever speaketh against the *Son of man*, it shall be forgiven him: but whosoever speaketh against the Holy Spirit, it shall not be forgiven him, neither in this age nor in the age to come." From this we learn that *any* thing that they might say against *him* would be forgiven, and so it was, for about the last utterance of Jesus on the cross was this earnest petition: "Father, forgive them; they know not what they do." It is therefore clear to my mind that up to that time they had not committed the unpardonable sin, else would he not have prayed for them, since John (1 John 5 : 16) declares that "there is a sin unto death; I do not say you should pray for it." Again, if my first proposition be true, viz., that the unpardonable sin was not possible under the Jewish dispensation, it is evident that those persons whom the Savior addressed had not committed it, since they were still under that dispensation. The question, therefore, arises as to why Jesus addressed them relative to such a sin. I answer that his language to those Pharisees was a prophetic warning, as much so as that which he uttered to the inhabitants of Jerusalem. I cannot think that he would allow them to commit that sin unknowingly and *then* inform them that their destiny was sealed forever; but upon the discovery that the tendency was toward rejecting the *Spirit's* pleading, as well as *his*, he warns them to be more considerate in the future, and then puts them on their guard, just as God did Adam and Eve in Eden, and the Israelites when the law was given unto them from Mts. Ebal and Gerizim. It was not the mission of Christ to guide humanity into the truth whereby they were to be saved; but only to make redemption possible. Hence, when Jesus left the earth, in his cloudy chariot, he left humanity in a similar condition to the mariner on the boundless ocean—in possession of chart and compass, but lacking the knowledge necessary to their use. He left his disciples only verbal instructions, with the command to "tarry in Jerusalem until ye shall be endued with power from on high." That power from on high was the Holy Spirit, for up to that time he had not come into the world, in his official relation to man, and therefore could not be sinned against. When he had announced the hour of his departure as being at hand, the apostles were greatly grieved, whereupon he addressed them as follows: "I will pray the Father and he shall give you another Comforter, that he may abide with you forever; even the Spirit of truth. These things have I spoken unto you, being yet present with you. But the Comforter, which is the Holy Spirit, whom the Father will send in my name, he shall teach you all things, and bring all things to your remembrance, whatsoever I have said unto you." (John 14: 16, 17). Again (John 16: 12-14), "I have many things to say unto you, but ye cannot bear them now. Howbeit when he, the Spirit of truth is come, he will guide you into all truth: for he shall not speak of himself, but whatsoever he shall hear, that shall he speak; and he will show you things to come. He shall glorify me, for he shall receive of the things of mine and shall show them unto you." From this Scripture we learn that the Spirit's mission was a *very* important one, viz: that of a guide into all truth that pertains unto life and godliness. Now, it is declared by Jesus that "ye shall know the truth and the *truth* shall make you free." The Holy Spirit, therefore, and not Jesus, is *now* striving with man, trying to lead him into the truth. Paul, in 1 Cor. 12: 3, says: "Wherefore I give you to understand, that no man, speaking by the Spirit of God, calleth *Jesus accursed:* and that no man can say that Jesus is the Lord, but by the Holy Spirit." We have often been accused of not believing in the operation of the Spirit in conversion; but I wish to emphasize the faith of the church, which is that there never was a conversion, since the knigdom of Christ was set up, that was not begun, carried on and completed by the Holy Spirit. When, therefore, persons come forward and confess their faith in Jesus Christ as the Son of God, they are led to do so by the Holy Spirit, without whom it would be utterly impossible for them to make that confession unto salvation. In Stephen's address to the Jews (Acts 7 : 51) he said : "Ye stiff-necked and uncircumcised in heart and ears, ye do always *resist* the Holy Spirit." He who resists the Spirit is committing sin which has a fatal tendency. Hence Paul (Eph. 4 : 30) says : "*Grieve* not the Spirit of God, whereby ye are sealed unto the day of redemption." Again, he says (1 Thess. 5 : 19), "*Quench* not the Spirit." These exhortations to *quench* not, *resist* not, and *grieve* not, are very significant to my mind, and impress me with the truthfulness of the declaration made thousands of years before, when God said: "My Spirit shall not always strive with man." I understand the Bible to teach that one can so act and speak (and thereby sin) against the Holy Spirit that he will go away from, and give him over to "hardness of heart, and reprobacy of mind." Paul very positively declares that this will be the result with

those who have no love for the truth.   In 2 Thess.
2: 9-12 the apostle says: "And with all deceiva-
bleness of unrighteousness in them who perish;
because they received not the love of the truth, that
they might be saved.   And for this cause God
shall send them strong delusions, that they should
believe a lie: that they might be damned who believed not the truth, but had pleasure in unrighteousness."   Jesus said, "I am the way, the *truth*
and the life."   Again, "Ye shall know the truth,
and the *truth* shall make you free."   Now, we
have learned that between man and the Savior,
who is the truth through whom they shall be made
free, there is an indispensable person, even the
Holy Spirit.   It therefore follows that if one so
acts as to grieve the Holy Spirit away, so that he
ceases longer to plead with him, he has committed
the unpardonable sin, or the sin against the Holy
Spirit.   John says (1 John 5: 16), "There is a sin
unto death: I do not say that he shall pray for it."
We have always contended that it is useless to
pray for *forgiveness* so long as people continue in
disobedince; and there is no need of my praying
for such, but rather persuade them to arise and
obey Christ, "that their sins may be blotted out,
when times of refreshing shall come from the presence of the Lord."

But if they refuse, and rush heedlessly on, they
will sooner or later reach and go beyond the deadline, beyond which hope is a stranger, and mercy

never comes; they cross the fatal Rubicon and
enter a territory where night is eternal; they go
into the dismal swamp out of which there is no
egress. That man may not make such a fatal
mistake, the Savior not only gave the warning
contained in our *text*, but admonishes him in such
language as, "Seek ye first the kingdom of God
and his righteousness." And, "Be ye also ready,
for in such an hour as you think not, the Son of
man cometh." Again, "*To-day* is the day of salvation, to-day if you will hear his voice, harden
not your heart." And in contemplation of such a
state of things as described, Solomon said: "Remember *now* thy Creator in the days of thy
youth, while the evil days come not, nor the
years draw nigh when thou shalt say, I have no
pleasure in them." It is a very significant and
impressive fact that only one out of a thousand
having passed their sixtieth mile-post on the journey of life, ever renders obedience unto our Lord
and Master. This shows that the older one grows
and the oftener he rejects the earnest entreaties of
the Holy Spirit the more nearly he approaches that
fatal line beyond which the Spirit's voice of en-
treaty is never heard. *This*, in the light of all
Scripture quoted, is what I regard as the sin
against the Holy Spirit. But, before closing this
discourse, I am asked to answer the question if it
be possible for church members to commit this sin.
I answer, Yes. A public acknowledgment of our

allegiance to Christ and a refusal to thereafter comply with his will in every particular is *sin*, and the Apostle Peter (2 Peter 2 : 20, 21) expresses his true condition in these words : " For if after they have escaped the pollutions of the world through the knowledge of the Lord and Savior Jesus Christ, they are again entangled therein, and overcome, the latter end is worse with them than the beginning. For it had been better for them not to have known the way of righteousness, than, after they have known it, to turn from the holy commandment delivered unto them." One so turning back seems to be more certain of passing over the "deadline" than one who has never confessed Christ. I am certain that it has been the experience of every minister of the gospel that it is far more difficult to re-enlist a backslider than to convert some of the vilest of sinners. " Let us therefore fear, brethren, lest, a promise being left us of entering into his rest, any of you should seem to come short of it," for :

> " There is a time, we know not when,
> A point we know not where,
> That marks the destiny of men,
> To glory or despair.

> " There is a line, by us unseen,
> That crosses every path—
> The hidden boundary between
> God's patience and His wrath.

" To pass that limit is to die,
    To die as if by stealth;
  It doth not quench the beaming eye,
    Nor pale the glow of health.

" The conscience may be still at ease,
    The spirits light and gay;
  That which is pleasing still may please,
    And can be thrust away.

" He feels, perchance, that all is well
    And every fear is calmed;
  He lives, he dies, he wakes in hell—
    Not only doomed but damned.

" Oh where is that mysterious bourne
    By which our path is crossed;
  Beyond which God himself hath sworn,
    That he who goes is lost?

" An answer from the sky is sent—
    Ye who from God depart,
  While it is called to-day repent,
    And harden not your heart. "

BIOGRAPHY OF H. A. NORTHCUTT.

H. A. NORTHCUTT was born near Hannibal, Mo., November 13, 1843. When he was eight years old his father, who was a farmer, moved to Knox county, Missouri, where he has ever since resided. Young Hosie, as he is familiarly called, like all other successful men, had nothing upon which to rely except characteristic goodness and energy. He too was reared in the rural district away from those contaminating influences of idleness and vice, and continually ate the bread of industry until he grew to be a young man of honesty, integrity and virtue (just such a man as God needs and wants to herald the good news of salvation). If Bro. Hosie ever uttered a bad word or committed a bad act, no one knows it. I but voice the sentiment of all who know him when I say that he is one of the very best men in the Lord's army. He had only the advantage of a common school education up to the time that he became a man grown. After he was 25 years old he attended the State Normal School in Kirksville during two sessions. He then attended Christian University, Canton, Mo., two years. Leaving college he taught school and preached for several years. When he

H. A. NORTHCUTT.

first entered the ministry no one ever thought he would ever be more than a mediocre in his chosen profession. His work was reasonably successful, and the field of his usefulness broadened year by year as he became more and more proficient in his work. He was always loved by those for whom he ministered, and they reluctantly gave him up as God called him into wider fields. His marvelous power over the hearts of men became more and more manifest as he engaged occasionally in evangelistic efforts. A few years ago he entered the evangelistic field, and gave himself wholly to that work. Everywhere he went grand meetings crowned his efforts. The State Board of Missions in Missouri were looking for another evangelist, and Bro. Northcutt was called to the work. In this field also he was marvelously successful. It was during this engagement that the greatest meeting of his life was held at Pleasant Hill, Mo., with 365 additions. He then received a call from the "General Home Mission Board," in whose employ he now continues. Under his ministry thousands have been brought into the kingdom of the Lord Jesus Christ. Bro. Hosie's wife died a number of years ago, leaving one child, a daughter, now an accomplished young lady, who accompanies her father and assists him in his evangelistic work, for which by nature and education she is well fitted. Bro. Northcutt's father has been a minister of the gospel in the Church of Christ for

18

more than forty years. Our beloved brother has
already passed the 50th milestone on the journey
through life, but still he appears as active and
enthusiastic in his work as one just beginning.
May he live to an old age to bless humanity with
his words of wisdom and good cheer, and when
his time comes to die may he

> " Gather the drapery of his couch about him,
>   And lie down to peaceful slumber,"

is the wish of his friend and brother.

H. C. P.

WHERE THERE IS LIFE THERE MAY BE GROWTH.

H. A. NORTHCUTT.

The earth bringeth forth fruit of herself; first the blade, then the ear, after that the full corn in the ear.—Mark 4: 18.

WHAT is life? I answer this question nega-tively first. It is not existence. The devil and his emissaries exist. The wicked shall ever exist, but will not have life. The smoke of their torment shall ascend *forever*. They will be cast into *everlasting* punishment; while the righteous shall go away into *life* eternal.

Many people exist, thinking perhaps they are living. Many a man and woman marry and exist, and are in hell long before they die. I never like to hear a man say he is not living, but just stay-ing here.

Life is growth. When life ends death begins. The world is *living* or *dying*. Life is a great con-tract between three parties: God, our fellow-men and ourselves. We are bound by every tie to carry out our part of the contract. We know God will do right; our fellow-men may not, but that does not release us from going on with our part of

(275)

the contract. Friends may prove treacherous, but that does not excuse us from being sincere.

Tennyson has developed this principle of life so beautifully in the life of King Arthur. He represents him as knowing his wife loved another better than she did him; she was unfaithful to him; yet never by word, look or deed did he betray this knowledge to her, but treated her with all the courtesy due a true wife. When her guilt became exposed she fled to a nunnery. He on his way to the battle in which it was predicted he should be killed, stopped at the nunnery and bade her good-bye. When he told her farewell he said, "Lo! I forgive thee, as the eternal God forgives. Do thou for thine own soul the rest."

A true life never seeks revenge, but ignores all petty personal attacks. When the rebellion of the South was broken, and the general of the South came to the general of the North and laid his sword at his feet, the fallen South received not a blow from the general of the North. He said, "Have your soldiers feed from our storehouses, and let them keep their horses to plow their farms." He denied himself the very thing that all other conquerors loved so much—the sword of his opponent. Surely the greatness of soul was never more manifest than in this, where revenge took no part, but mercy. When Napoleon took the sword of Frederick the Great, he said, "I would rather have this sword than twenty million dollars."

"Life should be a deep and earnest struggle. No malice in our hearts, no word born of hate, but love to all human kind; a sigh for every sorrow known, hearts tender as the petals of a rose, and a soul as guileless as the dimple of a prattling child."

Mrs. Barbauld, in extreme old age, wrote this beautiful stanza:

> " Life, we have been long together,
> Through pleasant and through cloudy weather;
> 'Tis sad to part when friends are dear,
> Perhaps 'twill cost a sigh or tear;
> Then steal away; give little warning;
>   Choose thine own time;
>   Say not good-night; but in some brighter clime
> Bid me good morning."

I have no ambition above that of living a manly life, dying a manly death, and taking a manly life up to God. If we thus live, white-winged angels will bear us up in hopeful triumph to glory, and heaven's gates will swing inward at our approach, and the music of angels will welcome us, and Christ, arising from the great white throne, will place on our brows flashing, blazing crowns, saying, Well done.

Sin destroys life and brings forth death. Hence whatever destroys life should be shunned, and if the disease is already destroying life, we should seek an antidote. Paul says, "The wages of sin is death, but the gift of God is eternal life through Jesus Christ our Lord." Why is death put down as the wages of sin? 1st. Because death is that which a sinful life legitimately works out. 2nd. Death is that to which a man may come, too, by himself without help. Man needs no help to die, but does need help to live. If you are sick you send for a physician to help you live. Jesus nor God will help a man die, but live.

Why is eternal life said to be the gift of God? 1st. Because no man can obtain it by himself. 2nd. Because God only has life. He is the author of life. If a man could work out eternal life, then he would need no Savior. Yet this life is a matter of choice. "I call heaven and earth to record this day against you that I have set before you life and death, blessing and cursing; therefore *choose* life, that both thou and thy seed may live." Deut. 30 : 19. "He who hath the Son hath life." If life was a commercial transaction, God would save all.

God has given us life—physical, intellectual, affectional and spiritual. Man's physical nature imbeds him in the dust, and yet he may hold fellowship with the stars, follow the comet in his immense excursion throughout the universe. He is a thinker. This part finds expression in the world of mind. The affectional capacity links him to home, country and God. His spiritual nature makes him a worshiping being. These endowments of man God has complemented. Man has but to reach forth the hand and partake.

These blessings God has not bestowed upon us

altogether in vain. We have somewhat to offer unto God in return. We can offer to him a better government than the world ever had before—more good men and women. It is *not* true the world is growing worse and worse. The Mississippi river at one point runs north, but the tendency is toward the south. So looking at the world from a certain point it may seem to be growing worse.

Infidelity says, " With mire behind me, and darkness before, I have nothing to long for or live for but death." There is a future for man. This life is but the alphabet of a future, the bloom of a golden fruitage. Eye hath not seen, nor ear heard the things that God hath prepared for them that love him.

Everything that has life may be improved, from the tiny insect to the elephant; from the pale flower which almost fades in blooming, to the oak whose life extends through thousands of years; from the oyster to the philosopher. The farmer delights in his growing crops, his lambs and his calves; not because of what they are, but because of what they promise to be. Why is the child of all things the most interesting? Because of what it may be. " It doth not yet appear what it shall be." The mother's joy increases from the time she presses her babe to her heart the first time until she closes its eyes in death. The soul has feasted constantly on the thought, " It is better farther on."

There is not a tree in the forest, nor a fruit that ripens in the orchard ; not a vegetable that comes to our table, but has been and may still be improved. All their excellences may be encouraged, and their faults kept in the background until their faults will finally disappear. The fine mealy potatoe that comes to our table every day was once a little knotty, stringy root, with but little nourishment in it. Cultivation has made it what it is. The beautiful double rose was once the single rose of the prairie. Cultivation has made it more beautiful and more fragrant.

There can be little doubt that dogs and horses were once as wild and almost as dangerous as wolves and buffaloes are to-day. Training has made them more intelligent and beautiful and useful. Who knows but the time may come when the buffalo will be as tame as the cow, and the tiger as domestic as the cat ?

If animals, under the training of man, lose their wild, ferocious nature and become like him who trains them, may not man, under the training and restraining influence of the perfect and holy One, lose his worst nature and become like Christ ? What is true of animals is true of man.

The horse does become like his master, and at times his attachment borders on affection. He will put his nose against his master's cheek, lick his flesh, bow his neck to have his mane stroked.

Man, left to himself, will never become better.

Flowers, fruits nor forests will ever become better unless cultivated. The animal will never grow better without a trainer. The wild Indian, if left to himself, will never improve. Vegetable life reaches down and lifts up the mineral, the animal reaches down and lifts up the vegetable, the mental lifts up the animal, the affectional lifts up the mental, the spiritual lifts up the affectional; but if there be no life above man's highest life, which is purely earthly, then what will lift his spiritual being? Man cannot get up without help, can't lift himself up.

If a star should fall from its place, it could never get back without help. The only means by which it could get back would be for the sun in some way to reach down and attract it again. Man is fallen, he cannot get up without help. He must be drawn. Hence God sent his Son down to earth to draw men. "I, if I be lifted up, will draw all men unto me." No man can come to the Father but by me. We are to-day what we are morally because Jesus has drawn us. Our constant prayer should be, " Closer to thee, my Savior, draw me."

We have said the world is growing better. I believe it. I am not a pessimist. 'Tis true man has fallen, but he can rise if he will. It is better to be a man that sins, but can rise again, than a beast that cannot sin nor rise.

The fact that man can fall very low is evidence

that he can rise very high.   Large weeds indicate strong soil.

We measure man's worth by the cross of Christ. Some one has said, "Calvary is man's eulogy, written by God in characters of his own life's crimson." The cross explains two things: 1st, God's estimate of man, and 2nd, his hatred of sin.

In what respect has the world grown better? The laws governing society are better now than at any other time. The weak were never so well protected before. Once it was thought better to be dead than to be weakly. Once weakly children were put to death, not because they lacked affection or intellect, but it was thought better to be dead than weakly.

Once the king and captain could use everything under them for their own selfish purposes. Women and children had no rights at all that men were to respect.

In the 7th century men could purchase a license to murder. Pay so much to murder a common man, so much to murder a man of a little higher rank, etc., etc. A full table of this may be seen in White's History of Eighteen Christian Centuries, page 152.

By and by, as time passed on, and men became better and purer, these crimes were prohibited. We look back on that age with horror and detestation; but we are not perfect yet. The next generation will look upon our license system as we do on these things. We license whiskey-selling, gambling houses, houses of ill-fame. Great God, is there not room yet? But we are coming out of the wilderness of ignorance and barbarism.

The day is not far distant when another Abraham Lincoln will issue a proclamation of emancipation of both blacks and whites from the slavery of passion and the demon of strong drink. Already the serpent's coils are being paralyzed. The white ribbon army is belting the world. God is spanning the floods and drawing the wires beneath the angry waves, and by and by we shall be delivered from the greatest curse of the age. It may be some who are now living will see the prohibition flag floating from the dome of the national capitol. You who have labored for this, if you are not living you will look down from above and strike a new note of praise on your harps of gold. Mary Bright Lucas, who now stands at the head of this white ribbon army, or some other woman blessed and honored of God and adored by men, shall with steady, firm tread climb to the capitol's dome and plant the white flag. Will not earth and heaven join in the grand chorus, "Peace on earth, and good-will to man?"

The poor were never so well cared for as now. Scarcely had the wires ceased tingling that brought the distressed cry from the fire sufferers of Chicago till help was furnished. Drafts for thousands of dollars were sent over the wires, trains were loaded with provisions and clothing. The yellow fever sufferers of the South had but to announce their wants, and money, and clothing, and provisions, nurses and doctors were furnished, and they had to say, We have enough. The waves that swept away Johnstown had not found their level till help was winging its way to the sufferers. Though the cry of distress comes from the uttermost parts of the earth, we hear it, and our throbbing hearts pulsate the wire or drive the engine wheel, and help is furnished. Even the sea may open her merciless jaws to swallow the shipwrecked mariner; a Grace Darling hastens to the rescue, takes her life in her hands and fights down the billows and saves the drowning. If one inmate in our states' prisons feels an inspiration of his better nature swelling his bosom, there is an Elizabeth Fry who is willing to leave her beautiful English home and help him.

Brethren, when the church grows to her full stature in good works, as God has designed she should, and as I verily believe she will some time, we will have no more need of Masonry, Odd Fellowship, fire or life insurance companies. The church will subvert them all. Christian fathers and mothers would never dread their children going to the poor-house. No, as long as one Christian has bread his child will, and it will never become homeless.

Two little sisters stood and watched while their

mother's grave was being filled. When they turned
their back on the mound that had been reared to
mark the place where mamma slept, the younger
clasped the elder sister's hands, while grief almost
choked her, and said, "Sister, where shall we go
now, we have no home?" A Christian man standing near by said, "You'll go home with me."
Yes, the church is a home; a part of it on this
side of the river and a part on the other.

The cardinal virtues of man are not what they
once were. Once the strife was for physical size,
fleetness and strength. The man who could knock
down and drag out most men on muster day was
the hero, and men worshiped him. In those days
might made right. Hence Homer wrote,

" No greater honor e'er has been attained
  Than what strong hands and nimble feet have gained."

" The Romans regarded a gladiatorial show about
as we regard a hunt. The news of the slaughter
of two hundred thousand of the Helvetians by
Cæsar, and a half million by Titus, excited in
their minds a thrill of triumph."

As the ages passed on man began to think, and
to appreciate the thinker. Then the hero was
the thinker. The world fell down and worshiped
him. This was a great advance over the Sulli-
vans and Kilrains of that day. I am not surprised that dogs in the form of men will fight—this
is their nature; but I am surprised that leading

men of our nation will countenance it, and that our leading newspapers will go crazy over it and seek to excite everybody else by giving two or three pages to its description. I believe the government ought to imprison for life the two men and prosecute the papers that report it, and never allow a man who witnessed it to hold an office, or a man who bet on it to vote again.

We are now in the twilight of the best age the world has ever seen, when strength nor intellect is the crowning virtue of man, but goodness.

Christianity is designed to bring the world upon a common level. That level is goodness, righteousness. It is in the power of the poor to be great. Greatness is goodness.

A few years ago this nation stood with trembling feet on the grave of Garfield, and rained their tears down on the dust. Why did this nation love him as it had not a president since the father of this country drew the drapery of his couch about him, and laid down to dream? Because he was a *good* man.

God led the world by successive stages, step by step, and thus prepared them for the Christian religion. He was four thousand years getting man ready for his kingdom. Once man's reward and punishment were temporal. God shook mountains, dried up rivers, fought battles. He could not reach man in any other way. Man has always sought to know God. He will not be satisfied without. His idea of God is often very absurd. In the absence of any revelation, man's idea of God is that he is material in form. My idea once of God was he was a great man, larger than father, or my school-teacher, and that made him very great. All idol-worshipers were seeking to know God. They regarded him a great being, of great power; hence they worshiped the sun, stars, waters, because they represented greatness. Such men as Homer, Virgil, Socrates, were grand men. They have furnished the world with valuable literature, and yet they were idol-worshipers. They remind us of men in a dark cave hunting for the light. They choose material things to represent to the mind God. Socrates once said, " God will reveal himself sometime more fully than he has ever done in nature." I am glad I live in that time when God has revealed himself in Christ.

'Tis a blessed thing that men can see God looking out of human eyes, speaking through human lips, toiling, sorrowing, weeping, dying. Once I thought of God on some far-away throne, ruling the world like a mighty king. He seemed so far away I could hardly approach ; but I am glad that I have advanced beyond that thought. I think of him manifested in his Son, that comes down to earth, takes hold of my hand and puts it in God's hand and beseeches me to be reconciled.

I believe in a personal Savior, one who walks the street with me, is with me as I pray, as I sleep.

He knows all my sorrows. I do not believe a single sorrow comes to the hearts of his children that don't first pierce his great heart. He is touched with a feeling of our infirmities.

Such men as Luther, Calvin, Wesley, Campbell, and Errett, men of great hearts, conscientious, doubtless would have been idol-worshipers had it not been for God's revelation. They lived and died rejoicing in that they saw God in Christ. This satisfied them. Philip uttered a purely human cry when he said: "Shew us the Father and it sufficeth (satisfies) us." The soul is never satisfied until it knows God.

Wherever there is life there can be growth. This is as true of the church as of the vegetable or animal kingdom. Religion is life, and life is growth. Where growth ends death begins. The principles of Christ's religion never change. In fact, principles have never changed. They remain the same. Plans and modes may change. The principles of locomotion have always been the same, but the manner or mode of applying them has changed.

Faith, *love* and *obedience* have always been conditions of man's salvation. These principles have never changed; but plans have changed. Once the sinner brought his lambs to the altar; he shed its blood; now he accepts Christ as the Lamb, and he comes with a loving heart, willing to obey, as did the Jew, but in a different way. The world has always been required to believe in God, love him and obey him.

The church at Jerusalem is a model church in its plan of conversion and can never be improved; but I am slow to believe it learned all about spreading the gospel, taking care of the poor, and a hundred contingencies that confront us. The early church was established and confirmed and perpetuated by miracles. These miracles, as another has said, " Were to the church what scaffolds are to a house." They are used while building the house, and when it is done the scaffolds are taken down. So when the church was fully established, miracles were withdrawn and the church since that time has depended largely on its merits. The church that does not merit life will die. If it does not work, if it does not advance, it will die. A church or a Christian ought not camp on the same ground twice.

We must grow, we must be in front of every good work; lead the van. The preacher or the church that does not keep up with the times, the age in which he lives, will fall by the way. Some good, honest people, Christian people, stopped twenty-five years ago, and have not advanced a step; the world and the church have gone off and left them. They think it is all going to the bad and are honest in it. I believe we preach as pure gospel to-day as they did. I believe we are as true to Christ. The difference is not in what we

19

preach, but the way. Modes of thought have
changed, and modes of preaching must too. I feel
sorry for these men and women; they honestly
think they are laid on the shelf by their younger
brethren. But it is not that. We are compelled
to change our tactics. We have moral questions
to meet to-day which no other age had, rather
questions in different forms.

The Ten Commandments given by Moses, while
they are true and right, do not contain the ideal
of a Christian to-day. Nearly every one of these
commandments is negative, and a negative life
is not our ideal of a Christian life. He must be
positive, aggressive. Fifty years ago the labor
question was very different from what it is to-day.
Then it was, Shall the laborer own his home? shall
he own his children? shall he own himself? That
form of the labor question is settled, but still the
labor question confronts us. We must meet it.

Too many of us have been too far removed from
the world. If I am to reach men I must be a man
among men. I must know their troubles, their
weaknesses, their homes, their hearts. Once people would listen two hours to dry theology, or dis-
cussions on dead dogmas, with a degree of grace,
but they will not now in these railroad times.
When people come to the Lord's house on Sunday,
tired with the cares of the week, discouraged, they
want to hear something that will inspire them,
something they can take with them and use in

their business to-morrow, something that will make them stronger to resist temptations, and that they can build in their lives. They want to be brought face to face with Christ, and feel his great heart beat against their hearts, leaving in them only love to God and sympathy for poor, fallen man. Let us live in the present. Ask God for light and grace to live by to-morrow.

Brethren, the contest is not over dead dogmas now, but over the crucified form of the Son of God. God help us to stand close to Jesus and preach to living men about living things. Let us make men feel, however sinful and discouraged they are, there is some good in them, and Jesus can save them if they will be saved.

I have no ambition above that of getting a pure heart and life beneath sinful men and lift them up to God.

We ought to study the best method of reaching the people with the gospel. The thing to be done is to get Christ enthroned in the hearts of the people. The command of Jesus is, *Go* and preach the gospel. God don't tell us how to go, but has left that to us.

I think we can become prejudiced against good things. I know we are always opposed to everything that is new; I suppose it is because we are egotistical; we don't like to acknowledge there is anything we don't know. I think we sometimes let our conscientiousness run into stubbornness. If we would sit longer under the cross of Christ we would be more forbearing.

When Paul said, " When I was a child, I spoke as a child, I understood as a child, I thought as a child: but when I became a man I put away childish things," he meant a great deal. He did not say when I became a man I quit speaking and thinking, but simply he quit thinking and talking and acting like a child. A change in the manner. Every nation, city, town, village and country has had its childhood period, then; manhood. So of the church. As a church, brethren, we ought to take on us the grave responsibilities of manhood. We have been but playing at many things. We have been playing at Sunday school work and missionary work. Let us cease objecting so much to every thing that is proposed and go to work. Some of us act as though we might have been "*born in the objective case.*"

The church of yesterday ought not be the church of to-day in her plan of work. No church can live on its past history. Nor is church succession the thing to be looked after so much as the church of to-day. We must not have stereotyped rules or cast-iron frames of thought. I am glad that that day of the church is fast giving way. The Roman Catholic Church says the people are not capable of thinking for themselves, so we, the priests and popes, will think for them. Some Protestant churches have tried to do the same thing. Hence these creeds of the churches. Men are throwing them off, and asserting their right to think. No church has a right to bind on its members cast-iron rules. Let this be the rule, "Where God speaks we speak, where God is silent we'll be silent." There is just one article in the creed of Christ's Church. This was placed there by the great Head of the Church. This must be believed or no salvation. Outside of this in matters of opinion we should grant each other the largest liberty. 'Tis a grand thing to be a free man—free to think for himself, think out the hard problems of life for himself. Without the right of free thought, free speech, free action, there can be no advance. If others are to do our thinking we become stagnant, and at the very best we only echo other people's thoughts. The one thing to be believed, or in other words, the one article of faith in the Christian's creed, is, "Jesus is the Christ, the Son of the living God." This should be the bond of union, and it is the only bond that can bind God's people. We are fast tending toward that. Creeds are becoming musty, and the religious world is rallying around Christ. This is a hopeful outlook. This is an advance, a wonderful growth in the last twenty-five years. What mean all these union prayer-meetings, union meetings, Church Congress, this fellowship between many churches and many more Christians? We are treading down these paper walls.

I believe all the religious world can unite on the simple yet very wise motto of *The Christian-Evangelist*, "In faith, unity; in opinions and methods, liberty; in all things, charity." In my mind a picture arises, not which fancy paints, but which faith sees. All God's children marching under the banner of the Christ, keeping step to the music of the cross, to the conquest of the world. May this thought soon echo in every Christian heart, and may the echo rise above the stars and mingle with the symphonies of heaven.

We are growing. We are not what we were fifty years ago. I am glad we are not. While I reverence the grand men who preceded us in this reformation, yet I am slow to believe they learned all there was to be learned. They did a noble work, but we should do a grander still. If I did not think I would be a larger Christian in heart and life twelve months hence, I would feel a little loath to live to see that time. A man once said to me, "You change so much." Said I, "It is for the better." He said, "Yes." Then said I, "Give us credit." But said he, "I don't like a turn-coat." I then quoted brother Franklin: "It does look a little bad to see a turn-coat, but I can think of something more ridiculous than a turn-coat. It is a man who puts his coat on wrong side out in the morning through a mistake, but through stubbornness wears it all day that way."

We have grown wonderfully in mission work,

both at home and.abroad. Men, women and children are catching the spirit. We love to give. What an army of workers! But the end is not yet. We are but children. We can yet devise new ways and means. In nature God shows us the little veins of gold, but we must dig deep, and crush the hard quartz to get it in abundance. A few pearls may be found near the shore and in shallow water, but we must dive deep, where the bright tinted fishes dart hither and thither among the wonderful flora of garden of waters, if we would find them in great numbers. God shows us a few stars, but we must build ladders (telescopes) and climb up if we would see the great star depths. So we must arise to the sublime heights of Christ's life, and love as he loved, if we would explore the wonderful heights that stretch out before us. Jesus says, "Love thy neighbor as thyself." Every man on earth to whom we can do good is our neighbor. Then the Chinaman, who joins lots with us eight thousand miles beneath us, is our neighbor.

We don't preach as we once did. We don't need to. It would be meaningless. We had to fight for every inch of ground we obtained. That was all right. We have always been very tenacious for the faith once delivered to the saints. We have collared every man who has come among us and demanded if he was right or sound in faith. Now we are asking as well if he is sound in love and good works. We once had preachers among us who had only one text, or at least it was made a part of every text. It was, "Arise and thrash." Now we are preaching one life, one death, and love and obedience to the one Christ.

Once if a little fire crept into the church, we cried out in holy horror, "Like other people! We don't want any excitement! Away with such a man!" Then it was said of us we only had a "head religion and no heart religion," and it did look like it sometimes.

Sometimes now (not often, I am glad to say), I go to hold a meeting for a church, am early met by a good brother who advises as to the best method. He says, "We don't want any excitement. Just reason with the people; there has been so much excitement in other meetings here lately, and we think best to have nothing emotional." I invariably say, then you have sent for the wrong man. I can't tell the story of Jesus' life, his sad, sorrowful death without feeling.

A scene that would blacken the heavens, cause the God of day to blush in shame, make the earth tremble, and cause the dead to turn in their dusty beds, surely would make our hearts bleed, while our lips would tremble with the words, "My God and my Redeemer." No person who has felt the power of Christ crucified in the soul, can tell the story without feeling.

God has ordained that preaching a crucified and

risen Savior shall stir men's hearts and cause them to cry out, " Men and brethren, what shall we do ?"

The cross of Christ is a restless and resistless agitator. What we need to-day is churches constantly fired with the story of Christ and filled with the Holy Spirit.

I could as reasonably expect an infant ten days old to live if thrown out in a snow-drift and left there, as that a young Christian would live in a cold church.

I know there is a wild fanaticism, a zeal without knowledge, which is dangerous; I don't mean that when I speak of enthusiasm. I mean the earnestness and zeal that control our entire being, and consecrate all we love to the service of God. Brethren, let your hearts be always on fire, and ever be desperately in earnest in persuading men to come to the Savior. There are two things which always excite me. One is when I talk about the sufferings of the Savior, and the other is when I see men going down to eternal ruin. Sometimes I almost become wild with excitement, and I can hardly refrain from taking hold of them and saying, I will not let you go.

There are many evils in the world, and many organizations for the suppression of these evils, Masons, Odd Fellows, Good Templars, White League Cross, W. C. T. U., etc. We almost forget at times that the church is a heaven-ordained institution for the suppression of these evils. As little as the world recognizes the fact, the church to-day is doing what none or all of these organizations are doing. They will accept good men and women, but do not seek to lift up the fallen. It is much easier to form than reform. But the church spreads the gospel net around all.

A few years ago a man who had fallen very low in drunkenness and its kindred crimes, one day felt an inspiration of his better nature, and resolved he would try to be a man, but thought he must have some help. Consequently he went to the Masonic lodge and asked for help. They appointed a committee to investigate his character; they reported unfavorably, he was black-balled. After a time he knocked at the Odd Fellows' door, and met the same fate. Discouraged, and ready to give up in despair, he thought of another organization, and sought help from them. It is hard for a man to reform without help. He needs sympathy and prayers. Yes, the world needs more sympathy to-day from us. 'Twas sympathy that drew the poor, the sinful, the children to Christ. See that homeless boy to-night at twelve o'clock; he is trying to sleep, he is lying on a few straws in a goods box. You approach him. His twitching nerves and uneasy frame indicate he is not resting well. Awake him roughly, tell him you have come to take him to the calaboose, or poor-house. He will arise and follow, but you have not touched the spring to his better nature. But suppose you touch him lightly, awake him tenderly, as he arouses tell him you have come to take him to a good home where he'll have a good bed and plenty to eat. And as you talk to him let him see the tears of sympathy falling down your face, and he'll tell you more of his sad story than you ever heard. Now you have led him to you, perhaps you can lead him to Christ. But we'll never lead a man to Christ until we first lead him to ourselves. What kind of persons ought we to be? This poor man of whom we were speaking, now applied to the church for help. What do you think she did? Like the father who saw his prodigal son away off, ran and met him, even in his rags. It was enough to know he had his son home safe again. So the church throws open her arms. She spreads a feast and all heaven rejoices. Oh, I bless God for the church. Shall I ever forget her? Yes, when mariner forgets the star that has guided him safely into harbor, when the flower forgets the sun that warmed it into life, or when love has gone out on the heart's altar, and memory has forever vanished—not till then.

> " I love thy kingdom, Lord,
> The house of thine abode;
> The church our blessed Redeemer saved
> With his own precious blood."

Brethren, let us continue to grow in faith, in grace, in love, in hope, in good works, in favor with God and man, in our missionary efforts, in our zeal for the Master's cause everywhere. If Christ fails to make men of us, no power can. One illustration and I will have done. I held a meeting in a certain town a few years ago, and among those who came to the Savior was a girl 15 years old, the only child of an irreligious father and mother. The father said a good many rough things about it. Before the meeting closed the girl asked me to take tea with her; I accepted the invitation. When we were seated at the table the father took occasion to apologize for what he had said. He said, "I had no objections to you as a man or preacher, nor to the church you represent, but," said he, "I knew our daughter was young and giddy, and I didn't want her to join and disgrace the church by backsliding." When he was through she looked him in the face, and in child-like simplicity said, "Papa, if I can't be a woman when Jesus leads me, what will become of me when he lets me go?"

Now, as the wheels of God and progress never turn backward, let us hope and labor and pray the time may come when every sea and lake and river, and every mountain, valley and field, and every living thing in heaven and earth will take up the high and glad refrain, One God, one Christ, one Church, one people, now, henceforth and forever more, worlds without end. Amen.

BIOGRAPHY OF W. H. BOLES.

W. H. BOLES was born June 23rd, 1850, near DuQuoin, Perry county, Illinois. While an infant his parents removed to Eight Mile Prairie, near Carbondale, Illinois, where he was reared to manhood.

At the age of four his mother died. Being left motherless, he and his sister went to their grandmother's to live. In November, 1862, when the subject of our sketch was 12 years old, his father was killed in the battle of Belmont, Mo. After a few weeks' attendance each fall and winter in the district school, at the age of eighteen he entered the Illinois Soldiers' and Soldiers' Orphan College at Fulton. Although he paid his way mostly by doing chores, he applied himself closely to study for nine months, and then came home and taught school the following summer, fall and winter of 1869 and '70. He again entered college at Ewing, Franklin county, Illinois, in the spring of 1870. Here he was aided by the late Hon. R. R. Link and Prof. John Washburn, who gave him work to do which enabled him to go to school ten months in this institution of learning. His early religious impressions were made by Methodism. But much excitement and conflicting experiences drove him into infidelity and further into sin, until near the age of seventeen he was converted by a Disciple preacher, Elder M. F. Wilson. He began platform speaking as a declaimer at the age of ten, so that at fifteen he was called the boy orator far and near. During the war he became famous for his abolition and war speeches. He was rescued from several mobs, and finally shot down on the streets of Carbondale by a mob of boys who were his political enemies, at a Fourth of July celebration, when he was fourteen years of age. He carries the bullet in his right thigh till this day.

When he was converted to the Lord Jesus he used these powers of speech at once in preaching Christ and him crucified to all his friends and enemies. He was now called the "boy preacher," and became noted at once all over Southern Illinois, and his labors were crowned with great success everywhere he went. Being reared on a farm and possessed with a strong constitution, he was well fitted for the work of evangelizing in the rural districts of Southern Illinois after the war.

He gave himself enthusiastically to this kind of work for several years, but was not ordained to the ministry until he had been preaching over three years. In April, 1873, he was united in marriage with Miss Duetta Ellen Baird. The union was a happy one, and blessed with one child—a boy. But death came and took both mother and child, and the happy little family was broken up.

In March, 1877, he was again united in marriage to Miss Lov Spiller. This union is a happy one, and has been blessed with three children—all living—one boy and two girls, aged respectively 12, 14 and 16. The boy is the youngest. Bro. Boles says that whatever he is or may be hereafter, and whatever his children may be that is good and useful, must be attributed mostly to the wise counsel of his good and faithful wife.

He had now been preaching, going to school and teaching (part of the time) for ten years. He had made for himself a splendid reputation as an evangelist over a large district of country, and in the last four years of the ten he had had remarkable success as a pastor—one year at De Soto, and three years at Marion, county-seat of Williamson county, Illinois, within twelve miles of his old home. At Marion he took hold of the work with twenty-five members, meeting in the court-house, and when, three years later, he resigned, the chuch had over 250 members and a new brick church that cost $5,000, all paid for except $600. The renowned Otis A. Burgess, President of Butler University, dedicated the church in July, 1877.

And while there he told Bro. B. that he had reached a grand climax in his work, and that now he should go off to school again. He and his young wife concluded at once that President Burgess' advice was good, and he resigned his work at

Marion and entered Butler University in September, 1877. Here he applied himself to study for two years, preaching for village congregations of Sundays.

But a long spell of typhoid fever, which he had before he left his old home in Marion, Ill., was not yet out of the system, and from which he never recovered till ten years later, and, hence on account of ill health he was compelled to leave college. This he greatly regretted, and still regrets that he failed to complete the college course. He removed his little family to Mooresville, fifteen miles south of Indianapolis, in the midst of the congregations for which he had been preaching during the time he was in the university. One year later he accepted a unanimous call to the church at Martinsville, Ind. He remained here three years, and accomplished a great work in strengthening the church and helping to drive saloons out of the city. In August, 1883, he accepted a call from the General Christian Board of Missions to take charge of the mission at Topeka, Kansas. He took charge of this mission with 90 members, meeting in a little hall which held 120 chairs. These had never all been occupied, except, probably, at a funeral. Two years later, when, on account of over-work and ill health, he resigned, he left them in the old Globe Theatre, with the fourth audience in the city, and the membership increased to over 250, and three fine lots purchased on Topeka Avenue, where the First Christian Church now stands, and several thousand dollars subscribed for the church building.

In July, 1885, he purchased a farm near Abilene Dickinson county, Kansas, and removed his family thereto, and began work as county evangelist. In this position he had remarkable success in strengthening the two churches in the county, Abilene and Bethany, near his farm, and also in building up two other strong churches in the county, viz: at Sutphen's Mills and Hope. At the close of this year, in the fall of 1886, he accepted a call from the Illinois Christian Board of Missions, to become State Evangelist for Southern Illinois. He began work at Marion, his old home, and removed his family there in the spring of '87. His labors were crowned with great success, gaining more accessions to the churches than any evangelist ever had done under the employ of the Board up to that time. In one year over five hundred were added, and all this work was done within twenty miles of where he was born and reared. His greatest meeting was held at Carterville, a town that had grown up in the old neighborhood where he was brought up. Two hundred and twenty were added during this meeting. In October, 1887, he accepted a call to serve the church at Du Quoin, near where he was born, as pastor, and removed his family there. In June of the following year he accepted the double work of State Evangelist and

20

Financial Agent of Eureka College, and in July, 1889, he removed his family to Eureka, where they still reside. He acted as financial agent of Eureka College, along with his evangelistic work and lecturing, for three years. His field began widening out into other States, and he resigned both positions, and since then he has held meetings in Illinois, Indiana, Iowa and Missouri.

His greatest meetings since the Carterville meeting, in '87, have been held at Cotton Hill, Petersburg, Pekin, Irving, Effingham and Tower Hill, Ill., Missouri Valley, Iowa, and Nevada, Mo. All these meetings have been well written up in our papers. Bro. Boles has been a reader and a student of history, science, the Bible, and all the living issues of the day, religious and political.

On the question of infidelity he is very strong. He has broken up some strong infidel clubs. His work in this field at Vienna and Minier, Ill., was pre-eminently successful. The great infidel and spiritualist lecturer and debater, Dr. A. J. Fishback, was converted by Bro. Boles in a meeting at Du Quoin, Ill. He delivered a series of lectures on the Evidences of Christianity during the meeting. On the question of temperance and prohibition he is thoroughly posted, and among the W. C. T. U. and prohibition workers he ranks among the best speakers on the platform in the United States. Ex-Gov. John P. St. John says: "I gladly commend W. H. Boles as one of the ablest speakers in the

United States." Mrs. Helen M. Gougar says: "I regard W. H. Boles as one of the most candid, calm, dispassionate, efficient and convincing platform speakers in all the ranks of reform."

Mrs. Clara C. Hoffman, President of the State W. C. T. U. of Missouri, says: "It has been my fortune to hear W. H. Boles, of Eureka, Ill., on several occasions. He is a power on the platform. He is logical, argumentative, humorous, fair and convincing. He is an honest man, chock-full of facts and figures which he uses with telling effect."

Many other such like commendations from workers in the ranks of reform we might publish.

On the question of economics he seems to be equally well posted, and the farmer and labor elements of the country in several States know of his able speeches all over Illinois and parts of Indiana in '89 and '90. The leaders in this army of reform have spoken highly of his work and ability. It is said by public men in Illinois that probably no man in the State has spoken to so many people upon so many different themes during the past ten years as W. H. Boles. He has lectured scores of times to great outdoor gatherings of from 1,000 to 6,000 or 8,000 people, so estimated by reporters of the great dailies of St. Louis and Chicago.

As a popular lecturer he is a decided success. He draws a large audience to a pay lecture, and never disappoints them. But his real forte is in

the pulpit and on the platform, handling the living
issues of the day. He hates sin, religious shams,
hypocrisy, drunkenness, the liquor traffic, gambling, and all the social evils of the day, and one
might as well try to dam the Niagara as to under-
take to get him not to be outspoken against all
these things in the pulpit and on the platform. He
hates meanness and stinginess in the church, and
woe be to those who are guilty of such things
wherever he goes.

He hates sectarianism and Catholicism, and woe
be unto both when he opens his mouth in a protracted meeting. He is not prepossessing in his
appearance. No one would, upon first glance,
take him to be a public man nor a man of any
more than very ordinary intelligence. But when
in the pulpit or on the platform he gets warmed up
he is a completely changed man. He always suc-
ceeds in carrying his audience with him, and for
weeks and weeks he holds an audience spell-
bound. The longer the meeting the more success.

He is particularly successful in getting men un-
used to attending any church interested. He converts the men. His work is lasting and permanent.
He holds Church Institutes often during a meeting, and drills officers and members in their duties,
settles difficulties and cleans up a church generally. His lectures on temperance, and to men only
and women only, clean up the town or city generally, and so he covers the whole ground. He has

a fine voice, never gets hoarse, always bright and cheerful, good company, uses logic, reason, facts, with humor, sarcasm, irony, and grows grandly pathetic in sermon. He is brave and lion-like, and yet tender and kind. A child in simplicity, yet neat in his dress.

CHRISTIANITY APPLIED.*

W. H. BOLES.

And whatsoever ye do in word or deed, do all in the name of the Lord Jesus, giving thanks unto God and the Father by him.—Col. 3: 17.

THE world has had enough of theory. It is too late in the world's history for social, political or religious dogmas. The voice of the dogmatist and theorist is lost in the noise of the busy practitioner. The old theories of the spherical shape and the rotary motion of the earth are no longer troubling ignorant priests and religious bigots. Thousands of people are going around the earth every year, and the globe is practicing the theory of rotary motion every day.

Watts' theory of steam no longer gives the philosophers any trouble. But the people are amazed at the millions of wheels and spindles in mills and manufactories; at the roar of thousands of railway trains moving along like long houses before a cyclone; at great steamboats going up

---

*NOTE.—The following sermon was delivered, in its present form, Lord's day night, Jan. 28, 1894, at Tower Hill, Ill., where the speaker was holding a protracted meeting, before a large audience. The effort was blessed by many souls coming to Christ.

and down our rivers, and mighty steamships, like great palaces, moving from continent to continent with great speed ; all rolling, whirling, whistling and moving by the practical application of steam. The theories of Franklin, Morse, Edison, et al, on electricity are almost forgotten, while the people are revelling in the enjoyment of the practical use and application of electricity. It heals our sick ones and electrocutes our murderers condemned to death. It moves little palaces upon the streets of our towns and cities.

It has established a personal communication between the people of nearly every neighborhood in the United States, and has brought into talking distance with one another all the civilizations of earth. By the telephone, business men send orders for goods, neighbors talk to one another, and lovers woo each other—all in human voice hundreds of miles away—as naturally as if by each other's side.

The theories concerning a western continent are dead and forgotten with the men who used to spend sleepless nights poring over them. These men and theories were only impersonated at the great World's Fair.

No longer do we hear the voices of Charles C. Pinckney and Patrick Henry in the House of Burgesses contending over the question as to whether the thirteen colonies are capable of withdrawing from England and sustaining an independent re-

publican form of government.   These and thousands of other theories are forgotten while people
are either putting them to practice or else have
long ago discarded them as impracticable.

And now, my brethren, the question presents itself, Has the moral and religious world kept pace
with the civilizations and human developments in
putting to practice what our Lord and Master has
taught us?

Some skeptical scientists have insisted that the
Bible is away behind the times with the theories
and developments of men.   But these skeptics fail
to see the unwise use that is made of God's revelation.   They fail, too, to discern the difference between Christianity and the Christian.

Thousands of years before Harvey discovered
the circulation of blood, God Almighty announced
through Moses, in Gen. 9 : 4, Lev. 17: 10-14, Deut.
12: 23-25 and Acts 15: 20, 29, that the blood is the
life thereof, and positively forbade any of his people from eating the blood of animals.

Thousands of years before medical science discovered the idea that habits and appetites, such as
theft, rapine, murder and drunkenness are trans-
mitted from parent to child through the blood,
God said, "I will visit the iniquities of the fathers upon the third and fourth generation." Ex. 20:
5, 34 : 7; Numb. 14: 18; Deut. 5: 9.   This is simply a fact that God makes known.   People have
found out that there is blood in their cattle, horses,

hogs and dogs; but they have been slow to find blood in their boys and girls.

The question that parents of America ask, when young men ask the hand of their daughters, is not, " What blood has he in his veins?" but "How much money has he in his pocket-book?" [A sensation.]

Dr. Keeley has found out that drunkenness is a disease. God told us that over three thousand years ago, and to keep the disease from passing through the blood into future generations he commanded the drunkard to be killed (Deut. 21: 18- 21), and prohibited the vender from selling intoxicants to his neighbor to make him drunk (Hab. 2: 15), and tells the drunkard, besides, that he can not inherit the kingdom of heaven (1 Cor. 6: 10.) If the twenty millions of Protestants, and the eight millions of Catholics who profess to believe in God and his revelation to man would put to practice the teachings of God, not a saloon, or a brewery, or a distillery, or a drunkard would be found in these United States within ten years. The trouble is not with God, or with his revelation, or with Christianity, my friendly skeptic. It is with these pretended Christians. Turn all of your battering-rams upon *them*, and not upon God and the Bible. I will say another thing just here: If the preachers, priests and members of these churches, in their pulpits, conferences, synods, counsels, associations and conventions had thundered forth their rebukes and denunciations against the conspiracies and robberies perpetrated upon the people on Wall Street, New York, on the Board of Trade, and in the legislative bodies of States, and the halls of Congress, as Jeremiah, John the Baptist and Jesus Christ did, against such like things among men in the counsels of the nation in their day, we would not to-day hear the millions of voices crying for bread. The devil is greatly rejoicing over the moral cowardice and conservatism of the pulpit and the pew of the American churches. There are some noble exceptions, but not enough to stop the onswelling tide of corruption and oppression. May the Lord Jesus walk among the churches and strike us with the thunder-bolts of his gospel. Applied Christianity, my brethren, is my theme. But now let us see how millions of the professed followers of Jesus are misapplying Christianity all the way through.

The text says: "Whatsoever ye do in word or deed, do all in the name of the Lord Jesus." "In word or deed." That covers all the ground of a man's life or the history of a church or a nation. "Do all in the name of the Lord Jesus." Here starts out a preacher into a town in which the Gospel was never preached. The inhabitants are starving for the "bread of life." He assembles a company of eager listeners. He announces that he is a minister of the "Great Methodist Episcopal Church."

He preaches to the people, setting forth Methodism. And soon another preacher comes and announces himself a Presbyterian preacher, and another comes and he tells the people that he is a Lutheran preacher. Another comes, and he is proud to announce that he is a Baptist preacher, and another comes, and with great pomposity and much assurance, he declares himself a Roman Catholic, and says that all the rest are heretics and can never be saved any more than the sinners can, if they don't repent and join the Roman Catholic Church. By the time each creed has been represented by a preacher before the people of that town, the people are more divided than before the preachers visited them. There is more hatred, more enmity, more backbiting and more prejudice among the people than before the reverend gentlemen appeared on the scene. Have I overdrawn the picture? I wish any of my audience to-night could say so. What is the trouble? The trouble is found in these preachers not "doing all things in the name of the Lord Jesus." If they had each of them gone there "in the name of the Lord Jesus" and had announced themselves as simply preachers of the cross and members of the Church of Christ, and had opened the Scriptures and preached the Gospel to the people instead of their dead dog–mas and creeds (sensation) they would not have confused the people. They undertook to build a tower up to heaven out of the brick and mortar of human creeds and dogmas, and God confused their language. That is all. O, Lord Jesus, thou that didst pray that the people might be one, help now thy people to be one.

Brethren, as disciples of Christ we have been going into these divided neighborhoods for about ninety years. We have gone in the name of Christ alone. We have pleaded for a return to the apostolic order of worship, taking Christ for our creed and the Bible as our only rule of faith and action.

God our Father has accomplished much in trying to get the people to lay down creeds, dogmas, and denominationalism, but no true disciple is satisfied with the results. We have been poor instruments and weak servants in his hands. But "God hath chosen the weak things of this world to confound the mighty." Christ and the Bible must be the only test of fellowship among his people. Our plea is right. The right will prevail. Let us not be discouraged. A noble few of the ablest preachers in the denomination are pleading for Christian unity. Praise the Lord for the few. Let us all thank God and take courage, my brethren. Union will come. Jesus prayed for it. John 17: 20, 21. Our God demands it and it will come.

How shall I receive the remission of sins? is a question that must be answered "in the name of the Lord Jesus." But when the preachers go to tell the sinners what to do to be saved, one tells it one way, and another another way, and the poor sinners are confused. The only remedy for all this is for each preacher to do to-day what each apostle and primitive preacher was commanded and did do when Christ first gave the commission to the apostles. Read Matt. 28 : 18, 19 ; Mark 16 : 15, 16 ; Luke 24 : 44, 45, 46, 47 ; John 16th chapter ; Acts 1st and 2nd chapters.

In Matt. 28 : 18, Jesus said, " All power is given unto me in heaven and in earth." Let us stop right here and make a practical application of these words of our risen Lord. I see before me Methodists, Presbyterians, Lutherans, Baptists, Christians and Catholics. Do you all believe that Christ " has *all* power in earth ?" Do you ? Be sure. Let us see. My Catholic friend, if you believe that, then why do you believe that the Pope and the priests have the power to forgive your sins ? [Sensation.] Why don't you go to Christ alone for forgiveness ? " Come now, let us reason together."

My Methodist, Presbyterian, Lutheran and Baptist friends, if you believe that Christ "has *all* power in earth," why do you have a human creed or a confession of faith as a test of fellowship among God's people, other than what Christ has laid down in his Word ? Why have you organized an ecclesiasticism unauthorized by the Word of God? Why have you set aside the offices of Christ's church and created new ones ?

O, my brethren, don't you see that you are rec-ognizing a power besides the *all power* given unto Christ?

Then again, do you believe that Christ has "all power in heaven?" If so, my Catholic friend, why do you pray to Mary? Come, let us reason together. Let us not forget that Christ has all power in heaven and in earth, and that Paul said that "Though we or an angel from heaven preach any other gospel unto you than that which we have preached unto you, let him be accursed" Gal. 1 : 8. Let every preacher, priest, officer and church member acknowledge that Christ has all power in heaven and in earth, and much of the great difficulty in the way of bringing God's peo-ple together and converting the world, will be re-moved at once. But in the next verse he says : "Go ye (the apostles) therefore, and teach all na-tions," or, as Mark puts it, "Go ye into all the world and preach the gospel to every creature." Mark 16 : 15. "Teaching them to observe all things whatsoever I have commanded you, and lo, I am with you alway, even unto the end of the world." Matt. 28 : 20.

Practical application : Are the preachers of to-day all preaching what Christ commissioned the apostles to preach? Are they preaching "in the name of the Lord Jesus?" Peter did not preach one gospel, John another, James another and Paul another. Each apostle and each preacher sent out by the apostles preached the same gospel of Christ. They each preached "whatsoever Christ commanded them to preach." In those days the apostles and preachers were stoned, imprisoned and put to death for preaching " in the name of the Lord Jesus " (Acts 3rd, 4th and 7th chapters), and the only reason why preachers are not stoned, imprisoned and killed to-day is perhaps because there are so few preaching what Jesus commanded, and "in the name of the Lord Jesus," that the devil has not yet learned that he has any particular opposition. Let all the preachers preach the old gospel and bring back the old days of the apostles and Christ and preach right out—telling people of their sins as they did, and we shall see some of the scenes enacted in their day repeated in our day. "Whatsoever I have commanded you." "Do all in the name of the Lord Jesus."

Now to the question in hand again. What did Christ tell the apostles to tell the sinner he should do in order to be saved? Answer: " Go preach the gospel to every creature." Mark 16 : 15. But in preaching the gospel to every creature what were the apostles to tell the sinner to do in order to be saved?

"He that believeth and is baptized shall be saved, and he that believeth not shall be damned." Mark 16: 16.

What else did he tell the apostles to tell the sinner he must do?

"Except ye repent, ye shall all likewise perish."
Luke 13: 3. "Then opened he their under
standing that they might understand the scriptures, and said unto them (the apostles), Thus it is
written, and thus it behoved Christ to suffer, and
to rise from the dead the third day: and that repentance and remission of sins should be preached
in his name among all nations beginning at Jerusalem." Luke 24: 45-47.

Here we find that Christ told the apostles to tell
the sinners to repent or they would perish. He
also put the command to repent in connection
with remission of sins. But did Christ leave any
other command for the apostles to tell the sinner
to do in order to be saved? "Also I say unto you,
whosoever shall confess me before men, him shall
the Son of man also confess before the angels of
God. But he that denieth me before men shall be
denied before the angels of God." Luke 12: 8, 9.

What else did Christ tell the apostles to tell the
sinner to do in order to be saved?

"And is baptized shall be saved." Mark 16:
16. Mark you, what is meant here by the Savior,
by being saved, is not salvation in heaven, but
saved now from all past sins. He is talking to
alien sinners. He is giving instructions to the
apostles to go "into all the world and preach the
gospel to every creature" and tell them the conditions of salvation and the terms of admission into
his kingdom. They are to tell the alien sinner

how to be born again (John 3 : 4, 5) of water and of the Spirit. And now, summing up, what did Christ tell the apostles to tell the sinners to do to be saved?

1. "Go preach the Gospel."

2. "He that believeth."

Here let us stop and have an understanding as to what the sinner was to believe. "But these are written that ye might believe that Jesus is the Christ, the Son of God; and that ye might have life through his name." John 20: 31. We see here that the thing to be believed is that Jesus is the Christ, the Son of God. The sinner is not to trouble himself over the theories and dogmas of men. "Believe on the Lord Jesus Christ and thou shalt be saved."

3. "Except ye repent ye shall all likewise perish."

4. "He that confesses me before men, him will I confess before the angels of heaven." "With the mouth confession is made unto salvation."

5. "And is baptized shall be saved."

Preach the Gospel to the sinners. And he that believes in Christ, repents of his sins, confesses the Savior before men and is baptized shall be saved from all his past sins. He is born again. Born of water and of the Spirit.

This was the commission of Christ unto the apostles. This was the divine programme laid down by Christ for the apostles to carry out after

21

he should leave them. And the apostles were to go into all the world—unto all nations, and preach these same conditions to every creature.

Now the question presents itself, Did the apostles do and teach what Christ commanded? Did they carry out the Divine programme laid down? Did they tell the sinners what to do to be saved? And if so, where did they begin, and when did they begin? And again, what means did Christ use by which to keep the apostles from falling into error—from forgetting a part of what he told them to tell the sinners they must do to be saved?

Where were the apostles to begin? "And that repentance and remission of sins should be preached in his name among all nations, beginning at Jerusalem." "But tarry ye in the city of Jerusalem until ye be endured with power from on high." Luke 24: 47, 49.

Jerusalem then is where they were to begin. When were they to begin? "Tarry ye in the city of Jerusalem until ye be endued with power from on high." "But ye shall receive power after that the Holy Ghost is come upon you: and ye shall be witnesses unto me, both in Jerusalem, and in all Judea, and in Samaria, and unto the uttermost parts of the earth." "Ye shall be baptized with the Holy Ghost not many days hence." Acts. 1: 5, 8. These words were spoken just before Christ ascended into heaven, as you will see by reading the latter part of the 24th chapter of Luke and the 1st chapter of Acts. According to divine arrangement the apostles were not to begin preaching till the power of the Holy Ghost came upon them. This power came on the day of Pentecost, as you will see by consulting Acts 2: 1-17. So the time for the apostles to begin work was on the day of Pentecost, a few days after Christ ascended to heaven. It was also arranged by Christ that Peter was to formally unlock the door of heaven with the keys of the kingdon that Christ had given him (Matt. 16: 19; Acts 15: 7) and offer the terms of salvation to alien sinners as laid down by Christ in the commission, the divine programme, given to the apostles. Having seen that the place where, and the time when, were at Jerusalem on the day of Pentecost, and that the Apostle Peter was the apostle chosen to do the preaching on that day, all eyes and ears must now be turned to the place, time and person. But let us not fail to see the provisions Christ made to guard against the apostles' forgetting any part of the commission they had received, or what they were to tell the sinners to do to be saved.

Jesus said: " The Comforter, which is the Holy Ghost, whom the Father will send in my name, he shall teach you all things and bring all things to your remembrance, whatsoever I have said unto you." John 14: 26, John 16: 7, 13. The Holy Ghost, remember, was to come and "guide" Peter and the apostles "into all truth." They could, therefore, make no mistakes. They could not forget anything.

Let us now turn to the account of the day of Pentecost and see how Peter proceeded to carry out the commission given by Christ to the apostles. Let us turn to the 2nd chapter of Acts. The first thirteen verses give an account of the baptism of the Holy Ghost promised to the apostles and disciples. None but them were baptized with the Holy Ghost, as you will see.

The roaring sound, as a rushing, mighty wind, which the Holy Ghost made when he came upon the apostles and disciples, caused thousands of people from different parts of the city to go to where the apostles and disciples were, to see what could be the matter. And when they arrived on the scene the Holy Ghost had assumed the shape of cloven tongues and lighted upon each of the apostles and disciples, and also these holy people were speaking in the different languages of earth as the Holy Ghost gave them utterance. These things confounded the multitudes. Some said one thing and some another. But none seemed to take the matter seriously, saying, that they were "drunken" men, "Galileans," etc.

But now comes the time for the sermon by Peter, according to the previously arranged divine programme. " But Peter, standing up with the eleven, lifted up his voice, and said unto them, Ye men of

Judea, and all ye that dwell at Jerusalem, be this known unto you, and hearken unto my words: For these are not drunken, as ye suppose, seeing it is but the third hour of the day. But this is that which was spoken by the prophet Joel." I have quoted from Acts 2: 14, 15, 16. These words are the beginning of Peter's memorable sermon on the day of Pentecost. He then quoted from Joel and David to show his audience that the outpouring of the Holy Ghost on that day was according to what their own prophets had predicted, and also Christ had risen from the dead, and had sent the Holy Ghost according to the predictions of the same prophets, and what Christ himself promised. Peter closed his great sermon with the following powerful words:

"Therefore let all the house of Israel know assuredly that God hath made that same Jesus, whom ye have crucified, both Lord and Christ." Acts 2: 36.

What effect did the sermon have upon the people to whom it was delivered? Read verse 37: "Now when they heard this they were pricked in their heart, and said unto Peter and the rest of the apostles, Men and brethren, what shall we do?"

These people, we see, were powerfully moved by the sermon. They were pricked in their heart. This brings Peter to the point now where he can tell these sinners what to do in order to be saved, as Christ told him and the apostles to do. They have asked him and the rest of the apostles what to do. Did Peter tell them? Let us see, verse 38: "Then Peter said unto them, Repent, and be baptized, every one of you, in the name of Jesus Christ for the remission of sins, and ye shall receive the gift of the Holy Ghost." Here we find that Peter told them to do just what Christ told him and the rest of the apostles to tell sinners, according to the commission. Peter carried out the divine programme exactly. He preached to them the Gospel. Thousands heard it and were pricked in their heart. Being pricked in their heart they believed the divine message from Peter, and then wanted to know what else they must do. Peter proceeded to tell them at once that the remaining conditions upon which they might receive the remission of their sins were to repent and be baptized, and that they should not only receive the remission of their sins, but the gift of the Holy Ghost also.

God, Christ, the Holy Ghost and the Apostle Peter having each performed his part, the question arises, Did any of the people on that day accept the conditions of salvation and act upon them? Read verse 41: "Then they that gladly received his word were baptized, and the same day there were added unto them about three thousand souls." Here we find three thousand people took the Lord at his word and complied with the conditions that Christ told the apostles to submit to dying sinners, upon which he would pardon all their past sins. Now we are prepared to ask another question. Did these 3000 people who "gladly received the word and were baptized" receive the remission of their sins? Were they pardoned? Did they, in common church parlance, get religion? Were they saved? If not, then I say, calling things by their right names, that Peter lied. And not only so, but if these people were honest and conscientious in their intentions (and there is nothing in the record to indicate that they were not) in hearing, believing, repenting and being baptized, and then did not receive the remission of their sins, Christ also lied. He told Peter and the apostles to tell the sinners to believe, repent and be baptized and they should be saved. Peter told these people just what Christ told him to tell them. And again, if these 3000 Pentecostians did not receive pardon and were not saved, then, the Holy Ghost also lied. For, remember that Christ sent the Holy Ghost to guide the apostles into all truth, and to bring all things to their remembrance, whatsoever Christ taught them. So that Peter could not be mistaken or forget anything he spoke as Christ, through the Holy Ghost, moved him.

Do you believe, my hearers, that Peter, Christ and the Holy Ghost lied? Those of you who deny that, when the three thousand people believed, repented and were baptized received, then and there, the remission of their sins, most assuredly say, right out, that Peter, Christ and the Holy Ghost lied. There is no other alternative. I believe that the three thousand received the remission of their sins. They had the witness of Christ, of Peter and of the Holy Ghost that they were pardoned. And I tell you to-night, dear friends, the same Lord Jesus Christ and Holy Ghost that spoke through Peter and gave the terms of pardon or salvation to the Pentecostians, on the day of Pentecost, speak to you to-night through this book (holding up the Bible solemnly) and the man or woman who says that if the alien sinner, to-day, believes on the Lord Jesus Christ, repents of all his sins, and is baptized, just as Peter told these people to do, will not be pardoned, saved, redeemed in the blood of the Lamb, from all his past sins, I say whoever says this gives Christ, the Holy Ghost and the apostles the lie. And they give the Scriptures the lie, and should be considered infidels along with Robert Ingersoll. Indeed, these people who are teaching that taking Christ and the Spirit's word for it goes for naught, as compared to seeing a red rag hung out of heaven, or a swan in the corner of the fence, or feeling some strong emotion at the mourner's bench, or somewhere else, as evidence of pardon, are teaching a worse phase of infidelity than Robert Ingersoll ever dreamed of. It is infidelity with the garb of religion thrown around it. It has the same effect Ingersoll's kind does, in that it teaches the subject not to trust God's word unless it suits his fancy. And, in addition thereto, it leads them off into a region of mysticism and fanaticism, receiving for doctrine the commandments of men, and the traditions of their fathers. This infidel trusting in the feelings of the flesh, mourners' bench system of religion, made an infidel of me once, and I hate it. I loathe it. I spurn it as from the devil. But I believe that good people are engaged in the use of this soul-destroyer instead of a soul-saver. Take God at his word, my friends. Let the Holy Ghost which guided Peter and told the Pentecostians to repent and be baptized for the remission of sins, tell you the same things to-night. Then gladly receive the word and be baptized, as they did, and God and Christ will take care of the rest. "The Spirit itself beareth witness with out spirits that we are the children of God." Rom. 8: 16. But how? By your fleshly feeling? Paul says: "Have no confidence in the flesh."

No, my friends, God's Spirit bears witness by telling you just as he did the three thousand through Peter, just what to do to be saved, and the same things the Holy Ghost tells you to-night. Will you take the Holy Ghost at his word, and go do as they did, and have the witness of the Spirit and Christ that you are saved? May God help you to trust him. You will feel all right when you do what Christ commands you to do to be saved. Feeling is not religion, any more than pain is a disease. Pain is a result of disease. Feeling and happiness and joy are the grand results of the religion of our Lord and Master. In the name of my Master and Savior I beg of you to take Christ at his word. Have the witness of the Spirit that you are the children of God, and let a most joyous feeling be the result. You may go through Acts of the Apostles, the book giving an account of many meetings which they and many other preachers held, and you will find that they all spoke the same thing. They told sinners what Christ told the apostles in the commission, and what Peter told the Pentecostians.

Why don't all the preachers tell the terms of pardon as laid down in the word of God to-day? What is the trouble? The only answer is, "They are teaching for doctrine the commandments of men and following the traditions of their fathers." Oh! shall we not take God, and Christ, and the Holy Spirit and the word of all these as given in the New Testament in preference to the doctrines of men and the traditions of their fathers? "If we receive the witness of men, the witness of God is greater." 1 John 5: 9. Lord, help us to believe thy testimony. Help us to "do all things in the name of the Lord Jesus."

We must now look at another side of our text. "And whatsoever ye do in word or deed, do all in the name of the Lord Jesus, giving thanks unto

God and the Father by him." These newly converted people who have been saved from their past
sins, in the blood of Christ, can't live on the
teachings of the first part of the commission. They
must be taught how to live the Christian life now.
Hence we must look through the sermons and actions of Christ, the apostles, and the letters
which the apostles wrote the churches, for practical every-day teachings of Christianity. New-
born babes must now learn to do all things in the
name of the Lord Jesus. It is not enough to believe and repent and be baptized in the name of
the Lord Jesus. They must continue to believe
and repent and live every day in the name of the
Lord Jesus. Oh how many professed Christians
are not doing this!

The Pentecostians continued steadfastly in the
apostles' doctrine, Acts 2: 42. Will you my dear
young babes in Christ "continue steadfast," or will
you take the view that many others have in all
the churches, that all you have to do is to go to the
mourners' bench and cry a little, or attend a protracted meeting and get greatly interested in hearing an evangelist expound the way of life to the
sinner, once a year, and then go away, and, the
rest of the year, be the same old cheater, defrauder,
liar, passionate, lustful old political hack, gambler
and drunken devil you were theretofore? And, if
you never was any one of these, will you remain
the same old cold soul you was, and have to be

warmed up every year? God help you. Better
that you had never started. That is *preacher* religion. If you can't "get" a better article of religion than *that*, the devil don't want any better
mortgage on your soul. Would that be doing all
things in the name of the Lord Jesus?

Come, let us make a practical application of
Christianity. "Do all things in the name of the
Lord Jesus, giving thanks unto God and the Father
by him." Can we take the name of God in vain,
in the name of the Lord Jesus, and thank God,
after we have rolled out a big oath, for the act?
Who can tell a lie, under any circumstances, in
the name of the Lord Jesus? Yet there are thousands of professed Christians who lie in their dealings, lie in political campaigns, on candidates, lie
right along every day. Can you cheat your neighbor in the name of the Lord Jesus? Can you take
advantage of a man's ignorance of the price of
that which he has to sell, and cheat him out of
what he ought to have had, and you know it—can
you, I ask, do this in the name of the Lord Jesus
Christ? Can you gamble on the board of trade,
on a horse-race, on an election, on playing at cards
in the name of the Lord Jesus and give thanks
unto God the Father for your success? Can you
rent your property for saloons, gambling dens
and houses of ill-fame in the name of the Lord
Jesus and give thanks unto God for the revenue
you derive therefrom? You old hypocrite! You

know you can't do these things and stand guiltless before God. Can you keep a drug store and sell liquor to make men drunk in the name of the Lord Jesus? You old corrupter of the morals of the community, you old destroyer of souls, you know better than that! Can you keep a saloon in the name of the Lord Jesus? You had as well ask if you can join one of the worst train-wrecking and murder gangs that ever roamed the Mississippi valley. Indeed, the saloon business is the worse of the two. "Who steals my purse steals trash; who steals my character steals my all." Jesus said, "Be not afraid of them that kill the body, and after that have no more that they can do." "But I will forewarn you whom ye shall fear: Fear him, who after he hath killed hath power to cast into hell; yea, I say unto you, Fear him." Luke 12: 4, 5. If the saloon is not a soul-destroyer and a body-killer I don't know where you will find one. Can you keep a saloon in the name of the Lord Jesus? Can you vote to license this body and soul destroyer, this robber of homes in your community in the name of the Lord Jesus? Can you afford to vote with a political party that declares for licensing this foul thing in state or nation in the name of the Lord Jesus? If the business is corrupting the morals of the community, and destroying the bodies and souls of men, which you do not deny or don't dare to deny, then how dare you, as a child of God, vote for a can-

didate or with a political party that favors licensing the business in any way? If you think you can
do so, take one of your dear boys into the voting
booth with you, and lay your hand on his head
and lift up your voice to heaven and ask God to
bless that boy with that vote, and then thank
God for the privilege of voting such a ticket! Not
a town or city in Illinois to-day would go for
license, if those who profess Christianity would
stand together against the saloon. The saloon
keepers have formed a secret political party and
declare that they belong to none of the existing
political parties, and that they will vote for no
party, or candidate for office, that does not favor
their business. In the name of God, my brethren,
how dare you any longer therefore vote the
same ticket, county, state or national, that the
liquor men vote, seeing that they will vote for the
party and the men that will stand by them, only?
God, my brethren, takes notice of a vote just as he
does of any other act. And he says, "Do all
things in the name of the Lord Jesus, giving
thanks unto God the Father by him."

The saloon men have elected a majority of the
congressmen for twenty-five years. They have
elected a majority of the members of the legisla-
tures of nearly all our States for over twenty
years. They have done this, not because they
have a majority of voters, but because they ma-
nipulate caucuses and conventions of political par-

ties and dictate terms, and because those who profess Christianity will let the liquor men do these things rather than rebuke their party leaders. Stand together, Christian men, and God will give you the victory over the greatest evil ever known. A practical application of Christianity is what this nation needs more than tariff theories. "When the righteous rule the people rejoice, and when the wicked bear rule the people mourn," is just as true to-day as in the days of the kingdom of Israel.

In conclusion, let me adjure you, brethren, "by the tender mercies of God, that ye present your bodies as living sacrifices, wholly and acceptable unto God" and that "whatsoever ye do in word or deed, do all in the name of the Lord Jesus, giving thanks unto God the Father by him." And to you, my alien friends, I would say, Come to Christ. Take God, Christ and the Holy Spirit at their word. Have each to bear testimony that you are the children of God. Trust not to yourselves for the evidence of pardon. Let the three witnesses in heaven—the Father, the Son, and the Holy Spirit—bear witness that you are the children of God. The true testimony can be obtained by your believing on the Lord Jesus Christ and doing what he told the apostles to tell the sinner to do to be saved.

Will you take God at his word? May God help you to come.

BIOGRAPHICAL SKETCH OF T. M. MYERS.

T. M. MYERS was born near Rogersville, Tenn., May 12, 1849. His father, Michael Myers, was an ideal type of the Southern planter, who had passed his entire days in the Sunny South. Tall and commanding in person, impulsive and brave in disposition, chivalrous and generous in character, he neither forgot an enemy nor forsook a friend. He was also an expert stock trader, and his natural love for a " splendid horse " was to some degree imparted to the subject of this sketch.

Like many of the men whose indomitable will and great courage brooked no obstacles save death, he literally exhausted a constitution that would otherwise have carried him to a good old age, at the comparatively early age of 54.

Minerva Phillips was the maiden name of the mother of this sketch, and through her came the blue blood of " Old Virginia," with all its slave-holding autocracy and imperial, though chivalrous, bearings. A Baptist in belief, and a devout Christian, she was a frail little body, of delicate constitution, and lived to see 35 years of the allotted three-score and ten. Seven children, six boys and one girl, blessed this union, and the subject of this sketch is the oldest of the six boys. The youngest of the boys, J. S. Myers, is now the pastor of the Christian church at Sedalia, Mo. Two of the boys are dead, and the other two are living in Oklahoma, one a sheriff of the county wherein he resides, the other one a merchant. The sister is now living in South Carolina, the wife of Mr. D. D. Little.

After their mother's death the children wandered away, and only once again did they ever meet together in their old Tennessee home, and this meeting was a sad one, so sad that the parting once more was for the last time for some—and for all from the old, old home.

T. M. Myers went to Lexington, Ky., and entered upon a theological course in the Kentucky University, where, for a little over four years, poverty and determination witnessed in him a daily struggle. By walking and driving cattle over the Cumberland Mountains, and working four hours out of each day, he managed to get a start the first year. As soon as he had gained a footing he preached on Sundays and received for this a slight compensation that enabled him to still more vigorously push his studies.

These, he says, were the hardest, and at the same time the best lessons of his life.

His ambition and his courage naturally made for him friends, who, recognizing in him merit and worth, were ready to assist when they saw help

22

would be appreciated, and that it gave promise of rich reward.

Hardship and hard study, however, told on the physical man, and for more than two years he paid the penalty of over-taxing his strength with spinal meningitis, and at one time his life seemed to hang in the balance.

This was a trying ordeal to him, for when he arose from his bed it was to learn that further trying to obtain the cherished diploma was impossible.

Work, however, he must. Home was but a memory, friends were few, and the world held out to him bread only "by the sweat of his brow."

Nothing daunted by his feeble frame and shattered constitution, he at once began upon the great calling of his life. While yet but a mere boy, and an exceedingly delicate one at that, he began the first revival meeting of his experience at old East Union, Ky.

This meeting was a famous one, attracting people from distances in every direction, and was talked about around the hearth-stones of every home in that country. Eighty-one additions were the fruits of that effort, a number that, at that day and period, seemed miraculous. One of that number, A. W. Kokendoffer, is now pastor of the church worshiping at the corner of Fifteenth Street and Virginia Avenue. 'Twas a "great meetin'," the people there said, and many were the words written and spoken about it during the succeeding months.

He has held since that meeting 149 revivals, spending much of the intervening years in this, his chosen work. Counting those who have been received into the church during his pastorate of churches and from revivals, he has taken into the fellowship of the body of Christ more than ten thousand souls during a ministry of a little more than twenty-two years.

He was married December the 26th, 1873, to Miss Mary C. Talbott, the only daughter of the Hon. Henry Talbott, of Bourbon county, Kentucky. Two boys, Henry and Thomas, aged 14 and 9, are the fruits of this union.

Mrs. Myers has resided with her husband in five of the States of the Union, and by her constant labors in the field with her husband, has won the well merited name, "a model preacher's wife," and, no doubt, much of the great work of her husband had its sowing from her hand.

His first important charge was at Carlysle, Ky., where he remained for a period of thirteen months, save the time spent at other points holding meetings. During this period he baptized at the various points over four hundred people, an unusual number in that early age of our growth.

His next charge was at Dover, Ky.; then at Vanceburg, Ky.; then at Tilton, Ky., and from thence to Jeffersonville, Ind., where he left as a monument of his labors an elegant church, the pride of our brethren to-day.

Three years of incessant toil at this point brought on a second attack of his old college affliction. He struggled against it, but uselessly, and he bade his loved and loving flock farewell, and took up his residence at one of the health resorts of North Carolina, a little place called Asheville. For three years he recuperated here, preaching most of the time, but not applying himself so arduously as in the past.

From here he moved West and took the field as Evangelist in the State of Kansas, with our noble and grand brother F. L. Cook, now of Montana, as his singer, and the churches of Lincoln, Ashland, Horton, Abilene, Independence, Emporia, Atchison and many others will long remember the work of these two faithful servants of Christ.

After serving the term for which he was engaged by the State Board, he moved to Kansas City, Mo., and in 1891 purchased the home where he now resides, 305 Walrond Place, intending to make it a kind of center for his future life work of evangel-ization.

While resting a little before starting out again into the field of active labor, he was invited to come over to the little church at Twelfth and Bales Avenue, by its board of officers, and preach to them on Sunday mornings. For two months he continued thus. In these two months the church began to quicken, interest was aroused, the members grew warm, and on November 1, 1892, a unanimous call was tendered him by every officer and member of the congregation, which he accepted.

Numerous calls from the best churches of our brotherhood have not inclined him in the least to forsake his present charge, and though he has held meetings since taking charge here, he has succeeded in adding about sixty to the membership, and put new life and vigor into every member of the church.

Tireless in his workings, and with his broad and matured experience, he is rapidly laying the foundations for what promises to be equal to the best work of his life.

Some of Bro. Myers' converts have in turn taken up his work, and to-day stand as beacons in their several midsts. Rev. Dickerman, at Napoleon, O.; the present pastor of the church at Boulder, Col., whose name the writer fails to recall, and J. S. Myers, at Sedalia, Mo., being some of the men of note who joined the church in revivals held by Bro. T. M. Myers. H. E. M.

FOOD FOR THE BODY AND FOR THE SOUL.

T. M. MYERS.

Give us this day our daily bread.—Matt. 6: 11.

THERE are said to be sixty-four chemical elements which go to make up every physical body in the known universe. These chemicals are oxygen, hydrogen, nitrogen, carbon, etc.

The heavens above, the earth beneath, "the waters under the earth," the rocks, the trees, the minerals ; "the fowls of the heavens," the animals of the earth, "the fishes of the sea," and the human body are thus formed. We are told by those who know that the reason that one body differs from another body in texture, form, size, color and durability is because of the different arrangement of these constituent ingredients. The difference in the quantity of any one or more of these, which may enter into that body, or the absence of any one or more of these chemicals, really causes the diversity. Thus eight-ninths of all the waters of "the mighty deep" are composed of oxygen.

Hydrogen is found to be a part of the blazing comet, and also it is in the illuminating gas, as

well as in the little candle. Carbon forms the
basis of charcoal. It also makes the diamond,
and is the most solid of all known substances.
Nitrogen forms nearly four-fifths of the common
air. These chemical factors, with all of their di-
visions and again their sub-divisions, are said to
be, and they truly are, the source from which is
formed everything that we see, touch, taste, smell
or hear. Stone in some parts is the same as water,
but by a difference in the quantity of some of the
components, and the absence of others, one is a
solid, and the other is a liquid, and may be evap-
orated into vapor. The human body and the earth
on which it walks are composed largely of the
same material. These bodies of ours are mostly
vapor, and at some time each one of them will return to its normal element, and it will be vapor
again. The part of the human body which is the
same as the " dust of the earth " will disintegrate
and enter into its native soil again. " Dust thou
art, and unto dust shalt thou return," Gen. 3 : 19.
We have also learned that all of these animal,
" vegetable and mineral bodies," are undergoing
a constant change. They are forming and they
are decaying. They are growing and they are dying. They are accumulating, and at the same
time they are " wasting away." Consequently
they all must be fed from some source, or the waste
would soon consume any or each of them. Bodies
like our own would soon pass away with every

other such transient existence if they were not
constantly supplied with such elements as sustain
them. Long before Jesus taught " the Disciples
how to pray," this same was the prayer of universal nature, and from the planets " which roll amid
the suns," down and down until we reach the little
animalcule, thousands of which can dwell in one
drop of water, the ceaseless cry of all created bodies has ever been, " Give us this day our daily
bread."   The tiny leaf, the blade of grass, the fragrant flower, the waving grain, and the tall forests,
are all said to eat and drink and breathe in their
own way. We know that when they are not supported in their mysterious way from the great
store-houses of nature, their natural decay
soon wears them away and they return to their
normal elements and to the "mother earth." Once
more they are oxygen or hydrogen, nitrogen or
carbon, or they are a part of some other body,
which in whole or in part is composed of these
subtle elements. They have not, as some have
said, " gone back to nothing." No existing body
of mind or spirit was ever annihilated, nor ever
will be. These chemical atoms which form physical bodies may be, as we are told, so small that
millions of them would not equal in size one grain
of sand, but small as they are, not more than one
four hundred millionth of an inch in diameter, yet
they are not mere playthings of the imagination.
They are real, positive existences. Clerk Max-

well says that though in the course of ages catas-
trophies have occurred, and may yet occur in the
heavens; though ancient systems may be dissolved, and new systems evolved out of their ruins,
yet the molecule out of which these systems are
built, the foundation-stones of the material universe, remain unbroken and unworn. Something
never comes from nothing, and something never
turns to nothing. In the presence of facts which
we know to exist, it is a thought " unthinkable "
that a material existence should ever be without an
existence in any form; that a dissolution should
mean the necessary end of anything. Hence the
most difficult belief is what is called " unbelief,"
or a belief that " death ends all."

This *cannot* be the truth concerning bodies composed of chemical ingredients, such as ours are.
The same number of these microscopic atoms,
gathered together and united with a given number
of another kind of these fractional atoms, such as
had been done at any previous date, would produce the same human body as they had produced
before. Like cause produces like effect, and this
is precisely what is affirmed in the promise made
to resurrect the dead, at least those whose bodies have been dissolved into their original elements. The Savior's resurrected body is the model
of that body of ours " which shall be," 1 Cor. 15:
37. That body will eat and drink and breathe.
It will live, and love, and speak, and it will know

and be known, as any other human being, and as was the Savior after his resurrection, and all of its gifts and joy will be perpetual. A spiritual body will never die, but it must have each day its daily bread.

These substances which compose our bodies may be undergoing a continuous change. They may be going back into space, or into other bodies. They are indeed moving in a ceaseless current, or they are revolving in a kind of endless cycle, but they never stop nor come to an end, but they go on and on without any known limit. These molecules, from whatever source they may come, are not raw material awaiting development. They are not crude and unfinished. They are rather like the stones of Solomon's temple, prepared and finished and polished ere the building was begun.

These material organizations may change, they may dissolve and pass away, but these elementary forms are always the same as far as science has discerned, and they seem to proceed immediately into the formation of other bodies. The judgment day will bring great changes for this world, and for the heavens above it, but nothing will be obliterated at the final judgment. "The heavens shall pass with a great noise away." The elements shall melt with fervent heat. The earth, also, and the works that are therein, shall be burned up. 2 Pet. 3: 10. But you may say the same at the

burning of a block of houses, or of a burning
ship in mid-ocean, or of the fuel which blazes on
your hearth.   It is converted into smoke and
ashes, both of which will form elements of earth
and air, and they will produce more timber, and
more coal, and at some time will make another
fire, another smoke, and generate more heat.
" There will be a new heavens and a new earth "
(2 Pet. 3 : 13) after the conflagration, and the dissolution of the old heavens and the old earth.
There have been transformations of this earth before, and it is not new to say that there will be a
transformation of this earth again. Geologists
tell us that there have been several distinct ends
to our earth, as it once was.   Though these end-
ings may have taken place slowly, yet if we pass
through the time embraced by the words, " In the
beginning" (Gen. 1: 1), we find that there was a
time when the earth was without its present form,
and we have no knowledge as to the length of that
time; only we know that it was very great. There
was a time when it was perfectly void of animal
or vegetable life, and darkness was upon the
face of the deep.   Gen. 1 : 2.   We are also in
ignorance as to the duration of this barren era.
" Deep answered back to deep " amid the darkness and the limitless waste.   There was then
another time, called the vegetable era, when vast
forests were produced to the exclusion of nearly
or quite everything else.   The submerging of

these tremendous timbers as they fell upon the
bosom of an ever-moistened earth, and the exclusion ever afterwards of the consuming elements of
air, caused a kind of petrifaction of this embedded
vegetation, and that has made our present coal de-
posits. In corroboration of this, we find the grain
of timbers and the veins of leaves running through
the lumps of coal. There was another period, or a
later era of this same vegetable period, in which
the monster mastodon, and other beasts of his
coarse and sluggish kind lived. Other animals of
more exquisite fiber could not have existed then.
A sufficient number of these monsters, when fallen, were submerged or embalmed by the natural
process of the then slimy earth to be preserved,
and to bring down to us a kind of silent story of
their time. Their tusks which rest in our mu-
seums are equal to great beams. Their grinders
are such in size as boxes of respectable dimen-
sions. Now we know that there was another era
in which a human being could live, and eat, and
drink, and breathe, and that which could sustain
so eminent a being as he with all of his attendant
animals, and fowls, and fishes, and " whatsoever
creepeth upon the face of the earth." He is now
enjoying this existence and environment. But
there will be another era after this, and in that
other era " righteousness shall dwell." There
shall be " no more sea." Neither will there be
any more sorrow or crying, for the former things

have passed away, and there will be no more
death, and "no night shall be there." For the
Lord God shall make it perpetual light, and the
race upon this coming and new earth shall reign
for ever and ever. Rev. 22 : 5. Thus we see that
chemistry and geology have at last risen up to be
a kind of silent commentary on the sacred Scriptures, the books of which, in their own way, told
of all these things thousands of years before human industry and genius had exhumed them from
the earth and air. On the new earth and under
the new heavens which we are yet to have, our
bodies will eat, and drink, and breathe, and look
upon scenes which, from our present angle of view,
are absolutely perfect. "The twelve manner of
fruit," which will be borne by the typical tree of
life, the leaves of that tree, "which are for the
healing of the nations" and the river of the water
of life (Rev. 22 : 1, 2), are all simply sources
from which we will be supplied in every possible
want, and with a sustenance which will completely
complement the wasting away. This has never
been true since our first parents were driven from
that tree of life to where they "must surely die."
Gen. 2 : 17. It is not true that every waste of these
mortal bodies is supplied, and those which are
supplied are not always furnished with a quantity
equal to their waste, hence "we all must die"
sooner or later, and is it not most natural that we
should pray for that bread of which if we eat we

shall never die ? Jno. 6 : 32, 33. " Give us this day
our daily bread," is the voiceless prayer of every
living existence.   There are inhabitants of the sea
which live for many centuries.   They wander
through " the paths of the sea " for ages of time, but
they are said to have very little waste of tissue.
There was a time when man approximated a thousand years of time in his " earthly pilgrimage."
But in that remote period he wandered about and
looked upon the face of the earth and of the sky.
He did little, and thought but little, and accomplished nearly nothing.   The annals which are
left us of their achievements are short and simple.
Methuselah and Lamech lived, in all, seventeen
hundred and forty-six years, and two short sen-
tences are sufficient to contain their biographies.
Men live and think and act more swiftly now, the
waste upon them is greater, and the supply is in-
sufficient, and if he lives up to

> " Three score and ten,
>   Ah, my pen !
> Sadly lingers,
> Wrinkles deep,
>   Icy creep,
> Death's cold fingers."

Again we remark that every physical body must
partake of the nature of the elements of which
it is composed, and it is not different from them
except in the sense in which a third element may
be produced by the composition of two or more

primary ingredients. Men of strong or weak constitution, tall or short of stature, light or dark of color, are all thus differentiated by the climates, the latitudes, and environments which would naturally produce these so-called races of men. Our father Adam was most certainly a red man. Moses and the Savior were most likely of dark complexion, for thus were their tribes and races. Tropical people, or those who have lived near the earth's equator, have ever been, both in life and language, a poetic, impulsive and a generous people, with great fluctuations in national and social habits. Their laws and language have alike been of a florid and of a figurative nature. The Scriptures, though they are righteously true, yet they must be interpreted from a tropical angle in which highly-drawn metaphors are continually brought into use. Geography and history are the best aids to the study of this book, which is so mysterious to some. The races whose habitation has been in or near the frigid zones have been the more hardy, the more enduring, persistent, and yet more conservative. Their language speaks what it means, and means what it speaks, but it is not so sweet in its cadences. These races have always excelled the tropical races eventually in the race for national supremacy. They have to live in harder climates, and this makes them more capable. God hath made of one blood all nations of men. Acts 17 : 26.

These "Torrid" and "Frigid" races of men differ widely now, but not more so than the student of physiology ought to expect. One land will produce giants and another will produce pigmies, if we will only allow time enough for the sun, and the air, and the soil, and the food, and other environments to change the original race into their own likeness. Ham was once as fair as Japheth, but the one will become fairer, and the other will become darker as the ages roll on. The swiftest horse will come from Kentucky, and the largest horse from Normandy, but the one will become swifter, and the other will become larger as they are continually developed, for there is scarcely any limit to the process of development. We have been told that the human race subsists off the animal kingdom; that the animal kingdom subsists off the vegetable kingdom; that the vegetable kingdom subsists off the mother earth, and that the earth itself subsists off the original granite rock. "Give us this day our daily bread" and give us of the kind that thou wouldst have us become as men and races. Joseph Cook has said that "on the origin of molecular life," the battle of a hundred years of controversy and investigation would be fought. May it not be true that in the uniting or bringing together of certain exquisitely assorted molecules or chemicals vegetable life is produced, and by the same process and in conjunction with other

of these elements, animal life is produced?
Did not the "Great Chemist" thus form man out
of the dust of the earth, and breathing into his
nostrils the "breath of lives," as the Hebrew has
it, impart to him a constituent element of life from
his own being which, like its giver, is without beginning or ending, and this in addition to the animal, whose first inhaling is from the common air?
Like produces like, and there would be little difference between the man and the animal, except
for the sources from which come the one and the
other, and this indeed is the difference between
men and angels. The one is made "a little lower
than the other" (Heb. 2 : 7,) but this will not
always be the case, for man and the earth on
which he lives are both passing through a refining
process, and at some time this man will be ac-
counted worthy "to judge the angels." 1 Cor. 6 :
3. This is not the case now, but at some period
we shall ascend above the angel. The angel can
rejoice, and consequently can sorrow, but "there
will be no more sorrow for man." Rev. 21 : 4. A
felicitous existence that will be!

> "We speak of the realms of the blest,
>   That country so bright and so fair,
>   And oft are its glories confessed,
>   But what must it be to be there?"

Let us ascend with this thought, and we will see
that all we have shown to be true of matter is also
true of the mind. The body is only an illustra-

23

tion of the spirit.   All that is seen is only a dia-
gram of the "Unseen."   "He who spake as never
man spake" (John 7: 46), said that the kingdom
of heaven is like this, and it is like that, and all
that he said was true.   Now we see through a
glass darkly, (1 Cor. 13: 12.)   We have to study
the earthly to understand the heavenly.

We are unable to divide asunder the soul and
spirit in our comprehension, nor can we tell where
matter ends and where mind begins, and yet we
"know" that mind and spirit do exist.   We cannot comprehend the human will, but we know that
it does exist from what we see it execute through
the instrumentality of human hands.   "The spirit
of man," together with his mind and moral attributes, are much the creatures of education and
of environment.   The existence of these lofty
faculties is perpetual and endless, but their kind
is conditional.   The Mohammedan would have
been a Christian, and the Christian in return would
have been a Mohammedan, if from the time of the
birth of each their residence and education had
been exchanged.   For the most part, a heathen
would have been a saint, and a saint would have
been a heathen if these could have exchanged
their surroundings and their mental culture.
Hence it becomes true and right that every individual and every nation alike becomes responsible
and is an ordained missionary, to carry to the benighted of his race any blessings of discovery or

of invention, or of light, and hope, and truth, of
any religion of which he may have become possessed in his more favored sphere. Selfishness,
the exact opposite of this, has stranded more souls
than any other sin. The truth is, when man is
born he is much like a vase, which vase is more
nearly empty, and at the same time more capable
than that with which any other animal is born.
We may plant in this vase either the "thistle"
or the "rose," and we may also cultivate either
of these. We may have the capabilities and the
defects when born which are found in the physical organization of our progenitors, and it may be
that in consequence thereof it is easier to develop,
and that we are more likely to develop in certain
directions. But it is truly in the planting, and in
the developing at last, that the mind and manners are made. Train up a child in the way he
should go, and when he is old he will not depart
from it. Prov. 22 : 6. Is it not true that "spirit
begets spirit," and that "mind begets mind ?"
and in some sense or in some degree, may this not
be independent of the begetting and being born
of which our bodies is the product ? "Like begets like." Sin begets sin. Virtue begets virtue.
Joy begets joy. Vice begets vice. A spirit can
be begotten within a human being, and can be
developed and born into the life of that being,
which spirit literally has no relation to the mind
or the spirit which dwells within the parents of

our flesh. This may be a slow or mysterious process of generation, but it is none the less the fact,
or none the less a mystery, than is the generation
and the birth of our physical or mortal bodies. If
a man reads Homer, he will get the spirit of
Homer. If a man reads Jesus, he will get the
spirit of Jesus. Why do the Scriptures admon-
ish us to lay aside all malice, and all guile, envy-
ings and evil speakings? 1 Pet. 2: 1. Simply
because a person literally becomes just what these
things are themselves, if he continues to subsist
on them.

A man in acquiring wealth, or even a small
competency, may become, while doing so, almost
an animal in greed and selfishness. A high school
in a great city leaves God and the Bible entirely
out of its curriculum. They teach clearly what
they do teach, but they have left an impious blank
upon the thousands of those receptive minds, that
the after culture of two worlds will hardly be able
to replace. O Lord! Do thou give us better bread
than this! A man may become an artist and at
the same time become godless and irreverent.
He may attain literary eminence, and at the same
time possess very little common sense. We have
more mouths than one to feed. The finer sensibil-
ities of the spirit within us may be calling at
every portal of "this castle of clay" within which
it is confined, with ceaseless appeal, to "give us
each day our daily bread," and if we starve this

virtuous soul, which came to us from some pious spirit, it will finally leave us, and often the last state of that man is worse than the first. 2 Peter 2 : 20. The real man or the real woman is actually formed and made within the family, or within the church, in society, or by business or books, and such an one is unwittingly the product of these and like environments. One may start very slowly in being allured by any vice, but as he goes on his speed will increase, and he will go more and more swiftly until he cannot be overtaken with the measureless speed of an angel's flight, nor be redeemed by the blood of a dying Christ.

The body can become so benumbed that medicine cannot affect it. The heart may get so hard that pity cannot move it. The conscience may become so seared that it can "quench the Spirit." 1 Thes. 5 : 19. There are places over which if the body or the soul should pass it will never return. "Gravity shifting turns the other way," and they are lost, lost, "world without end." The three most responsible positions known to human experience are said to be first, a parent, second a teacher, and third, to be a minister in spiritual things. A parent's mind, as well as the image of his body, may live in his child, and in his children's children, on and on, without limit or end. What a pity that some parents are not childless, and what a misfortune that other parents cannot be entrusted with all the children. " The hand that rocks the cradle is the hand that rules the world." Many children are never reared in any way, and many a soul will be lost over this awful fact.

> " Me thinks I heard some children say,
> I never heard my parents pray!"

Can a parent rest in heaven who has caused the ruin of a child by example or by neglect? Is not the penalty of a sin due in proportion to the amount of suffering which that sin really produces? Secondly, who are our teachers? We think the thoughts, speak the language, walk in the footsteps, and make the gestures of those who have been our teachers. We live their lives over again, when they are in the grave. Thirdly. It has been said that the ground upon which a minister walks "quakes with immortal realities." Think of the thousands and tens of thousands who are made and unmade before the pulpit. Of all men upon the earth's face, the preacher ought to be the most sincerely honest. Many may become wise enough but few ever become good enough to be entrusted with the confidence of the good people of this world, and with the tender mission of love and mercy which a humble minister has been sent to bear. If there is any " deeper doom " that " common sinners dare not meddle with," this " doom " is certainly reserved for the shepherd who, knowingly, misleads his confiding flock. We pray for the parent, for the teacher, and the preacher, and for the bread of life, or for the bread of death, which they shall give to this world. And may we at the last tell of the food which we think the soul should eat, as well as of the hand from which we know its bread must come? First, we mention its "thinking;" secondly, we mention its "association," and thirdly, we mention its "reading." We have been told that we could not control our thoughts, and that no thinking is wrong if it does not develop into action. Both of these statements are errors and they are alike untrue. If one cannot control his thoughts he is not a "free moral agent," and in consequence thereof he is as much of an automaton as if he could not control his actions, or as if it were not wrong for him to start (of his own volition) on the "broad road to ruin."

The will can be master of the mind, as well as it can be the master of one's habits. One can think pure, also one can think vile. We can meditate upon the lovely and the beautiful, or upon the painful and repulsive. "Charity thinketh no evil," 1 Cor. 13 : 5, and from these thoughts, which are the sources of all rational action, will come the men and the women which we are destined to make of ourselves for the here and the hereafter. Next, we say of the company we keep. No one who lives is free from the effect of his associations. This company is the bane or the blessing of the

whole life, and how much it is to be regretted
that we do not all know and feel this in the beginning of the long life of our habits. The mountains lay in ranges. The birds fly in flocks. The
cattle roam in herds. We go to heaven with a
"multitude that no man can number." Rev. 7: 9.
Or otherwise we wreck the soul with that company into which business, or choice, or chance may
throw us. "Evil communications corrupt good
manners." 1 Cor. 15: 33. How easy it is to place
ourselves with pure people or with Christians for our
associates, and thus to make the road to virtue, to
success, to happiness and renown comparatively
easy, if we would only do this. And on the other
hand how easily and how thoughtlessly we can take
up with the companion, or with the circle, or with
the business partner, the influence of whom, for
one year or for even a month, we could hardly be
able to efface in a thousand years. We are simply
ruined and easily ruined in this gradual way and
scarcely know it.

Those who nurse the children, who go to school
and play with them, or who may eat and sleep and
be with them when they are away from home, will
be either the "weal or the woe," the joy or the
sorrow of them forever and ever. While tracing
these avenues of eternal consequences, we are
made to think of the schools and colleges, of the
plays and sports, of the lines and allurements
along which runs the path of a short youthful

life. Last, as to the books we read, infinite care should be taken. For instance: All fiction is not bad, and all history or poetry is not good. Much of both is equal to the most deadly poison to the human spirit. Think of the millions who are incapable of discerning the right and wrong on the printed page. We positively tremble to see these unwitting souls descending these declivities to unending ruin. On the other hand, nothing is more helpful "to the angel of light" than is the dissemination of good books and good literature, and how easy it is for us in starting to learn to love the one or the other of these. A church people without a religious journal of any kind is much like a family without a Bible. We have seen both of these, and have seen them while thus destitute, both living and worshiping in the most elegant houses. Yes, we see the body both fed and clothed with bounty and elegance, while the poor soul is naked and hungry. We often bid farewell to this forsaken soul because it is the inhabitant of a "worldly being." We must hope to meet this soul in heaven, for it will never die.

We must do all that we can to save the soul, for we will never have another chance. It has within its depths "an aching void this world can never fill." No. Not with all its fleeting, uncertain, dying, disappointing and heart-breaking realities. It must have something more everlasting or it will weep and wander forever. We once visited the

Masonic Widows' and Orphans' Home at Louisville, Kentucky, and happened to be invited during the visit to see the hundreds of orphan children, while they ate their dinner. The dining room was long and wide. The many tables were placed in a long row, side by side of each other, reaching to the farthermost end of the room. The least children surrounded that table which was nearest us, and the next larger sat at the next table, and so on until the largest was reached at the last. Those nearest us scarcely reached the first round of the chairs with their little feet. They observed perfect order, and never asked for anything, but every moment the little hand of some one would be held perpendicular, and at that instant a youthful maid, dressed in white, with a platter in hand, would take some simple morsel of plain food to that little child. There! thought we, the "Lord's Prayer" is literally answered. "Give us this day our daily bread" seemed written on the fingers of every orphan's hand, and there was God's angel to answer the prayer, for she came "like light" at the motion of the hand when God's "little innocent" reached its arm toward heaven. We could count the very dimples on the child's dumpy hand, and number the tresses which fell across its little temples. Its motherless little body seemed to be well cared for, but the tears fell thick and fast when we remembered of all that number the multitude of little children who had neither a father, or a mother, or a home. There was no parent on earth who could throw the arms of love around their little forms and repeat the endearing words, "My child!" My own dear child. How I love thee, as only a parent can love. Oh! Will my own child ever eat "the bread of charity," and receive only the kiss and the care of a stranger? These thoughts sweep across the bosom of every parent on earth. But how like the orphan is the lost soul? The one is without a father and without a home in this cold world, and the other is without a God and without a "home in heaven."

EVANGELIST JAMES SMALL.

OF the great evangelists who have arisen in the Church of Christ during the last decade there are few, if any, superior to the subject of this sketch. He says of himself: "On the 21st day of December, 1859, I was born in the village of Seafin, or, as we would say over there, the townland of Seafin, County Down, Ireland. The nearest town to us of any importance was Belfast. Memory often with her swift wings carries me back to the dear old home, a little thatched cottage upon a beautiful mound overlooking the sea, and within a stone's throw of Giant Fin McCool's castle. Behind that little home was the sloping hill, its brow kissed by the morning sun, and the Mourne Mountains, Slave Donard being the highest of the range, twelve miles in the distance. The beech and elms lifted their stately heads in adoration, as the Irish sea sang its deathless hymn to Him 'who hath measured the waters in the hollow of His hand, and meted out heaven with a span, and comprehended the dust of the earth in a measure, and weighed the mountains in scales, and the hills in a balance.' I have sat in that little cottage watching the vessels. with their snowy sails, bearing

JAMES SMALL.

precious freight to the land of the free, and have heard by our fireside when a boy stories from friends who had visited 'Amerikay' until I longed for the time when I, too, might go to that favored land.

"My father had a small farm of twenty-one acres, and he worked besides at the carpenter's trade, and looked after the little farm himself before going to his work, to save 20 cents a day that would have been given to a laboring man. By hard work he supported eight of us, four boys and four girls, and gave us all a good 'national' school education. So perish my tongue and arm forever if I should ever reflect upon my precious father and mother. They have in their hearts to-day the refreshing consciousness of having done their duty to their children, who have now all left their old home to seek their fortune in this world of change."

At an early age James and his brother Matthew, now the able pastor of the church at Edinburg, Indiana, left their Irish home, and went to the great city of Liverpool, England, where they engaged in business. It was here that they both heard W. T. Moore preach the pure gospel, and after close and prayerful investigation they left the Presbyterian faith of their fathers, and were by Bro. Moore baptized into the likeness of Christ's death the last Sunday in September, 1881. They afterward sat under the ministry of M. D. Todd and A. Martin for a term of three years each, and came to this country as preachers of the pure gospel of Christ.

At the solicitation of Z. T. Sweeney, who had met him in England, Bro. James Small came to Columbus, Indiana, and entered upon the work of evangelist of Bartholomew County, in the autumn of 1887. In this capacity he labored for four years, and since then until recently has been in the general field. From the first his meetings have been a succession of brilliant triumphs for his Lord. In six years he has added 3,000 members to the saved. His largest meetings are Martinsville, Indiana, 387 additions, and East Des Moines, Iowa, 260 additions. He has held several meetings of 100 and more accessions. He is now settled as the beloved pastor of the church at East Des Moines, and he and his wife, who is a fit helpmeet for such a man, have a great work and a bright future before them.

Bro. Small is a fine specimen of the old Scotch-Irish race. He stands six feet in his stockings, and weighs about 170 pounds. His personal appearance is very striking, his voice strong and musical with a rich Scotch-Irish brogue, his language good and his manner very forcible. His fund of anecdotes and his store of apt illustrations seem inexhaustible, his wit is keen, his logic clear, and his pathos tender and powerful. As a popular speaker before the masses he has few equals, and perhaps no superiors in the West to-day. He is really a great preacher. He is affable in his ways, and has social qualities of a high order. Being but 34 years old, the best part of his life is probably yet before him. Long may he live to help weary feet on their way to the better land! He can truly say:

> " E'er since by faith I saw the stream
> Thy flowing wounds supply,
> Redeeming love has been my theme,
> And shall be till I die."

MAN'S DESTINY.

JAMES SMALL.

"What is man, that thou art mindful of him? Thou hast crowned him with glory and honor."—Psalms 8: 4, 5.
"How much, then, is a man better than a sheep?"—Matt. 12: 12.

MAN'S nobility, not his worthlessness, is indicated in the text. Man is more than what Watts, in his familiar hymn, calls a "worm." It nearly took my breath when I read the text from the Revised Version—" What is man that thou art mindful of him? Thou hast made him a little lower than God." Not than angels, as the Common Version has it; but a little lower than God. A mere man, in the eyes of the world, is a nobody. Jesus Christ teaches that man, as man, is greater than wealth or rank could ever make him. We have not yet understood the immense significance of the fact that Jesus Christ had no money; that he was one of the poorest men that ever lived, and yet the greatest. We can tell the value of man in the pains that God has taken to redeem him, and in the home he has prepared for him. When man had to be rescued, God himself came to the rescue.

In the light of these truths we can answer the Psalmist's question, "What is man?" He is a gem; rusted, indeed, by sin, but still a gem of infinite worth in the sight of Him who said, "What shall it profit a man if he gain the whole world and lose his own soul? or what shall a man give in exchange for his soul?"

The hope of reward is one of the strongest incentives to effort, activity and purity in this world. Life has its shadows, as well as its sunshine. It is marked by disappointments and trials for which the world has no solace; and sad would be the condition of this life if it were not for the everlasting consolation that we have a destiny beyond the control of anyone or anything in this world. There is a touching story of a young man who was rapidly and surely losing his eyesight. The physicians told him that he would be able to see but for a few months. At once, accompanied by a sister, he set out to travel over Europe, taking a last look at the beautiful things in this world before his eyes should be closed forever. He wished to have his memory stored with lovely pictures of mountains, lakes and waterfalls; of fields beloved, woodlands and meadows bright with daisies and primroses, so that, when he should no longer be able to see, he might have these beautiful visions in his soul to lighten his gloom. So, to-day, we are in the terrific warfare of life; and, as the soldier beside his lonely camp-fire, thinking of home, falls asleep and dreams of his dear ones, so the soldier of Christ, in the thick of the battle, foot-

24

sore and heart-sore, has beautiful visions of the
City that has everlasting foundations, "whose
builder and maker is God."

THE IMPORTANCE OF THE SUBJECT.

At the outset we are met with the importance of
the subject. "It is not the ordinary affairs of this
life, the fleeting or transitory concerns of to-day
or to-morrow ; it is not whether we shall live all
free men or die all slaves ; it is not the momentary
affairs of empire, or the evanescent charms of dominion ; nay, indeed, all these are but the toys of
childhood, the sportive excursions of youthful
fancy, contrasted with the questions, What is
man ? Whence came he ? Whither does he go ?
Is he a mortal or an immortal being ? Is he
doomed to spring up like the grass, bloom like a
flower, cast his seed into the earth and die forever?
Is there no object or future hope ? No God, no
heaven, no exalted society to be enjoyed ? Are all
the great and illustrious men and women who
have lived before we were born wasted and gone
forever ? After a few short days are fled, when
the enjoyments and toils of life are over, when our
relish for social enjoyment and our desires for returning to the fountain of life are most acute,
must we hang our heads and close our eyes, in the
desolating and appalling prospect of never opening them again, of never tasting the sweets for
which a state of discipline and trial has so well

fitted us? It is not what we shall eat and what we shall drink, unless we be proven to be mere animals; but it is, Shall we live or die forever? It is beautifully expressed by a Christian poet:

"Shall spring ever visit the mouldering urn?
Shall day ever dawn on the night of the grave?"

It has been said that a man is apt to recommend to others his own strong points. I confess that the subject which I have undertaken to discuss is the one subject, above all others, in which I am most interested. There has always been something in my very nature, to say nothing about revelation, that leads me to look on the bright side. I am an optimist, first, last, and all the time; and I cannot help it. I was born that way, I suppose. Conviction led me, not to despair, but to tears and to Christ; and from that time to the present I can say that I have cheerfully accepted the heart-aches, disappointments, and the discipline of life, and am willing to suffer for Him who has filled my soul with such a glorious hope.

With these introductory words, we come to the subject of "Man's Destiny." It is our purpose, first of all, to notice some mistakes concerning man, then to discuss what is man, what his destiny, and how that destiny has been secured him.

AS TO THE MISTAKES.

It is taught by the creeds, and by not a few preachers, that man is wicked through and through; that his nature, on account of Adam's transgression, is entirely depraved and that the regenerating power of God must be exerted before he can be saved or appropriate the offered blessings of the gospel. But if these views of man's natural condition be correct, it would follow that all men, by nature, are equally bad; sin would be in harmony with his nature, and a man in his natural condition could have no conceptions of good. But these are not the facts in the case. I do not care whether a man is a church member or not, whether he is a Christian or not, he has a conscience, a moral nature, call it what you may, that commends him when he does, in his judgment, what is right and condemns him when he does wrong. Again, how can the judgment of Christ be possible if man has lost all image of God? If a man had not his moral nature, he could say, in the judgment, "I have stolen, I have hated, I have sworn; but I did it in strict harmony with my nature." There could be no justice in condemning a man if he had a nature contrary to God's; a nature that did not condemn him when he did wrong and approve him when he did right. We do not deny man's wickedness and need of the Savior and of regeneration; but that he is so dead that a miracle is needed to enable him to believe the gospel, and that he cannot do right when the right is made known to him, is nowhere taught in the Scriptures. No

text of God's word can be fairly construed as
teaching that regeneration is accomplished prior
to faith and repentance. We do not deny, either,
the influence of hereditary descent. Man is what
he is largely by his social environment. We are
made better or worse by the friendships of life.
Two persons never meet and talk but they go away
either better or worse for the conversation. Man,
too, is what he is, to some extent, by his ancestry.
There is something in blood, after all; but not so
much as some people suppose. Heaven's aristo-
crats are "those who have washed their robes and
made them white in the blood or the lamb." The
only aristocracy of this earth are the sons and
daughters of the Lord Almighty, and the measure
of every man's greatness is the amount of humble
service he performs for the good of others. Let us
not take too much credit to ourselves for the positions we occupy. We owe a great deal more to
our social privileges and safeguards than we sometimes imagine.

But, to return. With all the influences of
hereditary descent and social environment, man,
in his moral activity, is free to the extent that he
is responsible. I know that I am free, and that
outweighs all metaphysical reasoning upon the
subject. But, last of all on this point, if total depravity be universal, then we necessarily make
conversion a miracle and leave the sinner without
responsibility for continuing in his sins until a

miracle is wrought, without which we cannot come
to God.   No one, I think, in the light of the New
Testament teaching, can believe this.   The apostles always addressed men as responsible beings,
and if there is any one doctrine that is clearly taught
upon the pages of the New Testament, it is the
essential liberty and responsibility of the individual.   And it is as true as that night follows the
day that in human nature, in man just as he is,
there is a capacity for God, as there is in soil for
seed.   And it does not follow, although he is said
to be " dead in trespasses and sins," that he is so
dead he cannot hear the gospel; and there is not a
grain of faith in a man's soul as big as a mustard
seed, that is God-given, that did not come by hearing the word of God.   Man is not dead in the
faculties of his being, but he is dead in character.
Man has still a heart to feel, a mind to think and
a conscience that can be impressed with guilt;
and there comes to him, in listening to this word,
as he believes it to be the word of life, this awful
and overpowering word, *ought*—I ought to be a
Christian.   More than this, he is conscious of possessing, under the faithful preaching of the gospel,
the power to turn to God and live a better life.   If
a man were totally depraved, if there were no
germ of good left in him, he would be totally lost
to the love of God and never would have been redeemed by Jesus Christ.   It is because there is
some trace of God's image left in him, however

faint it may be, that Jesus Christ said, " Go, preach the gospel to every creature." There are none so good that they do not need it ; there are none so bad that it should not be preached to them.

Of course, one has not the time in a single discourse to discuss every phase of total depravity, and we will dismiss this part of the subject and pause for a moment or two to answer the skeptic's question, Why didn't God make man that he couldn't sin ? We are inclined to answer this question by asking another. Would you have God to take away your will power and make you into a man or a sheep ? A man is that much better than a sheep in that he is free ; hence, virtue or vice in him is possible. This is man's crown of glory, but, true enough, his peril. But it is better to be a man that can sin than a sheep that can't. You say that was a marvelous thing to do. I admit it; but God assumed the responsibility and did it, and God always does the best thing. To say otherwise would be to take the position that he is not God. Again, we might ask our friend another question. Can you make anything better for seeing than the eye ? Can you make any thing better for hearing than the ear ? Can anything be made better for thinking than the mind ? Can anything be made better for communication of thought than language ? Who can measure the possibilities of the human soul ?   In themselves, every organ of the body and every faculty of the mind are good and noble and useful.   Sin is the abuse and excess of these. The extremes of our virtues are our vices, and it is one of the sad things in this great world that God's best gifts can be most abused.   Have we not seen, even in our own lives, that what is highest and greatest can, in its abuse and excess, be all that is most hideous ?   Combativeness and destructiveness are both, in themselves, right; but the abuse of these has turned many a man into a brute.   A noble pride and independence, if not kept within bounds, becomes offensive to our dearest friends; the lovely grace of modesty degenerates into self-opinion; high-hearted enterprise into a mad chase after fortune, in which we ride down everything that comes in the way of success.

Blessings are cruel to abusers, and most kind and indispensable to rightful users.   They serve us or rule us.   Fire warms our dwellings and consumes them.   Is not steam at times a servant and at times a tyrant ?   Is not the iron in the plow and ship necessary to man's happiness ? But are not the cruel sword and spear made of the same material ?   The mighty, throbbing locomotive, with its living freight of passengers—is it not a triumph of engineering skill ? But does it not, at times, plow the embankment, to the sadness and sorrow of men, women and children ?

You say that this was not the design of the
maker; this was only an accident, connected with
good. Very true, and the Scriptures inform us
that " God made man upright, but he has sought
out many inventions." Man can abuse his freedom and become a wreck.

As it is in the material world, so it is in the
spiritual. The Christian is the engine on the
line: the sinner is the engine off the line. The
powers that exalt us above the sheep and the
machine are the powers with which we sin; and
for God to have made us that we couldn't sin,
would have been to have made us more or less
than man. Take away the power to do wrong,
and you take away the power to do right.

WHAT IS MAN?

1. *Man is a thinker.* In one sense, a ship is
larger than a man; in another, it is smaller. It is
compelled to loan itself to our services. Man
made the ship and runs the ship. So of the earth.
In one way the earth is larger than we; in others,
it is a great deal smaller. You cannot measure
the worth of things by their size. A diamond in
a crown is worth more, sometimes, than the crown.
It is grander to think a world than to be a world.
When a good Christian lady was dying in Columbus, Indiana, she asked my wife to pull the cur-
tains aside and let her see, for the last time, a
sunset; and as the sun was sinking in the west,

she remarked, "This is a beautiful world." To
be able to rejoice in a created world and to conceive of a universe, is grander and greater than to
be a universe. "There is nothing great in this
world but man." This being true, the highest and
grandest service is service to humanity, and the
coming hero will be a servant, not a master. He
comes, not to be ministered unto, but to minister.

2. *Man is a feeler.* In this noisy, active, en-
terprising age, a man that is not intellectual is not
worth very much; but he is worth just as little
if he hasn't a heart. I would as soon cease to live
as cease to love and be loved. The Lord pity the
woman who marries a man who decides every
thing in the cold light of reason. Man has a conscience, a reason, a judgment, a memory and an
imagination; and he has these before conversion,
as well as after. He thinks, he feels, he acts. Man
is made in God's image in these particulars, and
God has to do this to make a being who could
enter into his thoughts, love and fellowship. It is
characteristic of man, and of man only, that "he
can think God's thoughts after him," and have his
heart warmed by the love of God. If this were
not so, revelation would be impossible. The
starry heavens, the blue sky, the green earth, covered with innumerable flowers and bedecked with
fair forests, excite our admiration and stir our
emotions. There is not such a thing in the Bible as
a worthless man. You say, What about the pub-

lican in the temple? To me, it is one of the most touching, far-reaching and grandest exhibits of man's worth on record. My own prodigal heart found great comfort in two verses of Scripture: "This is a faithful saying, and worthy of all acceptation, that Christ Jesus came into the world to save sinners," and the publican, smiting upon his breast, would not lift so much as his eyes to heaven, saying: "God be merciful to me a sinner." A miserable sinner, and yet addressing God in that imperative mode. A prodigal who has been out on the desert of sin, and still with such a sense of worth as emboldened him to pray, feeling that if God "heard the young ravens when they cry," he esteemed him enough to hear and attend to his penitent prayer. So worthless that he needed to pray; so precious in God's sight that it was of some use to pray. Take it for all that it is worth, it means that there is a pardon for the guilty, life for the lifeless, and grace for those who have wandered so far away that they think they can never return.

3. *Man is an actor.* I never heard, nor never expect to hear, a better division of the gospel than that given by our old pioneer preachers. "There are facts in the gospel to be believed, commands to be obeyed, promises to be enjoyed, and threatenings to be avoided." How royally God has treated us. There are faith and repentance for the intellect and emotions, and baptism for the

heart and will. That man can think, feel and act was assumed, too, in the provisions which God made for his salvation. First faith, then feeling, then action. A being that can think, feel, and act can be educated for heaven. It is the tendency too of life, and thought, and feeling, to take on the forms of life. What is a flower? It is thought materialized. What is a locomotive? It is thought materialized. The mechanic had the locomotive in mind like the creator who material-ized his thought. Back of the thought is the thinker; back of the plan is the planner; back of the design is the designer; back of the web is the weaver; and back of the law is the law-giver. Every flower and leaf is a marvel of beauty and a miracle of perfection, and proves there is a super-human thinker. Mental philosophers tell us there are three elements in mind: the intellect, the emotion, and the will. The function of the first is to decide; the function of the second, in the light of a clear judgment, to approve; the function of the third is to put one's self in harmony with what the mind has decided and the heart feels. Both Baptists and Pedobaptists sometimes berate the Disciples for teaching that baptism is essential to salvation; whereas, if I understand the Disciples, they are the only people who preach the gospel in harmony with the laws of the human mind. Baptism, with us, pertains to the conscience. The gospel comes to enlighten, first of all, the mind. Baptism, then, is an act of the mind. It is the surrender of the will. It is the sinner saying in his heart: "Jesus Christ has bought me with his own precious blood, but, alas, he has not my heart. I have never sought to obey his will; but now I am determined, of my own free will and accord, in the presence of God and man, to consecrate my time, thoughts, talents, body, business, money, life, my all to him. From henceforth I want only to be his, his slave, his chattel, owning no master but him; and I am persuaded that he is able to keep that which I have committed to him against that day." Fulfilling the conditions, he comes to the promise of salvation and seeks, through baptism, the assurance that his sins are washed away in the blood of Christ. The man who will reverently consult God's expressed will, learn his own conditions of pardon, and comply with them, can trust God's promise and feel secure. There is no poor sinner in this world required to carry his soul, burdened with sin, and his conscience with guilt, for months and years before he can appropriate the pardon of God in Christ.

WHAT HIS DESTINY?

It was a happy thought in Goldsmith to entitle one of his poems "She stoops to conquer." Christ accepted a sad and sorrowful life to reconcile man to his lot. He was born in a stable, cradled in a

manger, that he might have something in common
with the very poorest son of toil in this world, and
enable him to rejoice at last in the hope of the
glory of God.   Christ became a babe and slept
upon a mother's knee.   We become "babes in
Christ" and grow up into him.   And while it does
not appear what we shall be nor what we shall
have, yet it is a great truth that our present position is not our final position.

> " Nearest the throne and first in song
> Man shall his hallelujah raise;
> While wondering angels crowd around
> And swell the chorus of His praise."

Do we ever stop to think that everything in this
world but man comes to its highest possible
growth.   There is "first the blade, then the ear,
then the full corn in the ear."   After that what?
Nothing.   Man is like some kinds of fruit; it
takes *him* two seasons to ripen.   He is not ready
to be plucked yet.   No matter how much we have
grown, we have not yet come to the height of our
growth.   No man can grow to the highest possible growth in this world.   Some years ago, a
young man crossing the Atlantic, dropped over the
side of the vessel a diamond ring, and the next day
in the same way he lost a package of seed.   Now,
if you could rescue the diamond at the end of a
thousand years it would still be of the same
value.   Not so with the package of seed.   Rescue
it, sow it and re-sow it in fertile and favorable

soil, and at the end of a thousand years you could not compute the value and latent possibilities that are yet within the package of seed. So God views man; not so much in what he is now, but in what his nature is capable of becoming. Travelers to Palestine tell us that over there the cactus plant grows to the height of thirty and forty feet, and that they have seen bloom upon it numbering upwards of a hundred beautiful flowers. In that bright, balmy, sunny land, the cactus plant comes to its highest possible growth. So of man. The time of harvest is not yet. Wait until the winter's frost of death comes. Wait until we have been transplanted to the Summerland of birth. Wait until we have nothing to do but grow, and then we can show God and angels how much a man is better than a sheep, and what one may become.

As we have said before, we cannot tell, "we know not yet" all of the employments and enjoyments of the redeemed in heaven. Eye hath not seen nor ear heard (our eyes nor ears, at least) the things that God has in store for them that love him. It may not be possible for us to receive full instructions in regard to heaven, on account of the limitations of the human mind; but what we can learn and comprehend is full of interest and enjoyment, and enables us to "endure hardness" as good soldiers, and do our work with high thoughts. As we read of its jasper walls, its pearly gates and golden streets, we are assured that our Father in heaven is fitting it up in no niggardly way. We know enough to know, however, for a partial revelation has been made us, *that we shall not cross the river alone.* "Lazarus died and was carried by angels to Abraham's bosom." "Take heed that ye despise not one of these little ones; for I say unto you that in heaven their angels do always behold the face of my Father which is in heaven." We need a companion to accompany us on the long journey. Brick Pomeroy, in his "Saturday Night" sketches, draws a sweet and touching picture of a little girl dying. The little sufferer kisses her weeping mother farewell, turns around, raises her hands, embraces and kisses the angel that has come to take her up through the starry regions to the home of God's jewels. How sweet to know that

> " The eye that shuts in a dying hour
> Will open the next day in bliss;
> The welcome will sound in the other world
> Ere the farewell is hushed in this."

(2) *There will be perfect rest there.*

"Blessed are the dead that die in the Lord. Yea, saith the Spirit, from henceforth; for they rest from their labors, and their works do follow them." Rest is sweet when it is associated with toil and conflict, and heaven will be all the sweeter when we remember the past toils of this earth. Rest will be so sweet and the glory so great that we will not wish that the trials had been fewer or

the tribulations shorter or lighter. Oh, ye tired
mothers and brothers, look up, look up! Heaven
is as real as earth. The destiny that awaits us is
incorruptible, undefiled, and fades not away.
"Wherefore, lift up the hands which hang down,
and the feeble knees, and make straight paths for
your feet, lest that which is lame be turned out of
the way, but let it rather be healed." "Why art
thou cast down, oh my soul, and why art thou
disquieted within me? Hope thou in God, for I
shall yet praise him who is the health of my
countenance and my God."

> " Then why should I dream of the earthly abode,
> Of humanity clothed in the brightness of God?
> Were my spirit but turned from the outward and dim,
> It could gaze even now on the presence of Him.
> And what if my feet may not tread where He stood,
> Nor my ears hear the dashing of Galilee's flood,
> Nor my eyes see the cross which He bowed Him to bear,
> Nor my knees press Gethsemane's garden of prayer;
> Yet, loved of the Father, thy Spirit is near
> To the meek and the lowly, and the penitent here;
> And the voice of thy love is the same even now
> As at Bethany's tomb or on Olivet's brow."

Oh, the joy of that blissful hour when the toil-
worn pilgrim of the cross shall be able to lean his
weary head upon the bosom of God and weep his
sorrows away. Who but the Christian can say:
"Weeping may endure for a night, but joy cometh in the morning." The little Queen of England
was crowned when she was eighteen years of age.
When she was thirteen years old she took up the
court book that had in it the list of kings and
queens of the realm for many years past. She

saw that day, for the first time, that when her Uncle William died, she would be heir to the throne of England. In sweet surprise, she hied away to her mother, the Duchess of Kent, remarking: "Mother, now I see why you have tried to lead my youthful feet in the paths of truth and duty, and why you have been so anxious that I might grow up a good girl, superior in education, culture and attainments, to even that of my friends and cousins." "My child, why is it?" the mother replied. "Ah," said the young heir, "my destiny is higher than theirs." So the higher the destiny, the more imperative the need of the discipline of this life; and it is well to remember that the true philosophy of all affliction is that every condition of life is educational to a higher position.

(3) *It will be a place of activity.*

It used to be discussed as to whether rest or motion was the natural state of bodies. Now it is generally believed that everything is in motion, from the smallest drop of water that goes over Niagara to the mightiest planet in its orbit. Said Jesus: "My Father worketh hitherto, and I work." We shall rest in heaven, then, only from the pains and labors incident to the life that we now live in the flesh. Most of us would get tired doing nothing "forever and ever." Some one has truly said: "It is no more wonderful to live again than it is to live at all. It is less wonderful to continue to live than it is to begin to live. If God gave me a beginning once, he can certainly give me another beginning, or continue this beginning in another world." Hence, we conclude it is no more wonderful to suppose that he who created the powers of the soul has provided the highest exercise for those powers. We are only in training for work here. Heaven will be everlasting activity, without the weariness of this world. It may be that our activities will be in accordance with our different tendencies here. He who loves the music of earth will be baptized in heaven's music. He that searches for the beauties of earth will open immortal eyes upon the unfading beauties of heaven. He who seeks wisdom here will surely find it there. He who delights to meet God's people now will commune with them forever there.

HOW IS THAT DESTINY SECURED HIM ?

If I were asked to give an answer to this question, and required to give the answer in a short, single sentence, I would say: "It has been made possible through Christ." He is "all in all" as the object of the Christian faith. He is the "Alpha" and the "Omega," the beginning and the end, the first and the last; nothing came before him and nothing came after him. "He is the author and finisher of our faith." Jesus meets every possible need of the human heart. It is remarkable the different names that are given him in both Testaments, each of which expresses some

tender relation of Christ to his people. He is the
Bread of Life, which dying humanity may eat and
and live forever. He is the Rock in a weary land,
under which we can hide and be housed for eternity. He is the Lamb of God, who, by the offering
of himself, made man's acceptance with God possible. If we need a friend, he is a Friend of Sinners.
If we need a guide, he is an infallible one. If we
need a mediator, there is one mediator between
God and man, the man Jesus Christ. In the
sorrows of life we need a helper. The living,
loving, friendly, sympathetic Christ is the friend
we need. In our darkness and perplexity he is
our light. In our weakness, he is our strength.
There is not a need or a want of the soul that
Jesus does not supply. Christianity furnishes
wisdom for man's ignorance, righteousness for his
guilt, sanctification for his pollution, and redemption for his death.

(1) *Jesus died to reconcile man to God.*

Man has no confidence in a religion without
blood. There has always and everywhere been
some kind of intimation, whether from without or
within, whether from nature or revelation, that has
taught man that "without the shedding of blood
there is no remission." Now and then we meet
people who talk about and admire the beautiful
life of Christ, but reject the atonement. The mere
acceptance of him as a divinely appointed teacher,
the mere acknowledgment of him as a teacher, is

not Christianity. Any acknowledgment that fails
to take him just as he is is not sufficient. "It is
the religion of Cain, with its fruits and flowers,
without the blood. Grasping for the crown while
we ignore the cross is a sort of pious theft." "I,
if I be lifted up, will draw all men unto me." The
cross is what touches and tenders the heart; and
that cross proved two things—God's hatred of sin
and God's esteem for the sinner; and God's esteem
exactly matches man's worth. Whoever cheapens
man belittles the cross and makes the crucifixion
a waste of precious blood. Man's estimate of God
will maintain a certain proportion of his estimate
of man. A person who has a poor idea of man
has a poor idea of the Savior. Men are telling us,
now-a-days, that man isn't much of a sinner, and
doesn't need much of a Savior. Man fell up, they
say; he never fell down. But Christ tells us that
sin is real, and that it is the enemy, the curse, the
destroyer of mankind.

We have heard, too, of the skeptic who said, "I
will never accept a religion that comes upon the
suffering of others." I wonder if he would accept
a home that comes upon the sufferings of others.
I wonder if he would accept a country that comes
upon the sufferings of others. How many noble
souls have lived and suffered that the truth might
live. And we must remember that those who have
lived and suffered for the truth, have lived and
died and suffered for us. The rights and heritage

of Americans were secured them by the giving of the lives of their ancestors. Our inheritance in the new heavens and the new earth Jesus Christ secured by the sacrifice of himself.

I found myself lately studying with intense interest the biographies of Carey, Moffatt, Judson and Livingstone, and I came to this conclusion— that heroism is the abandonment of one's life for a good cause. Nothing else is worthy of the name of heroism. How the world loves those who have served it, and how little it cares for those who have ruled it! The world cares little for its masters, but it will never let die the memories of those who have helped it.

But if we go by the principle of our infidel friend, memory, with its swift wings, will never carry us back with gratitude to Paul and his co-workers of that generation; to John Howard, Frances Ridley Havergal, Florence Nightingale, Savonarola, Washington, Garfield, Moffatt, Carey, Judson and Livingstone. These men and women have been as angels of light to this world of ours. We are living upon the fruits of their sufferings, upon the result of their heroic self-denial.

(2) Nothing so touches and tenders the heart as suffering, especially when the suffering is borne, not for people in general, but for me. I once saw in Liverpool, England, Munkacsy's great picture, "Christ on Calvary." The room was darkened, while side-lights and foot-lights were placed

around and below. A feeling of reverence, mingled with fear and horror, stole over my heart while I gazed upon the life-size picture of the Son of God raised between earth and heaven. There were the thieves on either side. There were the mocking, the crown of thorns, the bleeding hands and feet; while the pale face looked heavenward and the broken heart cried out: "My God, my God, why hast thou forsaken me?" And as you gaze, you can see the elements grow dark, and an earthquake shakes the earth; and as I took the last long look at that sad scene, I repeated, with a full heart:

> " Ashamed of Jesus, that dear friend
> On whom my hopes of heaven depend?
> No, when I blush, be this my shame
> That I no more revere his name."

If a man has to be wooed and won by love and not driven by force, I am convinced that the innocent Christ, suffering "the just for the unjust, that he might bring us unto God," is the strongest appeal that God can make to win man from a life of sin; and if this sweet but sad story does not bring him to repentance, he is lost beyond all hope of redemption. Oh, my brother man, you are like the weary dove that flew sadly over the waste of waters, and found no resting place for the sole of its foot until it returned to the Ark from which it fled. Come back to God and all will be well; wander away from God and there is nothing before you except blackness, despair and death—a place of sadness where the light and love of God never come, and where hope is unknown.

This world is a poor portion for us without Christ. The best things in it do not come for money. "A man's life consisteth not in the abundance of the things he possesseth." Home love, the love of a mother, the sweetest love on earth, money cannot buy. It cannot buy that which man most needs. It cannot buy happiness, it cannot buy faith, it cannot buy pardon, it can not buy heaven. Matter cannot satisfy spirit. The world is full of the disappointed and unhappy, just because it is full of those who set their hearts upon securing that which, gained or not gained, can never satisfy the wants of the soul. They are trying to find what no one has ever found—peace without pardon and rest without coming to Christ.

What a grand thing it is to live and work for God, and know that we are ready to go when our time comes. "The other day," says A. C. Dixon, of Brooklyn, "I went to see a working man about forty-five years of age. I said: 'Are you a Christian?'" He replied: 'Yes, I have been trusting the Lord for about thirty years. Bright is it, bright as the promise of God; but I am in great suffering;' and he turned over from me, pain and agony filling every part of his nervous system until he could hardly endure it. He said: 'I am in pain, sir, but I have the peace that passeth understanding. My infidel doctor came in yesterday and said: 'There's no hope, sir; I have done everything I can for you.' I said: 'Doctor, your no hope is the brightest hope I ever had. Sure as you live, sir, that is the sweetest sentence you ever spoke at my bedside. I have been lying here in pain. In a few days, if your are right, I shall soon be beyond the reach of pain.'" The infidel's no hope is the dawning of hope to every Christian man. It is the dawning of the hope that

There's a home in the skies where the weary will rest,
A glorious home in the land of the blest;
There tears will be wiped from the sorrowful eye,
And the broken heart will forget to sigh.

From earth, such a barren and desolate waste,
We may long to that happier world to haste,
For though this planet seems lovely and gay,
Like shadows, its pleasures are passing away.

They linger not here, but away to the skies,
Like the offerings of youth, in the morning they rise;
The heart once so light is now burdened with grief,
And vainly it looks to the world for relief.

It may find in the smile of a loved one a charm
That may, for a season, its sorrows disarm;
But it knows that e'en love shall lie cold in the grave,
And its pleasures be lost in affliction's dark wave.

But, oh! there's a home of eternal delight,
Where smiles on the faces of Christians are bright,
Where the angel of beauty, immortally brsght,
Are floating forever on pinions of white.

No pestilence rides on the wings of the air,
No wave of affliction or sorrow is there;
In darkness that region shall never be furled,
For the smile of the Lord is the light of that world.

O blessed Christ, thou Son of the living God, keep me faithful until I shall stand redeemed in thy presence, and realize, as I cannot here, what there is in this great salvation for me.

BIOGRAPHICAL SKETCH OF J. V. UPDIKE.

J. V. UPDIKE was born in Celina, Ohio, January 23, 1850. His mother's name was Lincoln, and he bears the full name of his father. He was an only child, his father dying in October, 1849. He was obliged to commence life for himself at the age of twelve years. He followed in the footsteps of President Garfield in that he spent some years on the tow-path of the canal. He made the confession of faith in Christ in the month of March, 1867, in a series of meetings held by a local preacher of the United Brethren Church, by the name of Lewis Johnson. Not liking the discipline of the United Brethren Church, he refused to remain with them, but took membership at Fairview Bethel, near Neptune, Mercer County, Ohio, with the people known as the Church of God (nicknamed Winebrennarians). Six months later he preached his first sermon in a schoolhouse near Celina.

His first charge was in his twentieth year, and was called the Williams County Circuit. He had nine different preaching places in this circuit, and all his protracted meetings were very successful. He traveled this circuit two years, usually preaching four times each Lord's day, and many times

J. V. UPDIKE.

through the week. Hundreds of people were converted, new churches were organized, and houses of worship erected.

In 1872 he was appointed to what was called the Maumee Mission. Here he took up new points, had unusual success in all his meetings, and at the end of the year he had twenty different appointments with large ingatherings. From here he was appointed to the best circuit in the State, called the Wyandot Circuit. He lived in Upper Sandusky, Ohio, during this charge. He had the most wonderfully successful meetings ever held in that entire country by any preacher of any denomination. When the Eldership moved him from there to Findlay, Ohio (the only station in the State at that time), the people of Wyandot County offered objections, but the rule was to change preachers every three years at most, so he must go. This proved to be a very fortunate move for young Updike, who was known as the most successful preacher in the whole Church at that time, for here is where he came in contact with U. M. Browder, with whom he began to discuss the plan of salvation, but with the least thought in the world of being converted to the views of the Disciples. He contended strenuously for "foot washing" as an ordinance in the Church; for the "Lord's Supper" in the evening; for the "mourner's bench," etc. etc. But U. M. Browder successfully explained the teaching of the Word of God, so that the young preacher could not, with any honesty, meet his scriptural arguments. Yet he would not surrender at that time. He went to work to investigate the different positions held by the various religious bodies. He thoroughly investigated the "sanctification theory," "getting religion," etc., and concluded that the modern sanctification, sinless perfection theory, as advocated by its ablest and warmest supporters, was simply the "mourner's bench gone to seed." Then he took up the "Dunkard theory," read their theology, papers, etc., and came to the conclusion that the Disciples were right on the weekly communion question. Then he investigated the Seventh Day Adventist theory, and found that the Disciples' position was the only correct and scriptural position; that the whole trouble with the religious denominations was that they did not know how to "divide the word of truth." He studied night and day, and preached as he went, debating with and converting the people. He has held several oral debates with representative men, always to the entire satisfaction of lovers of the truth, whether professed Christians or not.

He was changed from the Findlay station to the McComb, Ohio, circuit, in the same county. He moved his family to McComb, ten miles from Findlay. His meetings grew more and more successful. He always had large audiences wherever he went. McComb was the first place he ever found a Church of Christ organized after the primitive order, and now the real struggle began. The members of the Church of Christ in McComb would always hear him and tell him he was in the wrong pew. His position in the Church in which he was a member kept him back, for, as he said, he must treat them honorably. He was missionary collecting agent for Mansfield Mission; a member of the standing committee for the Ohio Eldership—was first clerk of the same; was secretary of the Ministerial Association of the State; was secretary of the Ohio State Sunday-school Association; wrote the Ohio letter for the *Church Advocate*, published at Harrisburg, Pennsylvania; took care of churches; dedicated meeting-houses; assisted other ministers in special ordinance meetings; and was a delegate to the Ohio Eldership in 1878, to the General Eldership of the Church of God in the United States held at Syracuse, Ind. In all these offices he was kindly and honorably treated. He has always had a good feeling for that people, and hopes that they may see the way of the Lord more perfectly, and join with us in our efforts to unite all God's people upon the Bible and the Bible alone.

He wrote out his reasons for withdrawing from them as a people, and sent them to the Eldership by M. C. Skates, and many tears were shed when the letter was read.

On the 19th day of September, 1879, in a hall

where the Disciples met in McComb, Ohio, after a sermon by Q. A. Randall, an invitation was extended, and he and his wife went forward and took the right hand of Christian fellowship, and he has never seen the day that he regretted the step. He commenced preaching there for the church in McComb, and was more successful than ever before.

He has held one hundred and seventy-three protracted meetings up to December, 1893; has never held a meeting, since he came into the Church of Christ, that continued over more then seven Lord's days. He has never failed yet, and never will, if the Church with which he works will follow his instructions. He is not afraid to attack any hard place. His most successful meetings, up to the present writing, have been as follows.

East Liverpool, Ohio.......4 weeks, with 143 additions.
Toledo, Ohio...............4   "   "   152   "
Columbus, Ohio............4   "   "   160   "
Emporia, Kansas..........5   "   "   167   "
Ft. Wayne, Indiana....,..5   "   "   177   "
Paulding, Ohio............6   "   "   196   "
Ft. Scott, Kansas..........5   "   "   218   "
McPherson, Kansas........5   "   "   222   "
Springfield, Ohio...........6   "   "   226   "
Hutchinson, Kansas 5   "   "   386   "
Wichita, Kansas...........6   "   "   387   "
Des Moines, Iowa..........6   "   "   563   "
University Place Church, DesMoines, Ia.,   253   "
San Jose, California,...... 5 weeks, with 376   "
Toledo, Ohio, 1st...........4   "   "   121   "
   "   "   2nd..........4   "   "   196   "
Payne, Ohio...............10 days,   "   100   "
Massillon, Ohio ....5 weeks,   "   255   "

In 1870, when twenty years of age, Bro. Updike was married to Miss Annie E. Houts, a talented and devoted Christian lady. Five children have been born unto them—three boys and two girls. One boy died in childhood. Their older daughter is the wife of Pastor Sims, now pastor of the Central Church of Christ in Wichita, Kansas. His second daughter is married to Mr. Carrie Blount, of Ft. Wayne, Indiana.

Bro. Updike's preaching is notable for its simplicity, sincerity and directness. He is eminently a preacher for the masses. He is the very soul of logic and powerful reasoning, and yet so clear and simple are his statements that the "common people hear him gladly." He is emphatically a Bible preacher. His sermons are replete with quotations from the Scriptures. He says he believes the old Book from back to back, and he presents its great truths with a positiveness and confidence that can not fail to carry conviction. His illustrations are drawn largely from his own rich and varied experiences. He has excellent descriptive powers. His addresses often sparkle with irrepressible wit. He occasionally introduces pathos, but not often. He regards laughter as more serviceable than tears in leading men to a knowledge of the truth. It is a very common thing for him to convulse his audience with laughter by some happy hit or mirth-provoking anecdote. He sometimes rises to the loftiest eloquence. He is an exceed-

24

ingly interesting speaker, and usually holds his hearers for one hour with no apparent restlessness on their part. His themes are practical and scriptural. His constant effort is to lift up Christ before a lost and dying world, and bring sinners to him through a knowledge of the truth.

Men, women and children alike are convicted under the preaching of this powerful revivalist. In one of his meetings he delivered an address on Lord's day afternoon to men only, touching upon various phases of the social evil. In his audience were four young men, college students, who had planned for a visit that night, for the first time, to a house of ill-repute. But so thoroughly were their consciences quickened under Bro. Updike's heart-searching words, that they abandoned their evil plan, and instead of making their contemplated visit, came to hear Bro. Updike again; and when the gospel invitation was given, all stepped forward and made the good confession. At another place Bro. Updike went to a bank to get some money exchanged. The cashier handed him the amount demanded, but added more to it. Upon counting the money he discovered what he supposed to be the banker's mistake, and promptly called his attention to it. The latter replied: "Your meetings here have been worth more than that to this bank. One man has returned five hundred dollars which he had dishonestly held from us, and it was your preaching working upon his conscience which caused him to do it. You are a good collector, sir." Persons who could not get into the house because of the crowd have been known to reach their hands through the open windows and make the good confession. And others have come forward, at the close of a pay lecture on a partly secular theme, and professed their faith in Jesus preparatory to Christian baptism.

Personally, Bro. Updike is a genial, good-natured, companionable man. He is remarkably free from eccentricities—is just a plain, practical, everyday man. He has a wonderfully vigorous constitution, weighs about one hundred and sixty pounds, eats heartily, sleeps well, and, in short, conducts himself as should any well-poised man. He loves children, delights in visiting the poor, speaks to everybody. He sincerely hates shams, hypocrisy, and evil in every form.

He is especially severe upon sin in high places. Dancing, card-playing, theater-going, and all evils of like nature receive terrible blows from this fearless man of God. One day, while driving, a friend pointed out to him the beautiful residence and lawns of a wealthy and popular man, who makes no pretension of godliness, and whose family is not noted for the purest morals. "Well, let them enjoy it," said Bro. Updike; "it's all the heaven they'll ever get." He has a strong voice, and his enunciation is good. It is always a pleasure to listen to him. His voice is as clear at the end of a long meeting as at the beginning. He presents a splendid appearance upon the platform. He at once impresses an audience with the fact that he is a man of extraordinary ability, and this, too, without any studied effort. He seems absolutely free from everything like affectation. He prides himself in being a *man* in every sense of the word.

In conducting revivals his greatest power, next to his preaching the unadulterated Word, consists, perhaps, in his generalship. He knows how to run a meeting. He seems to read men and situations at a glance. He is possessed with powerful and nearly always correct intuitions. He has the faculty of putting people to work, and inspiring a practical enthusiasm. He believes in judicious advertising. He believes in planning and praying for great things. But withal he is conservative. He is cautious about divulging his proposed course in any given meeting, and in this he shows superior generalship. He can not be taken unawares. His favorite expression in closing his " Afternoon Workers' Meeting " is, " Go out, now, and bring some one to Christ to-night." He has a very high appreciation of the necessity and power of personal work. Sometimes he reminds the pastor and church officers, in a very forcible manner, that he is present and conducting a meeting for them. He cannot brook carelessness or indifference on the part of those who profess the holy religion of Christ. He has been known to abruptly dismiss an audience and retire quickly through a side door, leaving the people in amazement, and causing them to realize as never before their lack of energy in the great work of saving souls. The largest houses, tabernacles and tents are usually too small to hold the vast assemblies that always desire to hear him. He seldom stops for anything. Some of his best meetings have been held in the hottest weather, in presidential campaigns, and in times when few preachers could be successful. He has engagements ahead for several years. He receives letters almost daily from all over the United States, pleading with him for meetings. He is very kind and thoughtful about answering letters, and seldom neglects a correspondent, even though he can give him no encouragement with reference to his assistance. He writes many letters, both with his own hand and by proxy. His correspondence is too heavy for his own good, but there seems to be no help for it.

He is now considering a proposition from London, England, about going there to hold meetings for the Church of Christ for one year. He has all that he can do. He has never had two weeks vacation since he began preaching. He will be forty-four years old January 23, 1894, and says that he never felt better in his life than now, and only wishes that he could live 150 years to work for Christ.

Heaven be praised for such a man! In this age

of general looseness it is refreshing to find a preacher who is able to draw the lines with a tightness that knows no defeat. Long may he be spared to go up and down the busy highways of this sinful world, and call men to a godly, sober and righteous life. Long may he live to present to a creed-glutted world the great fact that the Bible is its own best interpreter, and that man's highest business is to get right with God in accordance with his Book. H. C. PATTERSON.

Higginsville, Mo., December 27, 1893.

WHAT AND WHERE IS HEAVEN?

J. V. UPDIKE.

The whole family in heaven.—Eph. 3: 15.

THERE is a natural longing in the human heart for another, a higher and a better life. There is nothing in this world that gives so much joy and satisfaction in the midst of the trials and difficulties of this inconstant life as to be assured from the Scriptures of Divine Truth that there is a home for the soul.

"Home of the soul." In our visions we have thought about it, we have talked about it, we have written about it, and we have dreamed about it, and our souls are filled with bright anticipations as we look forward to the time when the light of heaven shall be round about us, and when in the city of the living God our souls shall thrill with joy at being surrounded with the redeemed of the Lord, and when we shall be everlastingly satisfied in his everlasting kingdom.

The subject to-night may be considered upon the part of some as being speculative. I have heard people talk about its being speculative; that we can know but little about it, and that when we talk about it we are talking about something that we know but little about. So far as this life is concerned, it may be true that we can know but little about it; but it is also true that we can find out a great deal about heaven. It is not all a dream. Not all a dream, my brother; for when we come to inquire if there be such a place, the answer comes: There certainly is. God has not created us in vain. We are not put in this sin-cursed world to suffer a few weeks or months or years, and then go out and be nothing but food for earth-worms forever, and not have life beyond the tomb. Oh, no! God never makes any mistakes; and there being a God, that God has created us for a higher and a nobler and a better purpose than simply to have heart-aches and pains and tears and sorrows, with but a few joys mixed with them, and then to die and be no more forever. Oh, what a mistake that would be, my friends! We believe that God is all-wise, and doeth all things well. We believe that he has prepared something better for man than he now enjoys.

I would not leave the impression upon your mind that I am dissatisfied or discontented with the place in which we are now living. I am not dissatisfied with this world so far as the world is concerned—with its hills and valleys, its beautiful trees and beautiful lakes and streams and rocks, and all that is grand and glorious! No, I am not dissatisfied with these; but I am glad, since it is true, that we cannot always stay here—that there is something better for us.

That old question that sometimes comes up in our minds, don't you think also arose in the mind of Job when in that country in which he lived and in the age in which he lived? "If a man die, shall he live again? All the days of my appointed time will I wait until my change comes." He was going to change this world for a better one. And in the language of my text to-night it seems to me that there is something about it that satisfies the mind in regard to that place called heaven. "Of whom the whole family in heaven and earth is named." There is but the one family of God, part of them in heaven, and part of them on earth. And this family is named of him, and for him, and to glorify him.

And when you ask me to-night if I have any good evidence upon this subject, I answer you in the affirmative, I certainly have. "Well," you ask again, "have you any testimony from anyone who has ever been in heaven; any record made by anyone who has been there and told us anything about it?" I answer, Yes; yes I have. "Is it a matter of history placed upon record upon the part of those who have been in heaven?" Yes; yes.

We are going to call just a few witnesses to-night. The first one I shall place upon the witness-stand, to prove to you that there is such a place as heaven, is the Lord Jesus Christ. He

claimed that his native place was heaven, and that
he was going back to heaven. He told us that it
was certainly a beautiful place; and he said to his
disciples: "Lay up for yourselves treasures in
heaven, where moth and rust doth not corrupt, and
where thieves do not break through and steal."
He talked very much of heaven. He rejoiced at
the thought that he would soon return there.
When he came near to his own death, he rejoiced
at the thought that he would soon be through with
this sin-cursed world, and be at home in heaven.
And when his disciples were sad and cast down,
lamenting the fact that he would have to leave
them, he gave to them this grand evidence: "Let
not your heart be troubled. Ye believe in God, believe also in me. In my Father's house are many
mansions. If it were not so, I would have told
you. I go to prepare a place for you. And if I
go and prepare a place for you, I will come again
and receive you unto myself; that where I am,
there ye may be also." So Jesus declares that
there is such a place. He makes the declaration
that if there were no such place, he would have
told them. We have this evidence from Christ,
and Jesus Christ is the Son of God, and a messenger from heaven. Then, my brother, it is true that
heaven is a different place from this; it is a place
of holiness, a place of happiness, and a place
where the redeemed of God are now. And so he
said to his disciples: "If ye love me, ye would

rejoice, because I go to my Father." He looked
forward to the joy that awaited him in heaven.
He endured the cross, despising the shame, looking gladly forward to the heavenly city beyond.
So, my friends, Jesus makes a first-class witness
in the case.

The second witness I will put upon the witness-
stand is that man we sometimes call Saul of Tarsus. He had the blessed privilege of having a
view of heaven. We might call it a bird's-eye
view. God meant that Paul should make a record
of the matter. He had the privilege of being
caught up, not into the first or second heaven, but
into the third heaven—even into paradise. He
said he saw things that were not lawful for him to
utter. Then Paul tells us there is such a place. If
he is to be relied upon in other questions, we must
rely upon him respecting the place called heaven,
and we must believe that he was there; but then
he doesn't say himself that he was there. Let us
sum that up a little. Saul, or Paul, said that "he
knew a man in Christ above fourteen years ago,
whether in the body or out of the body I cannot
tell. God knoweth; how that he was caught up into
paradise,' or the 'third heaven.'" Now, then, the
question is, does that mean Paul? I say it does.
Everybody that has examined the matter says it
does, and how are we going to settle it satisfac-
torily? If you will take your Bibles and look
into them carefully, and see where he was fourteen

years before, or about fourteen years before he wrote this, you will find out about what they were doing with him. Where was he then? You remember how he went down to Lystra and preached the Gospel to the people, and how they were ready at one time to worship him, and make a god out of him, nearly. He was a wonderfully popular preacher for a little while; but his popularity did not last very long. They soon became desirous of getting rid of this wonderful preacher, and so they stoned him and dragged him through the streets— took him and dragged him outside of the city, leaving him for dead. They believed him to be dead. They believed it when they dragged him through the city. Well, so far as we know, he was dead, for the spirit was separated from the body. And while they were pounding the old body of Paul, and bruising it and beating it, Paul was having a good time up in heaven. Oh, what a glorious time he was having! If he had had time to look back and see them pounding his old body, he would have smiled and said, "Well, if they can get any satisfaction out of that, they can have it; I am having a good time." But you know that he came back and entered into that same old beaten body, and got up and walked twenty miles the next day. And then did he say to the people that they must be careful about preaching Christ? If you are not careful you may get stoned? No, he just preached harder than ever. They never stopped *him* with stones, or stripes, or bruises, or threats. They couldn't do anything to stop him, only to take his head off; and he had done so much before his head was taken off, that he preached louder after he was dead than before. When they put him in prison to keep him from preaching, he would write, and write, and write, so that his writings might go to all the world. I don't know whether we would have the beautiful epistles of this wonderful writer if it had not been that they shut him up in prison. When he was out he had no time to write. He had to preach. When he was in jail he couldn't preach, so he had to write. So he was a busy man.

You never knew a Christian man yet who was not a busy man. There are some people, I am afraid, who will not get to that heavenly world. Lazy people will not get there. It is no place for lazy people. I think, my friends, that we want to be very careful about that. Saul's was a very active life. He was a zealous, wide-awake preacher—weak physically, but strong spiritually. When they beat him, he could go up to heaven and stay. When he got through, he made a record. He becomes a witness in the case before you to-night, that there is such a place as heaven, or Paradise.

You remember that when the thief was dying upon the cross he said to the blessed Christ, "Lord, remember me when thou comest into thy kingdom;" and the Lord said, "To-day shalt thou be with me in Paradise." Where was Paradise, then? Jesus didn't go to heaven when he was crucified, when he died. No, for after his resurrection from the dead he said to Mary, "Touch me not, for I have not as yet ascended unto my Father." Where had he been? In Paradise. Where was Paradise, then? It was what was commonly understood on the part of the Jews as the "intermediate state," where the spirits of the righteous went until after the resurrection of Jesus Christ. When Christ arose from the dead, he took captivity captive. He conquered the unseen world, conquered hell, and took the spirits up to heaven, and made the way accessible. If I die to-night, I will be in heaven in the morning! If the Christian dies in the faith and the hope of the Gospel, he dies on safe ground now, under the Christian dispensation. Why? Because Jesus has made atonement in heaven. He has made the way accessible. He has opened up a new and living way. He has conquered death, and conquered the grave, and conquered hell. When we read of Paradise, we read of its being the third heaven. Paradise, where God is, and where the angels are! We do not read of Paradise as being an intermediate state after the Christian dispensation came. That matter has been changed. Why? Because until Jesus went into heaven with his own body and blood, as a sacrifice, as a great High Priest, to make atonement in heaven for men, men could not enter heaven. The blood of bulls and goats would not suffice to take away sins. Without the blood of Jesus Christ, there could be no remission of sin. But when that was done, when that work was performed, that ended it completely, and opened up a new and living way, so that heaven is the home of the redeemed now. And Brother Paul tells us that "the whole family in heaven and earth is named for him." Jesus taught them to "lay up for themselves treasures in heaven." Why lay them up there, if there isn't much hope of getting there? Why not lay them up in the "intermediate state," if that is the place you are going to get to first? No, my friends, I don't care; if *you* want to go there, you may. But as for me, I don't want to go around on any side track, so far as I am concerned. Jesus Christ has opened up a new and living way, with a strait gate that takes us right up into heaven. "Strait is the gate, and narrow is the way that leadeth unto life, and few there be who find it;" but "blessed are they that do his commandments, that they may have right to the tree of life, and may enter in through the gate into the city."

So the city is prepared, and we have our Master's evidence in the first place, and Brother Paul's in the second place. Now, we want another— Brother John. You will remember that God didn't select Paul to make a record of heaven and tell us all about it; he gave him a thorn in his flesh that he might not get proud over it. That's the reason Brother Paul had that thorn to contend with. God told him he would give him grace to bear it, but he would not take it away from him, for fear he might get proud because he had been to heaven once. That is a good thing sometimes. Some preachers need thorns sometimes to keep them from getting proud. Paul had it for that very reason, and it was a grand, good thing, and he was satisfied with it. He believed God; and he said that "his grace would be sufficient." And he went on believing that his grace would be sufficient for him.

But now John was to be the revelator, or at least to make a record of the revelation of Jesus Christ. The last book of the Bible is the book that gives us a history or description of the heavenly city and heavenly world. And Brother John was selected of all the apostles to record a vision of heaven. He had a vision of it. He had a vision of the Church, too, in this world, and that book is meant to tell us of the trials and triumphs of the Church of the living God, and to give us a description of the Heavenly city, the New Jerusalem. Brother John tells about the city, that the walls are of jasper; that each gate is of pearl; that the streets are of gold; and that the river of life is as clear as crystal, flowing out from the throne of God. And he tells us three times of the tree of life being there. And they who do God's will shall be permitted to enter and partake of the leaves of this tree, which are for the healing of the nations. God drove Adam and Eve, as I said once before, from the tree of life in the Garden of Eden, and transplanted that tree of life over in Paradise. Through disobedience to the will of God, man was driven away from the tree of life. Through obedience to God they get back to the tree of life, and hence, when we get back to the tree of life, and eat of that fruit, we shall live forever.

John gives us a description of the New Jerusalem. He tells us that the walls are fifteen hundred miles long, fifteen hundred miles wide, and fifteen hundred miles high; there will be plenty of room for all of mankind who will enter there. Will there be a good many people in that city? Oh, it will be a large city. They can number the cities that are in this world to-day; but John, in giving a description of this heavenly city, said he saw them standing before the throne and before the Lamb, clothed with white robes, and with palms in their hands, a great multitude that no man could number, of all nations, and kindreds, and peoples, and tongues. There they stood, before the throne and before the Lamb. It is not going to be just a little company that get to heaven after all. Think a moment. When you consider that the great majority who die in this world die in infancy, and that all who die in infancy die in safety; also that all irresponsible persons who die in this world are, of course, saved; and all who obey God's divine truth will be saved; when you take all this into consideration, there is going to be a great number in the city of the living God, the New Jerusalem. The New Jerusalem is to be brought down by God out of heaven.

But enough of this, so far as place is concerned. We have no trouble in settling that by these witnesses who have made a record in the inspired Book. We have the evidence, then, from people who have been there and seen with their own eyes, and heard with their own ears, and have made a record with their own hands, so far as John and Paul are concerned. Revelation is clear. There is such a place as heaven.

Now, then, where is heaven? Which way, up or down? Well, this is to be treated a little differently, possibly, from what a great many would treat it. How far is it above us, if above? We always speak of it as above; you cannot speak of heaven to a little child but what it will think of "above," "up," always. Say anything about hell, and their mind goes "down," every time. We speak of people "losing heaven" when they have never been there. They have lost heaven just by not getting it; and some people never will lose heaven any more than I will lose a million dollars to-night. I can't lose a thing I haven't got. That would be impossible. And you will never lose heaven if you don't get there. You will simply *miss* it; and hundreds of people are missing it; at least they are going to miss it.

But now, when we come to the question in regard to where heaven is, we take up the sciences that we have to-day, and we will find a wonderful study there. Take up astronomy, for instance, and see what we will find. If you were permitted to stand on one of the golden rings of Saturn, you would see another firmament of suns, moons and stars stretching overhead, and all around. Then could you go on to the nearest fixed star, Alpha Centura, with its two suns, shining with a light equal to forty-six times the intensity of our sun, and stand on one of the beautiful planets there, you would behold the firmament of the Polar Star system, whose light is forty-six years reaching our earth. From thence you would see Vega, which shines with a light equal to four hundred and forty of our suns. Could you then pass on up the silent aisles of the heavenly temple of the shining monarchs of Vega, you would see the glittering firmament of Capella, blazing with several suns. From the golden brow of Capella, you would behold the firmament of Arcturus shining with a light equal to five hundred and fifty of such suns as shine in the blue vault which surrounds us. Could you stand upon one of the planets in the bewildering firmament of Arcturus, you would not then be beyond the reach of the telescope, or the calculations of bold astronomers. Above you

27

would discover glorious Alcyon sending forth a flood of light equal to twelve thousand of our little suns. But this is only the beginning—the mere vestibule of the starry temple. There are celestial systems lying beyond, some of which, we have every reason to believe, contain upwards of twenty-two thousand suns each—and think— each system is a firmament with a family of revolving planets a million times larger than our own. It is affirmed by those who have spent a lifetime in the exploration of the starry heavens, that there are no less than eighteen million suns shining in the firmament, within reach of Lord Ross' mighty telescope! Well may we ask, where are the frontiers of the boundless heavens—the last remote spot, beyond which no star glitters on the dark bosom of eternal night—where is the verge of the universe? Where are the highest heavens, the home of the redeemed? Who dares to say that he could count the grand total of heaven's millions of firmaments, one above another, even though he could count a million years at the rate of five hundred per minute? Could you fly in a straight line with the velocity of light from the edge of Alcyon, the sixth firmament beyond ours, it would take you billions of years to reach the highest heaven. Nay, if you were to travel through all eternity, you would never reach the outer bounds of Jehovah's vast and beautiful temple, beyond which no suns may be found exploring their way through the infinite heavens, burning into the dark concaves of night.

Now if the home of the redeemed is beyond the stars, as many imagine, it will never be reached, *for there is no beyond.* If Adam and Eve had started from the Garden gate of Eden six thousand years ago, they could not have reached it yet. They never can, if it is in the region beyond all the stars. Then where is it? Is there such a place? We answer, yes, yes. Then where is it? Above us? The idea with us is that it is above the stars, and above the moons, and above the suns. No, my brother. Heaven is not far from every one of us to-night; and if we had the spiritual hearing that we some day may have, it is possible that we could now hear the music of the redeemed in heaven. It is not far, not far. It is described to us as being so far away, but no; it is not far.

You will remember that Jacob had his ladder extending from earth to heaven, and he saw the angels of God ascending and descending upon it. And then you remember of reading where the angels of God came to Daniel while he was praying—came from heaven to Daniel while he was praying. And then you remember that the angels came to direct Lot to go out of Sodom. And the angels came when Jesus was born and sang the cradle song of the Lord of life and glory. The angels were there with him after he had been

tempted of the devil. The angels came from
heaven to roll away the stone the morning of his
resurrection. The angels were with him when he
ascended into heaven. And he said before he
died, "In my Father's house are many mansions;
if it were not so, I would have told you."

Then it is not faith in astronomy, but it is faith
in Jesus Christ, faith in the Spirit of God, faith in
divine revelation that there is such a place as
heaven. And it may be the center around which
the universe of worlds revolve; or it may be that
the planet upon which we live is very near that
planet, or that great center around which the universe of worlds revolve. And if we had the hearing, as I said before, which we some day may
have; the spiritual hearing which even Huxley
says it will be possible for man to have, such that
the growth of a petal will make a noise like the
rumbling of a wagon crossing a corduroy bridge,
and such that when you go into a silent cave,
where the silence is so great that the blood rushing through your veins and coursing through the
arteries will sound so loud that it will become
painful to you; if we had that hearing now, my
friends, heaven would not seem so far from us
after all.

Then the music of heaven! I remember a good
old sister who had been faithful in the service of
Almighty God for so many years, nearly fifty
years. We were holding a series of meetings in

the place where she lived, and she sickened and was about to die. She had been to a number of the meetings, and she was always ready to get up and speak in regard to her hopes of heaven, and the joy of heaven. And when that night I stood beside the bed of that noble women of God, her husband, whose hair was gray with many years, having been fifty years a member of the Church of Jesus Christ, asked her, " Mother, shall Brother Updike pray with you?" She nodded assent. We prayed, holding her by the hand. Then he asked her, "Mother, shall we sing?" And she shook her head, "No." And then she made a powerful effort to speak. She was a woman who would tell the truth. She was dying, and she knew it; and she would tell the truth then, surely. She said, "No, I hear sweeter music—the music of heaven." Those were the last words that that grand old saint, good old Mother Gordon, uttered. "The music of heaven." When we went out of the room that night, the stars were shining brightly, and all was so clear and' silent, and the gentleman who was walking along by my side, who was not a professed Christian, said to me, " Mr. Updike, it seems to me that the air is full of heavenly music." Oh, yes, the music of the heavenly world! And I have no doubt, as Dr. Nelson, in his "Evidences of the Christian Religion" suggests, that the people of the Living God, dying in faith, and conscious of it, are permitted, even before they pass, sometimes, from this world, to hear the music of heaven, and to sing and to be permitted to enter into the spirit of that worship that awaits the redeemed of the Lord. I believe it from the evidence I have had from personal observation, standing by the bedside of dying saints of God.

I stood by the bedside of another saint, whom I knew to be true, who would never lie for anything or anybody. Her husband stood at the foot of the bed, and the little boy stood beside the bed, the only child they had, a child that I brought into the family of God. They stood there weeping over her, and said, "How can we give you up?" She said, "If you only knew the joy I have in my soul; if you could only hear the sweet music that I hear, and if you could only look forward to the home to which I am going, I am sure you would be glad that I will soon be there." Do you believe that a person who has consciousness, and who has faith in God, and faith in his word, will lie about music that they hear in the dying hour?

So, my friends, we haven't any trouble, it seems to me, in settling the question in regard to its not being far to the center, possibly, around which the universe of worlds revolve. God is there; and in the second place, Christ is there, for he ascended into heaven. Christ is there. And in the third place, we have the holy angels there. Yes, "there is more joy in heaven in the presence of the angels over one sinner that repenteth, than over ninety

and nine just persons who need no repentance."
There is the joy of the angels in heaven, but is
that all there is there? No; the redeemed of the
Lord are there. The saints of God who have died
in the triumphs of the living faith have entered
the heavenly world. We have children there,
possibly. We have fathers and mothers there.
Possibly you have sisters there. Or possibly you
have a wife there, or a husband, or some one who
is very dear to you indeed, has crossed the river.
They are in heaven to-night. Part of the family
in heaven, and part of them on earth. "The whole
family in heaven." The family just divided by
the narrow stream of death, and that being the
only division, it is not far above, and it will not
take us long to get there, when we get a good start,
when we come down to the river.

Now, my brother, that soul who gets out of this
life into the eternal life, sweeping through the
gates, washed in the blood of the Lamb, will
beckon us there. Oh, what a grand thing to beckon to-night! What a grand thing to urge on to a
better and holier life! When we begin to think
of heaven and where it is, and the joy that awaits
us over there, our souls are thrilled beyond expression.

When I was a boy I remember that heaven
looked to me like a place filled with strangers.
No one there that I could think of. But by and
by I stood by the bedside of a saint of God, my

grandmother. Then by the side of an aunt. And then by the side of an uncle. They died in the triumphs of the living God. They had the promise of the life which now is, and also that which is to come. By and by I had a family of my own; little ones; and as I was leaving home one day, my little boy, Harry, whom I loved as dearly as I loved my life, crawled to the door, and his last words to me were, "Papa, papa, good-bye." The next time I saw him he was in the spasm of death, and lived but a few minutes after I arrived home, having been dispatched for. And when I saw our darling pass away, and I found that we must give him up at last, oh, what joy to my soul to know from the Word of God that there is a home beyond! And it is only the little flower plucked from our own family flower garden, and placed in the great bouquet of God in heaven, near by the throne in the eternal home. Home! Home! Thou darling, stay thou there! Stay thou there! God helping me, I will go to you. He is free from this sin-cursed world. Saved through the blood of Jesus Christ! Redeemed forever, and placed near the throne of God! Oh, stay there, my darling; I would not call you back to this world! Thus my loved ones have been crossing the river. Some of my best friends are already over the river. They are in heaven to-night, and they are beckoning for me to come, for you to come, for all to come.

I remember, years ago, in a part of the country

where railroads were not in use, some of the old preachers would start out on a trip of three months. They could not get news very quickly or easily, as we can now. One minister, of whom I am now thinking, had a darling child who used to watch and wait at the gate just about the time she supposed her papa would return home, glad to greet him. One day, while the father was gone, the death angel came to the home, and took the child on to the heavenly world. The father knew nothing of it until he came home. He came on horseback, watching the gate as he came to see his darling child. But the child was not there to greet him and welcome papa home with her usual kiss. No, she had crossed the river. He hitched his horse and went into the house. The wife met him with tears in her eyes; and he said, "What is the trouble? What is the trouble?" She said, "Sit down and I will tell it all to you." And then she related the sickness and death of the child. And just before she died she had said, "Mamma, I guess papa will not be home before I go to heaven; but you tell him when he comes that I will be at the beautiful gate, watching and waiting for him; that I will beckon for him there." Oh, that would be enough to make a man faithful to God! Many are at the beautiful gate to-night, with beckoning hands, watching and waiting for *you* there. The beckoning hands of mother; the beckoning hands of the darling child; the beckoning hands of loved ones; and, above all, the beckoning hand of the Lord of Life and Glory. There are so many beckoning for me to-night, so many beckoning for you to-night; and as these loved ones over there are beckoning us to come, let us resolve, God helping us, to live better lives, and try to meet them over there.

I am going to ask Brother Hawes to sing my favorite song, "Beckoning Hands." The song was sung by Prof. Hawes.

BEAUTIFUL BECKONING HANDS.

Beautiful hands at the gateway to-night,
Faces all shining with radiant light,
Eyes looking down from yon heavenly home,
Beautiful hands that are beckoning, Come.

CHORUS.

Beautiful hands, beckoning hands,
Calling the dear ones to heavenly lands;
Beautiful hands, beckoning hands,
Beautiful, beautiful beckoning hands.

Beckoning hands of a mother, whose love
Sacrificed life its devotion to prove;
Hands of a father, to memory dear,
Beck'ning up higher the waiting one here.

Beautiful hands of a little one, see!
Baby voice calling, O mother, to thee!
Rosy-cheeked darling, the light of our home—
Taken so early—is beckoning, Come!

Beckoning hands of a husband or wife,
Waiting and watching the loved one of life;
Hands of a brother, a sister, a friend,
Out from the gateway to-night they extend!

There is another question, and I am done. Shall we know each other there? That mother asks, Shall I know my child in heaven? If I see my child in heaven, shall I know my child? Why not? Why not? Is heaven going to be a place filled with strangers? It will not seem like heaven to me, it seems, if I am not to know those whom I have loved and been associated with here. Why, my friends, certainly I believe we shall know each other there. The mother will know her child. And why not? As you cross the river you shall know them. That will be heaven to know that you are safe forever—forever beyond the reach of harm.

Let me urge upon you to get ready, and to get ready, too, to-night, and enter into the work of God with all your heart. Young man, you cannot afford to miss heaven at last. You may gain the whole world, but if you lose your own soul, where is the profit? Young man, what have you gained? Young woman, what have you gained? If you have all the pleasures of this life, but by that miss heaven at last—miss that grand home, prepared at so great expense by such a great Savior as the Lord Jesus Christ—what have you gained?

Now, I want you to come, all of you that will have heaven as your home, God helping you. Come, give me your hand to-night. Come, like honest men, and honest women, and honest boys, and honest girls. Take your stand upon the side

of God. "Blessed are they that do his commandments, that they may have right to the tree of life,
and may enter in through the gates into the city."
You have no home if you have not heaven. The
sinner who dies has no home to go to. The Christian only has a home.

> " Home in heaven! What a joyful thought,
>   As the poor man toils in his weary lot."

God help you, my brother, to come.